The
Fiercest
Kind

A Volume in the Series

AFRICAN AMERICAN INTELLECTUAL HISTORY

Edited by
Christopher Cameron

The Fiercest Kind

FIVE BLACK WOMEN IN ART,
PERFORMANCE, AND RESISTANCE, 1937–1965

H. ZAHRA CALDWELL

University of Massachusetts Press

AMHERST AND BOSTON

ISBN 978-1-62534-932-3 (paper); 933-0 (hardcover)

Designed by Jen Jackowitz
Set in Adobe Caslon Pro
Printed and bound by Books International, Inc.

Cover design by adam b. bohannon
Photo by unknown U.S. naval officer, *Pianist Hazel Scott making a guest appearance
at the Naval Training Station, Great Lakes, Illinois*. December 17, 1943.
Official U.S. Navy Photograph, now in the collections of the
National Archives. (2016/07/05)

Library of Congress Cataloging-in-Publication Data
A catalog record for this book is available from the Library of Congress.

British Library Cataloguing-in-Publication Data
A catalog record for this book is available from the British Library.

The authorized representative in the EU for
product safety and compliance is Mare Nostrum Group.
Email: gpsr@mare-nostrum.co.uk
Physical address: Mare Nostrum Group B.V.,
Doelen 72, 4831 GR Breda, The Netherlands

This is dedicated to the beginning, middle, and the end of me
—my mother, husband, and son.

Contents

Epilogue
162

Illustrations

Acknowledgments

I stumbled upon the May 1956 issue of *Ebony* magazine in my undergraduate department's library. The bright red cover featured Hazel Scott in a gold lamé dress with an irreverent caption that read "I Found God in Show Business." As the resident work-study student, I could not resist returning to this cover over and over. I was fascinated and intrigued. Little did I know that, at that moment, the seeds of this book were being planted. I would carry Ms. Scott around in my psyche for the next several decades, gathering other performer-artist-activists along the way. The entire Black Studies Department at the State University of New York at New Paltz deserves my respect and appreciation for any and all successes throughout my long academic journey. It was in their department that I first discovered the depths of Black history and its myriad legacies. The exploration of those legacies became my life's vocation.

I first want to thank UMass Press for the wholehearted support, time, patience, and energy they put into my project. A special shout-out to Matt Becker and Sally Nichols is warranted. Dawn Potter deserves kudos as a meticulous copyeditor as well. I have many archivists to thank at institutions across the country whose help was invaluable: The Special Collections Research Center staff at Morris Library, Southern Illinois University at Carbondale, was remarkable in their level of assistance and guidance; the archivists at the Performing Arts Reading Room at the Library of Congress performed miracles; the staff at the Vivian G. Harsh Collection at the Woodson Regional Library in Chicago also provided fantastic support; Lisa Moore at Amistad Research Center was especially diligent and kind; Researchers at the National Museum of African American History and Culture were amazing; the Billy Ireland Cartoon Library and Museum staff at Ohio State University were of great help; and the staff at the Schomburg Center for Research in Black Culture pointed out additional resources during my several visits that would have otherwise eluded me, and created a stronger book project as a result.

Many people generously provided interviews and primary assistance over the several-year project. They include Hazel Scott's son, Adam Clayton Powell III, who selflessly opened up his mother's archive; Katherine Dunham's daughter, Marie-Christine Pratt, who shared photos and special memories; the artist Elizabeth Catlett, her son, Francisco Mora-Catlett, who welcomed me into their home, and Jackie Ormes scholar Nancy Goldstein, who fielded a decade of emails. I was indeed blessed to access these folks and their memories, memorabilia, understanding, expertise, and research.

I understand that it is customary and appropriate first to thank the various people and institutions that have assisted in the academic endeavor. This seems important but wrong somehow. My journey could not have been possible without the support of mentors, family, and friends. Two special women deserve singular praise and thanks—my mother, Gene Caldwell, and Dr. Margaret Wade-Lewis. My mother was the true inspiration for my project and is my reason for being. She has been an unparalleled model of strength and resistance. Academic semantics would do poorly in describing her model of Black womanhood. Dr. Wade Lewis, in life and in spirit, provided limitless support and encouragement. She was the truest embodiment of a Black feminist scholar activist I have encountered. I express my gratitude to elders and mentors who saw my potential as greater than I could see it myself, including Dr. Charshee McIntyre, Dr. A. J. Williams-Meyers, Dr. James Turner, Dr. Ronald Walters, and Dr. James E. Smethurst. Though many have passed into the ancestral realm, how lucky I was to have them in my corner from a student to my present.

My circle of sister fam, a.k.a. "the Ladies Salon," supported me through this arduous process: Allia Abdullah Matta, Rani Varghese-Funk, Shelly Perdomo-Ahmed, Hye-Kyung Kang, Cruz Caridad Bueno, Diana Yoon, and Anna Rita Napoleone shared wisdom and love, wiped away tears, read and commented, celebrated successes big and small, and staged needed interventions, all while managing their own careers, raising their own families, and living their own full lives near and far. I will cherish our friendship always. Manuela Picq, beyond being a friend, acted as an eagle-eyed editor and motivator in critical hours of need. Most importantly, I have nothing but gratitude for my husband and family, Deroy Gordon, Nefer, and Samori. I can only strive to shine as bright as these young men do. Each demonstrated love, grace, patience, and boundless faith in my possibilities and capabilities. Lastly, Black women, their ways of being, and the history they create really deserve appreciation and acknowledgement. I hope that this book will make a small contribution to that effort.

The
Fiercest
Kind

Introduction

In 1943, the production of the Columbia Pictures film *The Heat's On* ground to a halt for three days due to an on-set protest by its featured performer, Hazel Scott. In a departure from the script, the assistant director, Robert Saunders, had instructed the makeup department to spray oil and dirt onto the aprons of Black women extras and dancers who were scheduled to appear in a scene in which they would bid farewell to their soldier boyfriends heading off to war. Scott immediately and furiously opposed the stereotypical classist, sexist, and racist implications of sullying the white, pressed aprons worn by these African American women. After all, these characters, like many real-life women, were seeing men off to a war that was purportedly being fought to "preserve democracy and freedom abroad."[1] At the same time, a fight was raging against the racism, discrimination, and segregation being practiced at home. In the scene, Scott herself would not wear an apron but be dressed in full uniform as a member of the Women's Auxiliary Corps. So David Lichine, the film's choreographer, responded with force. He did not understand how "Negro" domestics could be dressed in aprons that "looked too new."[2] A screaming match ensued. Indignant, Lichine asked, "What do you care? You're beautifully dressed. What's it to you?"[3] The choreographer's response was worse than an insult; it blindly separated Scott's experience from the whole of African American women. Such characterizations were one tool of many that were meant to subvert Black Americans' social and political power.

Until now, Scott's relatively recent foray into film had been a welcome and unexpected opportunity. She was just twenty-two years old and had lately become a new addition to the Black specialty acts within Hollywood films of the moment. After being cast in three films in 1942 as "herself," she was signed to an additional three-picture deal with Columbia. Casting executives had sought her out because of her mesmerizing performances as a classically trained boogie-woogie stride pianist. Yet while she understood the power and import of her own character's image in *The Heat Is On*, she was unwilling to participate in a scene that would perpetuate the debasing imagery of Black women. Such stereotypes denied them sophistication, branded them as unclean, and entombed them as perpetual domestic servants. Scott understood the depth and width of this insult: "I insisted that no scene in which I was involved would display Black women wearing dirty aprons to send their men to die for their country." Her one-woman strike would last until "black women in the film were given proper costumes and not depicted seeing their sweethearts off to war wearing dirty Hoover aprons."[4] Hemorrhaging money by the hour, the studio was forced to relent.

Negative portrayals of African American women not only insulted Black womanhood but were also elements of a tense political debate in the years before, during, and after World War II, as African Americans again sought to secure full citizenship from the nation. Hindsight reveals the folly of this objective, for America instead doubled down on racism, racial exclusion, and racial violence, a reaction that continues into our present era. Yet in the moment, Scott could not and would not allow her individual presentation to be isolated from the larger national social and political context.

With her victory, she went further to ensure a more affirming image. The night before the final shoot, she called together the Black female extras, demanding, "Tonight, I want every one of you broads into the hairdressers. Tomorrow morning at nine, I want you on this set, immaculately turned out."[5] She recalled, "Each of them looked at me as if they were taking a last look before the lid closed for the last time."

Admittedly, the final cut of the scene still suffers from the limits of Black popular construction in the white imagination. The setting for the musical number places an upright piano conveniently and ever so oddly on an impoverished street surrounded by dilapidated tenements. Scott, dressed in uniform, begins her boogie-woogie rendition of the army's "Caisson Song" as Black male dancers, dressed in full uniform, march in, toting guns. Their female sweethearts and others in this imagined community eagerly greet the soldiers. The couples dance to Scott's upbeat rendition; and as the tune turns unexpectedly melancholy, the soldiers exit the stage as if on their way to war.

Still, despite the many circumstances beyond her control, Scott's protest had a transformative effect on the scene. The female extras wore clean, chic clothes and carried themselves in ways that engendered the dignity of the African American women whom Black moviegoers would encounter in their home communities. Scott's scene revision contextualized African Americans as part of a modern world, whereas its original conception would have rehashed antiquated Aunt Jemima and mammy tropes as well as blackface minstrelsy. But Scott paid a steep price for her remonstration. Although her star had been ascending quickly, she was soon effectively barred from American film. The troubling episode echoed what many Black women activist artists and performers confronted in oppressive, tightly racialized, and gendered spaces in the United States and abroad, but it also revealed the adroit ways in which they chose to navigate them. In later decades, Scott often relayed this tale in interviews and made it a feature in her unpublished biography. She was clear about its significance, given that many backstage and off-the-page struggles of activist artists and performers, particularly those of Black women, had gone unrecorded and unacknowledged as critical sites of resistance in larger movements for Black freedom and equality. Her stance testifies to African American women's repeated demands that they be treated as worthy and fully human, be it on film, on stage, in the home, or in political arenas.

In this book, I unveil the multi-terrain struggle waged by highly visible African American artists and performers positioned at intersecting forms of popular culture, fine art, and various social and political movements during the mid-twentieth century. These battles were a fundamental component of the larger, longer struggle for African American freedom and equality. The book centers on five Black women at the top of their craft in this period: the dancer Katherine Dunham (1909–2006); the pianist Hazel Scott (1920–81); the graphic artist, painter, and sculptor Elizabeth Catlett (1915–2012); the cartoonist Jackie Ormes (1911–1985); and the singer Lena Horne (1917–2010). From the late 1930s to the mid-1950s, they were among the most popular and nationally known Black women in their respective areas of cultural production: film, television, print media, and fine art. Grouping them links them across imposed boundaries of cultural production (popular culture and fine art), geography (North, South, Midwest, the United States as a whole, and abroad), and movements (the popular front and civil rights) and joins their contributions to those of other Black women activist artists in the 1930s through the early 1960s. Bringing together this extraordinary ensemble allows us to explore the possibilities of resistance within diverse cultural fields of expression for Black women.

Each artist is a giant in her field, yet their lives intersect figuratively and literally throughout the book. Because I have grouped them as activists, I examine their agency and resistance collectively. This has allowed me to better examine their resolute Black feminist and activist practices under America's fickle, ephemeral, and perilous popular public spotlight. Though their cultural locations are distinct, by the mid-1940s they formed a web of highly visible women activist-artists and performers. Certainly, I could have included various other contemporaries, such as the dancer Pearl Primus, the pianist Mary Lou Williams, the actors Fredi Washington and Ruby Dee, and the artist Augusta Savage. All are powerful activist-artists in their own right. Yet Dunham, Scott, Catlett, Ormes, and Horne had a distinct impact on Black women's forms and representation in national popular culture and fine art, due to their often undervalued cultural reach, their early and ongoing lean into activism, their geographical stretch, and their singular legacies.[6]

A CONSIDERATION OF LAYERED RESISTANCE

Layered resistance refers to the multifaceted and multileveled forms of weaponized opposition that Black women employ to survive compound sources of oppression. Across historical eras, Black feminist scholars have delineated, via many terms, the insidious and intricate manifestations of oppression that face Black women.[7] The central threads within these descriptions are the experiences that arise from the interlocking of those oppressions.

In 1949, Claudia Jones penned the now well-known essay "An End to the Neglect of the Problems of the Negro Woman!," published by the National Women's Commission of the Communist Party USA. In it, she condemned the party and the country at large for what she saw as their inattention to and misuse of Black women. Chiding the party for dismissing the enormous value of Black women, her essay brilliantly outlines the contemporary and historical roles they played in the Black family as well as their "militancy" in the labor and civil rights struggles. All the while, "Negro women—as workers, as Negroes, and as women—are the most oppressed stratum of the whole population." Jones showed that the postwar period held "not equality, but degradation and super-exploitation" for Black women.[8] Her essay lays bare the heinous imprint of sex, race, class, and gender-based repression and its endless nexus within the lives of Black women. The result has been enduring abuse, exploitation, mistreatment, lack of access, invisibility, and the abiding need for a layered resistance from Black women en masse.

As Jones described, Black women across the spectrum have engaged in shared tactics against repression. However, the layered resistance of cultural laborers has been articulated in particular ways. In her influential cultural history, *How It Feels to Be Free: Black Women Entertainers and the Civil Rights Movement* (2013), the historian Ruth Feldstein insists that "a fuller understanding of black activism and feminism requires expanding the realm of political activity."[9] Her work dissects the performance and intersecting activism of several Black women entertainers during the civil rights era, including Lena Horne, Nina Simone, and Cicely Tyson. In this book, I work to further expand the definition of resistance by integrating artistic labor with off-stage activism to reveal the deft layered resistance of Dunham, Scott, Catlett, Ormes, and Horne as a Black feminist practice within cultural and political spaces.

I have conceptualized their particular resistance as four separate layers. First, they claimed and manipulated popular and fine-art cultural spaces in the name and likeness of Black women. During the period, this was no small feat. With rare exceptions, performers and artists who garnered national exposure and attention were white and predominantly male. Thus, each woman in this study maneuvered herself into the public spotlight despite a racist and sexist media environment and projected images and representations that were seldom seen nationally and were articulated as political acts. Then, once they gained access to highly coveted cultural spaces, they strategically wielded a measure of agency over the productions, representations, and images they honed, created, and broadcast.

Second, the women combined resistance within performance and/or visual representation with on-the-ground social and political activism. Each contributed to contemporary political and social movements beyond their artistic creations, and all came to understand their creative labor and representations as extensions of social-political movements, including the cultural front and civil rights movements.

Third, they strategically crafted representations of Black womanhood that directly challenged the grotesque stereotypical tropes sprouting from the white imaginary. All tenaciously defied those assigned to African American women, including the acquiescent mammy, the hypersexual Jezebel, and the bullish Sapphire.

Fourth, all chose to live their lives in unorthodox and feminist ways. They took nontraditional approaches to marriage and motherhood (or not), valued their economic and artistic independence from men, exhibited irreverent personal conduct, and thwarted the expectations of ladyhood. All grappled with, engaged in, and were heavily impacted by what the historian E. Frances White calls the "politics of respectability."[10] White argues that African Americans sometimes create overly restrictive narratives and covenants to counter oppressive and racist constructions of blackness. This standard has been particularly and historically applicable to Black womanhood. The activist-artists I study adhered tightly at times to gendered expectations in relation to their lived lives, image, and representation. At other times, they resisted and reimagined them. Like life, their choices could be messy and uncategorizable. I do not suggest that Black women ever strived or were meant to fit into constructions of womanhood as joined to whiteness. Neither do I suggest that all Black women have expressed womanhood in the same way. Still, these particular activist-artists stand apart from the many gendered expectations across race and identity. When employing layered resistance, each engaged in her own distinct form based on her location. Thus, although extraordinary, they were emblematic of African American women's unique approach to resistance.

The lives of African American women easily illuminate the political implications of resistance to all forms of oppression. Historically, they have relied on various forms of layered resistance due to the juncture of multiple oppressions. Among the women under study, the principal form of struggle was cultural resistance. All five constructed a spectrum of affirmative personas, representations, and imaginings to challenge the stereotypes of African American women in mainstream white American cultural spaces. To this they coupled progressive political activism during pivotal eras in the African American fight for freedom and equality, and they garnered a notable reaction from state and federal agencies during the anti-communism/anti-radicalism epoch that followed World War II. Their combined FBI files include more than

2,500 pages of documents, a number that speaks volumes about governmental distrust of their activism.

In this book, I loosely examines links in their personal, artistic, and political lives from 1937 to 1965. I believe that the sweep of their lives and art illustrates their black feminist practice and the layered political, social, and cultural resistance they embodied. The year 1937 marked the start of key events in their careers: Katherine Dunham opened her New York dance and drama school; Hazel Scott established herself as a New York radio attraction; Lena Horne got her start as a film star with the shooting of *The Duke Is Tops*; Jackie Ormes began her entry into popular culture as a cartoonist; and Elizabeth Catlett, after graduating from Howard University's fine arts program, began her work as a sculptor and teacher.

In the following year, the House Un-American Activities Committee (HUAC) was formed. For most Black activists and artists, HUAC was an ominous specter from the late 1930s into the late 1950s. This entity would impede the careers of all five women under study by acting as a main engine for anticommunist, antiradical forces within the U.S. government. For some, it altered the course of their careers. For others, it caused different sorts of irreparable damage. Unfortunately, the transgressions of this committee were as significant to their narrative as their cultural production was.

Yet these women were just five of the many African American women who were transforming the American media, political, and social landscape. At a time when a sudden emphasis on the rhetoric of equality and democracy filled the nation, Black women from all walks of life inserted themselves into the country's consciousness. They co-opted the era's rhetoric of democracy, humanitarianism, and egalitarianism into their own goals of equality. They made unique contributions to this period of the freedom movement.

Americans often view World War II and its aftermath as a watershed moment in its history, one that broke the stranglehold of the Great Depression and propelled the country into decades of sustained economic growth, security, prosperity, and military superiority. For African Americans, however, this period is equally important for its continuously reconstructed counternarrative of African American history. In Black communities, the war's onset prompted a second wave of the Great Migration from the South to the North and West, a demographic shift that had begun before World War I and would help African Americans make marked economic gains. A diversity of groups existed within the varied and intersecting strata of these communities; and some, such as women and the working class, engaged with this historic moment in innovative ways that yielded critical gains for their cohorts. In addition, wartime mobilization led to significant changes in all of African American life, including an eventual shift from rural- to urban-centered communities, increased access to economic advancement and stability, an occupational shift away from agricultural work and domestic service, small gains in education, and a passionate and renewed focus on civil rights protest that would begin the modern civil rights movement.

Black women organized women's political councils and other groups to press for the integration of public facilities such as hospitals, swimming pools, theaters, and restaurants and for the right to pursue collegiate and professional studies. Women like Rosa Parks and Ella Baker, whose names would become synonymous with the modern civil rights movement in the 1950s and 1960s, helped lay its foundation in the World War II era.[11] Playing a major role in this struggle were African American women artists and performers who garnered national exposure during the war and the postwar period.[12] The most visible architects of African American women's images, such as Catlett, Dunham, Horne, Ormes, and Scott, labored in the art, music, and entertainment industries. They understood that, whether they desired it or not, they represented African American womanhood on national and international stages. An abundance of stereotypical images showed African American women as excessively compliant servants, brutal aggressors in domestic and familial relationships, or lascivious romantic partners. These tropes continually undermined their fight for equality. The unsinkable tropes of the mammy, Jezebel, and Sapphire continually undermined Black women's societal standing. Thus, there was an inherent political debate and tension within portrayals of African American women during and after the war.

The representation of Black women was important both within and outside the Black community. Wrongly or rightly, it was a significant societal signpost of Black progress and so-called worthiness for citizenship. Yet the impact of the five women under study was systematically hindered. By the late 1950s, the collective's cultural contributions were waning, due to many forces. The year 1957 marked the last run of Ormes's *Patty-Jo 'n' Ginger* cartoon as well as Scott's exodus to France to evade the blacklisting of politically progressive artists. Still, their work as activists was not done, as evinced by Horne's 1963 activism at the March on Washington. That legacy that absolutely stretches into our modern moment.

THE CANON OF BLACK WOMEN ACTIVIST ARTISTS

Dunham, Scott, Ormes, Catlett, and Horne were part of a milieu of women activist-artists and performers in the 1930s, 1940s, and 1950s whose resistance can be understood through a Black feminist lens. As I have mentioned, actors such as Ruby Dee and Fredi Washington, dancers such as Pearl Primus, and artists such as Augusta Savage were also part of a core group engaged in layered resistance as they battled negative representations and second-class citizenship, a struggle dating back to the nation's colonial days. Over time African American women artists and performers repeatedly fought for the right to create in the arts, to express themselves through dance, and, by the late nineteenth century, to perform on local and national stages. More importantly, they fought to make work that reflected some level of agency over image and Black womanhood. The women under study were exceptional in this regard because of their national and sometimes international visibility. They not only joined contemporaries like Washington and Primus but also added to a lineage of activist Black women artists and performers for whom layered resistance was a fundamental part of their lives.

What does a chronicle of their activist and cultural narratives offer to scholarship on contemporary Black women's activist and cultural labor? First, each of the women in this book is only now beginning to be fully acknowledged within these histories. My study expands on their influence, sometimes via biography but more vitally by probing their layered resistance against repression across genres, geography, and the political landscape. Second, such a study can serve as a lens through which to see their contemporaries, thus adding to a larger conversation about the cultural, social, and political resistance among twentieth-century African American women activists, artists, and performers.

The late 1950s through the 1960s have been closely scrutinized by scholars of African American and women's history, particularly in terms of the civil rights, Black power, and second wave women's movements. This has often obscured the resistance waged by African American women in the first half of the twentieth century. Their activism has been viewed as either the beginning of the civil rights movement or the end of the radical popular and cultural front movements that began in the 1920s Harlem Renaissance. The women I discuss, however, straddled these eras and thus operated in a related but distinct social and political atmosphere. As bridges between adjoining eras and movements, all offered valuable insight into the continuity and substance of Black women's resistance strategies and struggles against an array of oppressions in the twentieth century.

Black women artists and performers have often been left out of histories recounting the many phases of the long movement for Black equality and liberation. Writings about African American artists often confine themselves to cultural histories that focus on artistic production or art-based activism. By subordinating activities off the page, beyond the stage, and outside of the studio, such studies create artificial separations among popular performance, fine art histories, biographical studies, and movement histories. Under these constraints, the layered cultural, personal, and political resistance engaged in by Dunham, Scott, Horne, Ormes, Catlett, and others becomes invisible. But the peculiar and overwhelming conditions oppressing African American women throughout American history require a critical consideration of their resistance from all angles and intersections.

Still, a growing body of literature is developing directly around Black women artists, cultural production, and their social and political resistance. In addition to the aforementioned work by Feldstein, Farah Jasmine Griffin's *Harlem Nocturne: Women Artists and Progressive Politics during World War II* (2013) surveys the art and activism of three women artists during the era: the dancer Pearl Primus, the writer Ann Petry, and the pianist Mary Lou Williams. These three are contemporaries of the five whom I study and extend the notion that Black women labor for freedom in intersecting layers, as their oppression is also layered.

Feminist scholars have also released in-depth studies of some of the women I feature in this book. In *Black Women in Sequence: Re-inking Comics, Graphic Novels, and Anime* (2016), Deborah Elizabeth Whaley examines how Jackie Ormes's comics unexpectedly "place[d] a Black [woman's] voice within the discourse of late World War II leftist culture and the Negroes People's Front."[13] Melanie Anne Herzog has written the comprehensive, art-focused biography *Elizabeth Catlett: An American Artist in Mexico* (2005). Although there are numerous texts devoted to Dunham's tremendous contribution to dance, Joyce Aschenbrenner's *Katherine Dunham: Dancing a Life* (2002) and Joanna Dee Das's *Katherine Dunham: Dance and the African Diaspora* (2017) extensively detail her life as both a dancer and an activist. Karen Chilton's well-researched *Hazel Scott: The Pioneering Journey of a Jazz Pianist, from Café Society to Hollywood to HUAC* (2010) is currently the sole biography on Scott. Such interdisciplinary examinations of Black women's resistance to dominant racial and gender narratives, including popular challenges to tropes and off-stage political activism, may be the best way to accurately unveil the breadth of their contributions.

GEOGRAPHICAL, POLITICAL, AND SOCIAL BACKDROPS

As I have noted, in the first half of the twentieth century, Blacks fled the South looking for better employment and living conditions, an exodus that came to be known as the Great Migration. A significant result was the creation of dense Black urban spaces in the North and Midwest that functioned as bases of concentrated Black social and political power. These regions were not free of oppression by any metric. However, they nonetheless opened unprecedented opportunities for Black political activism, exchange of ideas, transnational exposure, and more liberated cultural production. Without such spaces, the lives and achievements of this core group of women could not have unfolded as they did. Thus, it is important to consider the influence of the places in which they were raised, where they lived or worked, or to which they traveled. Their narratives serve as a bird's-eye view into the communities and social and political spaces that African Americans inhabited around the country and the world during this era: Harlem, Chicago, New Orleans, Los Angeles, Pittsburgh, Paris, Mexico City, Haiti, and more.

The Great Migration gave birth to Black urban neighborhoods and spaces in which African Americans survived and sometimes thrived by inventively hurdling the many obstacles of racism and segregation. It also sometimes flung African Americans into transnational cosmopolitanism. In particular, New York City's Harlem neighborhood became a key geographical space, and both local observers and distant admirers have romanticized it as a utopia, an image that derives from the yearning dreams of immigrants and migrants as well as the privileged conceptions of the neighborhood's elite. Just as European immigrants in the nineteenth century viewed America as a paradise free from economic exploitation and social repression, Black people around the world viewed Harlem in the early twentieth century as an idyllic refuge. In this way, they helped to construct a Black cosmopolitanism that located Black people in the modern world. But Harlem was just the most visible part of a broader transformation that would eventually include similar Black urban spaces in Chicago, Los Angeles, and Pittsburgh, all of which figure prominently in this book.

These spaces provided unique opportunities for African American women. While most still tended to work in servile domestic positions, some began to see possibilities for other types of work (and time away from work) as well as for cultural production and political involvement, none of which had been feasible in the South. Of course, African American women had always been key political workers and community builders in the South since enslavement, and they were indispensable and often primary organizers in Black southern movements during Reconstruction and into the civil rights era. However, the layered politics of resistance in which many Black women artists and performers engaged were not typically possible in southern spaces.

The political engagement of women artists was substantially manifested in their involvement in movements, beginning with the popular and cultural fronts during the 1930s. My study draws heavily on the classic scholarship that has defined these movements. In his landmark work, *The Cultural Front: The Laboring of American Culture in the Twentieth Century* (1996), Michael Denning defines the cultural front as an arm of the popular front, a loose coalition of communist and leftist groups that endorsed radical and democratic ideals within the United States. In his words, it was a "terrain of cultural struggle" consisting of a set of "cultural industries and apparatuses" involving the alliance of radical artists and intellectuals.[14] Bill Mullen's *Popular Fronts: Chicago and African American Cultural Politics, 1935–1946* (2015) and Mary Helen Washington's *The Other Blacklist: The African American Literary and Cultural Left of the 1950s* (2014) position Black folks within these movements. White political radicalization during this era was most often a result of economic collapse, whereas African Americans were constantly engaged in political struggle. Left-leaning political organizations filled a void for disenchanted workers and provided many Americans, across race, with ideas about alternative governmental and social structures. Both the popular and the cultural fronts swept up Black artists, treating them as essential to gaining and maintaining relevance and effectiveness among working people.

The ethnomusicologist Monica Hairston suggests that the popular front was made possible by the cultural production of Black women (for instance, Billie Holiday) and that the movement both celebrated and rendered them invisible.[15] Yet, as I will show, many Black women artists hijacked it for their own uses. Chief among these interventions was their promotion of complex, sophisticated, and visible representations and images of Black women, which they linked to social and political fights for the benefit of Black people as a whole.

PEOPLE, PLACES, AND SPACES

A number of physical places and progressive spaces helped fashion and nurture the Fierce Five as artists, intellectuals, and activists. If one were to map their creative and political labor and their travels and traverses, these spaces and places would reveal themselves to be critical midcentury hubs of Black progressives and radicals. The women often shared membership in local, national, and international organizations such as the Civil Rights Congress, the NAACP, and the National Negro Congress. Some were acquainted with or belonged to the Communist Party; for as the Black feminist historian Dayo Gore attests, "the growing emphasis on culture allowed the CP to count among its supporters or 'fellow travelers' . . . a plethora of Black women cultural workers."[16] At times, the women shared tangible space; at others, they entered a space just as another had left. Some, like Hazel Scott and Lena Horne, became dear friends. In fact, Horne's impression of Scott while working together at New York's Café Society is the inspiration for this book's title: Horne remarked that Scott had the "fiercest sort of racial pride."[17] The café was a far-left venue and the city's only formally integrated club. Dunham, Scott, and Horne were all performers there simultaneously, and Catlett was a regular patron during her time in Harlem. Yet others in the web of women, such as Ormes and Catlett, only knew of one another, though ironically both were very involved with Chicago's historic South Side Community Arts Center.

Notable individuals made repeat appearances across their lives. Paul Robeson, an actor and humanitarian, had a personal connection to almost all of the women. He had been mentored as a boy by Cora Calhoun Horne, Lena Horne's grandmother, and later became a friend and valued advisor of both Horne and Scott. Catlett was also acquainted with Robeson, who served on the board of directors of the George Washington Carver School, where she worked. Dunham and Catlett shared a relative, the artist Frances Dunham Catlett. The widow of Dunham's brother, Albert, Frances later married one of Catlett's uncles.[18] This familial link demonstrates how activist-artists moved in overlapping circles, building friendships, connections, and deeper relationships. Ormes was a good friend of the writer, composer, and activist Shirley Graham Du Bois. The writer Langston Hughes was also a personal friend as well as a colleague at the *Chicago Defender*. Hughes was Catlett's neighbor while she lived in Harlem and was also friendly with Scott and Dunham. Ormes hobnobbed with innumerable intellectuals, artists, and celebrities at Chicago's Sutherland Hotel, a go-to spot for the "it" crowd. She lived on the premises with her husband, Earl Ormes, who was the manager. Other luminaries, such as the civil rights leader Medgar Evers, the actor Harry Belafonte, and the uncategorizable firebrand Gloria Richardson also made appearances in the women's lives. Their interlaced narratives establish how closely knit the circle of Black activists, leaders, artists, celebrities, and intellectuals truly was in the 1940s and 1950s and how their overlapping efforts shifted Black life.

A NOTE ON RESEARCH AND METHODOLOGY

Readers will notice that the chapters, like the five women they outline, do not follow any one formula. For some of the women, I use specific life epochs or particular cultural productions to illustrate their expressions of layered resistance. For others, I lean into their extraordinary biographies. This is purposeful. Each woman has important tales to tell, though not in the same way. My delineation is not meant to set boundaries on the Fierce Five's resistance or that of other Black women.

This book represents fifteen years of engaged research. During that time, I interrogated the artists' life stories and cultural production, studying archives, first-person interviews, newspapers, biographies, cultural and political histories, FBI files, and a spectrum of Black, feminist, and political scholarship. Among the archives, I consulted the Schomburg Center for Research in Black Culture in New York City, the Katherine Dunham Papers (1906–2009) at Southern Illinois University, and the DuSable Black History Museum in Chicago. At the time of my research, Hazel Scott's substantial archive was privately held by her son, Adam Clayton Powell III, but has since been moved to the Library of Congress. In the case of Ormes, much of her political and artistic record is contained in her comics, which I have treated as crucial archival material. During this long process, I have gathered a personal collection of more than 4,000 documents, excluding expansive FBI files, dedicated to these five women.

I had the opportunity to conduct three first-person interviews. Two were immediate relatives: Katherine Dunham's daughter, Marie-Christine Pratt; and Hazel Scott's son, Adam Clayton Powell III. One was the artist herself: Elizabeth Catlett. All shared powerful statements about work and resistance, making it clear to me that each woman deserves a dedicated book. Powell recalled Scott's management of motherhood, her hectic performance schedule, and how she flew home on weekends to be present for him. Despite her advanced age, Catlett evinced a fiery and unapologetic dedication to Black women's representation, and her intrigue with their image remained evident during our hours-long conversation. At the close of our interview—sadly, one of her last—she reached out to touch my hair, which was twisted in long locs. She asked, "Is that all your hair?" I assured her it was. I realized that as I had been prodding her with my questions, she had been taking me in through her keen Black feminist artist's gaze. As she palmed one of my locs, I could see her deliberate on how to re-create them in sculpture or on canvas. The artist was observing her favorite subject: the Black woman.

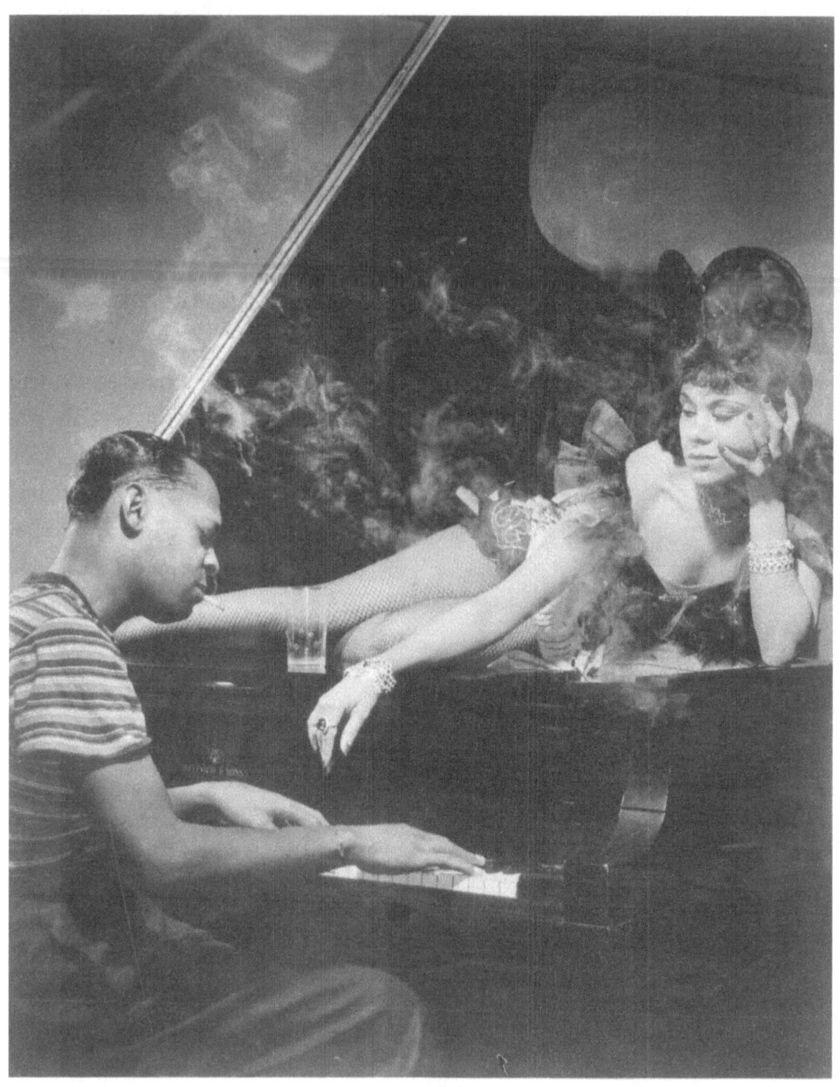

FIGURE 1. Katherine Dunham sizzles in *Le Jazz Hot*, c. 1940s. Courtesy of Special Collections Research Center, Morris Library, Southern Illinois University, Carbondale.

"Whole New Vistas Were Opening"

Katherine Dunham, Resistance, and Black Modern Dance

On March 7, 1937, with the help of fellow dancers Edna Guy and Alison Burroughs, the Chicago-based Katherine Dunham Dance Company premiered before a New York audience.[1] Recognizing that New York was a crucial market for nationwide touring and legitimacy within the world of dance, Dunham had been wanting to broaden her troupe's access to concert venues so had corresponded with Guy, Burroughs, and concert organizers and had agreed to perform.[2] Titled "The Negro Dance Evening," it was held at the Theresa Kaufman Theater at the 92nd Street Young Men's Hebrew Association, at that time a popular venue for white modern dance concerts. This performance, however, was meant to showcase the emerging soloists, troupes, and choreographers of cutting-edge Black dance.[3]

Expectations for immediate earnings were slim. Guy wrote to Dunham, "None of us will get big money out of this concert. The expenses are too high, and the income too small, even if we sell every ticket." However, "the future holds great rewards for us all if we are willing to make some small sacrifice at the beginning." The program included a mix of traditional and modern styles. Guy asked for some "outstanding traditional Haitian dances, about six, or a suite of Haitian dances for the historical part of the program" and "one modern dance of yours for the modern part of the program."[4] The night included a dance performance by Clarence Yates, the director of the Works Progress Administration's Negro Dance Unit, who choreographed and danced *Songs of Protest* and *Because I Am a Nigger*. Burroughs performed *Scottsboro*. Guy brought down the house with an original performance titled *Spirituals*.

The organizers wanted the lineup to encompass a range of Black dance forms that would challenge the demoralizing misrepresentations of Black dance that had limited artistic creativity and denied Black contributions. The program traced a historical narrative, beginning with dances from the African continent, then illustrating the evolution of Black dance in the Caribbean, and ending with popular dance in America's Black urban and rural centers. Each act hoped to counter the discriminatory perception of Black dance as the natural expression of a "dance-inclined" race and instead reveal its place within the realm of high artistic expression.[5] As a result, the emphasis was on Black modernists. Modern dance had come into vogue in the late 1920s and was changing the rigid landscape of dance by allowing much more freedom in movement and themes than was permissible in traditional forms such as ballet. Yet while expression in this form was relatively unrestricted, participation was not: white women dominated and controlled the medium as dancers and choreographers, making it yet another racially segregated space for Black folks. According to the dance historian Julia Foulkes, "if white women found modern dance a means by which to work within modernism and refute conventional images of femininity, African American men and women had less success working around modernism's fundamental rift between high and low culture, which mirrored and reinforced social experiences of racial discrimination."[6] Reflecting the dominant view of the rest of American society, the dance community understood Black culture as exclusively based on a vernacular expression of "low culture" that lacked actual artistic value. This delegitimization of Black dancers as artists led to their exclusion from newly formed modern dance troupes.

Americans linked Black dance, particularly that of women dancers, solely to popular musical entertainment rather than to prestigious forms of artistic production. Still, staged Black dance did enjoy brief popularity in the 1920s during the Harlem Renaissance. Celebrated performers and dancers such as Nina Mae McKinney, Josephine Baker, Bill "Bojangles" Robinson, and Florence Mills appeared in various Broadway revues during the decade. At least nine productions were staged with all-Black casts.[7] Though Black dance formed the foundation of American popular dance during this era, it was not seen as a complex and nuanced art form until much later in the century. Regardless of their phenomenal talents as dancers and choreographers, Black performers were not viewed as contributors to the development of dance as an art form and even today have not received full acknowledgment of their imprint on American dance. In the United States, the work of the best Black dancers was confined to well-choreographed popular dance, and the artists were treated as progenitors of passing novelties. By the late 1930s, the national conception of African American women as professional dancers was dominated by images of light-skinned chorus girls such as those at the segregated Cotton Club in Harlem. Dunham, light in hue herself, and other Black women dancers of all kinds were aware that they were inheriting judgments based on a paternalistic white Victorian morality.

Edna Guy's experience with discrimination was a prime motivation for staging the 92nd Street Y event. As a teenager, she had studied for several years with the lauded modern dance innovator Ruth St. Denis. But although she was one of St. Denis's best students, Guy was unable to tour or dance at public concerts with the school's troupe because she was Black. Fed up with her teacher and, more generally, with the racial prejudice in dance schools and companies, she was happy to help organize the performance. She and her co-organizers had long recognized that they needed to create their own opportunities to stage Black concert dance. In 1931, they had participated in an event titled "The First Negro Dance Recital in America," which the condescending white press referred to as "the outstanding novelty of the dance season." One reporter snarked that there were "eighteen dancers, the majority of them husky young athletes, attempting to move with something approaching primitive vigor."[8] These were the racist notions with which Black dancers had to contend. The 92nd Street Y performance was part of a long effort to expose the beauty and brilliance of Black dancers on the concert stage, despite formidable odds.[9]

The inequity and suppression of Black artists in modern dance were transparently evident in the 1920s correspondence between Guy and St. Denis. Guy wrote, "My dearest Miss Ruth, each day I get up with wild hope. I visit this office and that. I dance before this man and that one, and even though they like my work, someone else not half as good gets the call." She deduced, "They win because of their light skin and flashing eyes" and asked, "Brown skin is as lovely to look upon as light skin, isn't it?"[10]

St. Denis responded, "Edna dear, it seems wise to me that you do not attempt for a moment to get into the cheap shows here in town. There are thousands of young, attractive, very pretty colored girls who are storming the stage doors of those productions. You could neither stand the life that those girls live, nor are you pretty enough or light enough in color.[11] St. Denis's belittlement conveyed both racism and colorism, making difficult to discern whom she was denigrating more: Guy or other Black women dancers. The exchange reflects the dominant white sentiments expressed toward Black women dancers; they were seen as inelegant, inexpert, lacking in virtue, and regulated by color and skin tone.

Like African American women before them, Guy, Burroughs, and Dunham practiced self-definition as a tool of resistance, staging their own performances and working to upend the false narrative of Black women in and through dance. Thus, the 1937 performance was a tremendous break for Dunham and her dancers. However, the troupe nearly missed the show. Forced to drive for fifteen hours through a terrible snowstorm, they arrived in New York just in time to change into their costumes and perform the planned Haitian "ceremonial dances" and a modern ballet. While the Chicago dancers did not present the standout performance at the recital—that honor went to Guy—they were well received by a demanding and savvy New York audience. At the show's close, the company was invited to a house party thrown by a new acquaintance, the dancer Archie Savage, who would eventually become Dunham's performance partner. In celebration, the dancers partied through the night, falling asleep anywhere they could—sofa, floor, even an empty bathtub—before heading back to Chicago the next morning.[12]

The show provided Dunham with badly needed exposure and, eventually, funding. It marked the beginning of her professional career in Black dance, a field in which she would become a transformational force. By combining African, Caribbean folk, European ballet, and Black popular dance with American modern dance, she would create a hybrid space for Black dance centered on Black creativity, African-derived forms, and Black innovation. Reflecting on her career, Dunham later said that she had sought to "develop a technique that will be as important to the white man as the Negro. To attain a status in the dance world . . . and take our dance out of the burlesque—to make of it a more dignified art."[13] Her goal of taking Black dance "out of the burlesque" was a reaction to the strict identification of Black dance with low culture, sexual expression, lack of sophistication, and the objectification of Black women's bodies. By attaching modern conceptions of Black dance to the bodies of African American women, Dunham was dignifying all Black dance, whether it was performed by chorus girls, social dancers, or burlesque artists. Her layered resistance challenged the fraught landscapes of American dance, which clung to racial binaries and relied on eugenics in conceptions of artistic expression.

Part of what distinguished Dunham from other modern dance innovators was her long career, which added to her national impact and visibility. Her troupe toured in some form or another from 1937 to 1956, giving hundreds of stage performances worldwide. They remain the longest-touring unsubsidized American dance company and were the longest-touring Black concert dance company until Alvin Ailey emerged in 1958.[14] This achievement granted them unprecedented public exposure in the world of Black concert dance. Ultimately, Dunham redefined that genre and the national representation of African American women in dance, even as she fought numerous battles against racism, sexism, and Jim Crow. As an activist-artist and an innovator in her field, she was truly a transnational figure and had the most international exposure of any of the five women under study in this book.[15] Her breakout 1937 performance was the culmination of a longer journey yet only the beginning of a lifelong vocation that uncompromisingly combined dance and activism on and off the concert stage.

BEGINNINGS: JOLIET TO CHICAGO

Born in 1909, Katherine Dunham was raised in Joliet, Illinois, a suburb of Chicago. In the memoir of her childhood, *A Touch of Innocence*, she disassociated herself from the early pain and abuse in her youth by writing about herself in the third person. She later told an interviewer, "It was too close to me, I was too tender, to be objective."[16] In the memoir's introductory note, she spoke of family upheaval as a reason for writing the book: "Perhaps from their confused lives may come something that will serve as guidance to someone else."[17] Even by the standards of the time, Dunham's father was extremely strict and abusive, and his approach to fatherhood alienated his family. Remarks by her brother, Albert Dunham Jr., hint at the conditions in their home. The two siblings were exceptionally close; and after fleeing the house after his high school graduation, he sent a letter to Dunham and his stepmother: "You know how hard it is to live with a person who 'treats 'em rough.'" The letter includes a separate postscript to his father: "You have told me many times to clear out. We can't get along together—so long!"[18]

Dunham's unyielding drive was apparent early on, regardless of the strife in her household. Even in high school, her interest in dance was linked to an uncanny ability to claim and manipulate public space. After convincing her conservative church to allow her to stage a cabaret-themed fundraiser, she took charge, showcasing her enthusiasm for secular jazz and blues dancing and acting as writer, director, and star attraction. After the show, many of the church elders expressed disapproval, but their discomfort seemed to be tempered by the $32 she'd raised for the church coffers. The fundraiser would conclude her staged dance career in Joliet.[19]

For some in the community, the show earned Dunham the reputation as a "wild" girl, but she was undeterred from her focus on dance.[20] After finishing high school in 1928, she followed her brother to Chicago, which by now had a national reputation for its rich artistic and intellectual communities. The city was considered by many "the preeminent site of African-American activism, exchange, and affiliation with the organized Left in America in mid-century."[21] During the late 1920s and 1930s, Dunham would spend time with artistic and intellectual luminaries such as the writers Frank Yerby, Richard Wright, Langston Hughes, Gwendolyn Brooks, and Margaret Walker; the artists Charles Sebree and Charles White; the musician W. C. Handy; the intellectuals St. Clair Drake and Charles Johnson; and the actors Rose McClendon, Canada Lee, and Ruth Attaway. Several of this radical elite, among them Hughes, Sebree, and Attaway, became lifelong friends and helped her form and articulate her political consciousness. She recalled that, during this early period in Chicago, "injustice of man to man became a dominant theme in my life."[22]

Like other American urban communities, Chicago during this period played a role in extending and constructing what Alain Locke, the midwife of the Harlem Renaissance, called "the New Negro Movement." In her reminiscences, Dunham clearly identified with that movement:

> We took so much for granted, but we worked hard for our freedom. . . . We were the prime motivators of the "New Negro" rage. It was more than a vogue. In Chicago, we were inundated by media waves—films and lectures, and photographs from Paris and New York. Picasso and the Cubists, Gershwin and Handy, Nancy Cunard and Noble Sissle—even without realizing it, we were touched by them. More than that, we felt *ourselves* to be the New Negro.[23]

Nonetheless, her approach to thought and resistance can be better understood as a combination of New Negro ideas and cultural front notions that grew out of labor-oriented radicalism in Chicago in the 1930s. Both the labor movement and the Communist Party were affiliated with sundry progressive groups, and throughout her long career Dunham was affiliated with several of these left-leaning organizations and institutions. For example, within a few years, she became a key choreographer for the Federal Theater Project and collaborated with the International Garment Workers Union.[24] But she often had mixed feelings about the efforts of such organizations, describing their attempts at interracialism as "heavy-handed" and sometimes involving "deception and hypocrisy."[25] Nevertheless, communist and socialist forces remained an important and ongoing progressive presence.

The excitement and activity of the radical left did not improve the lives and upward mobility of most Black Chicagoans, who in those years were concentrated on the city's South Side. Juxtaposed alongside the lively arts and letters scene were crumbling neighborhoods vacated by Whites and left for the African Americans who were steadily fleeing the South. Dunham had spent a few years of her childhood living with her aunt in Chicago so had long been familiar with this pattern. As Richard Wright wrote, "Chicago is the city from which the most incisive and radical Negro thought has come; there is an open and raw beauty about that city that seems either to kill or endow one with the spirit of life."[26]

Dunham's brother Albert, who was studying philosophy at the University of Chicago, helped her considerably in her transition to adult life in Chicago. His connections enabled her to take a civil service test, which led to a job at a library during her early years in the city. He also helped her pursue her true passion. He had recently co-founded the Cube Theater Club, an unusual interracial venture dedicated to "all forms of modern art." The theater became an important space for Dunham to experiment artistically.[27] She was hoping to parlay her small amount of dance experience in high school into an avenue for generating income and to build some kind of career. Striving to make up for what she saw as precious lost time, she took modern dance and ballet classes and performed on stage at the Cube. In 1931, she debuted at the Chicago Beaux Arts Ball, appearing in *A Negro Rhapsody*. Acting on a suggestion from one of her friends, she began teaching dance to earn extra money and, in time, moved into a poorly renovated stable that doubled as her studio.

The year 1934 was pivotal for Dunham, marking the moment when Mark Turbyfill and Ruth Page, dancers and choreographers at the Chicago Opera, decided to back her new enterprise in dance. Friendships such as these opened even more opportunities. For instance, she was asked to arrange the "Negro Dance" portion of the Chicago World's Fair. Soon Dunham would also be a student of anthropology in the newly formed department of anthropology at the University of Chicago. It was liberal and unorthodox by contemporaneous standards. Another anthropologist later described the department as "holistic, in tune with the interdisciplinary atmosphere at the university. Liberal humanism was the philosophy, and racial equality and cultural relativity were its first principles."[28] Dunham's personal papers include undergraduate report cards indicating that she often earned straight *As*.[29]

She would integrate the principles she learned in these studies into her social and political thought, eventually developing a field that she called dance anthropology, which intersected the disciplines as a method for studying and understanding human communities. Yet despite her earnest studies, her extracurricular participation in performances with the Cube were what allowed her to conduct the groundbreaking fieldwork for which she would become famous.[30]

For Black women in the 1930s, watching Dunham transform from small-town girl to college student in a soon-to-be-renowned department at a prestigious school was like witnessing a shooting star. Miraculously, this academic success took place alongside her burgeoning dance career, which she continued to pursue passionately while working and studying. In time, these parallel pursuits became crafted elements of her layered resistance. Her pursuit of education, the arts as a vocation, and a future shaped by her own desires were outrageous goals for any woman in this time, especially a Black woman. Dunham resisted the expected and defied racial and gendered boundaries.

FIELDWORK, SELF-DISCOVERY, BLACKNESS, AND TRANSNATIONALISM

In 1935, Dunham had an opportunity to advance her dance anthropology fieldwork, one that also served as an early demonstration of her mastery in gaining access to and manipulating public space. That year the board of the Rosenwald Fund, which often provided fellowships to Black artists and scholars, was so impressed with her work that it asked her to give a research proposal presentation.[31] Conflicting narratives exist about this interview. Some claim that she stripped off her street clothes to reveal her costume beneath and asked the committee if she could dance her objectives rather than verbalize them. In later recollections, Dunham herself dismissed this version, saying that she would have been much too modest to engage in such behavior and was instead focused on earning the committee members' respect and esteem. She insisted that the interview had consisted of a conversation and an academic presentation.[32] But the apocryphal story adds to her mystique.

The board's response was overwhelming. They agreed to fund her project; and after a few months of intense training with the famed anthropologist Melville Herskovits (also a great mentor), Dunham was on her way to the Caribbean to undertake fieldwork. Her research took her first to Jamaica to study in Accompong, a Jamaican maroon settlement, and then briefly to Haiti, whose people, she believed, retained a great number of African-influenced traditional dances. She continued on to Martinique and Trinidad before returning to Haiti for a nine-month sojourn.[33] Dunham focused on African influences because she felt they had been widely devalued on the world stage. This fieldwork became part of what would become a lifelong goal to foster greater reverence for Africa's indigenous cultures and dance as well as the cultures and people that comprise its diaspora. She was concerned that many African Americans had rejected their African ancestry and that others, such as the New Negro cultural nationalists Countee Cullen and Aaron Douglass, had romanticized it. She wished to recognize it in its multifaceted dimensionality. Her success in this endeavor would be her intellectual and professional legacy.

Dunham fused Black modernity with traditional African culture via dance. Her ethnographic work during her initial Caribbean research trips helped change understandings of the relationship between African Americans and Africa and their identification with a global Black community. She located Black women in particular as the locus of this dance heritage and its modern evolution. As a student of Herskovits, her fieldwork emphasized the value of African retention in anthropological work within the Black diaspora. What we might now see as her Black feminist understanding of the world gave her an advantage. Several qualities set Dunham apart from other ethnographers, who were traditionally white and male, and they helped her avoid the conventionally exploitative nature of anthropological fieldwork. For example, she was herself a member of the African diaspora that she was studying. She brought an appreciation for African history and culture forged by the New

Negro cultural nationalists with whom she had spent time in Chicago. She was very aware of her membership in a global Black community governed by systems of segregation, apartheid, and colonialism.

Dunham later explained, "A good field technique, I found, was to establish the relationship between my ancestors and theirs. They thought of me as an American, not as a Negro, until I talked to them about our common African ancestors. Then they accepted me."[34] In Jamaica, this approach had a significant impact on the maroons, who referred to Dunham as "one of the lost people of 'Nan Guinea' and revealed their secrets to her so that she could inform her people."[35] Although she was a foreigner in many aspects, they recognized her common ancestry. Her ability as a dancer further connected her with individuals and communities, despite her social and cultural distance.

Dunham's gender was both a hindrance and a benefit in her research. She was a woman entering traditional spaces in which gender played a key role and in which women possessed knowledge of the most sacred dances and rituals. Yet the repressive narrative of gender roles sometimes limited her access to study. She described how the Haitian elite, for instance, adhered firmly to nineteenth-century French society's gender roles. Women were discouraged from participating in public meetings, political events, or even leaving their homes.[36] So Dunham had to navigate carefully when doing fieldwork among the peasantry while simultaneously interacting with the elite. She applied her political savvy to the problem. In Haiti, she creatively negotiated a system of barriers that differed from the more familiar rigidity of the Black-white binary in the United States. Haitian society's multipart caste system, based on class and complexion, had developed from a history of exploitation, capitalism, and slavery that had divided a small mulatto upper class (lighter in skin tone and descended from French and African parentage) from the darker-skinned, largely impoverished peasant majority descended from the enslaved population.

In this system, Dunham was identified in Haitian terms as mulatto, but she found ways to circumvent and distance herself from the island's rigid class narrative. Herskovits had provided her with several letters of introduction to facilitate her research, and she used these carefully so as not to attach herself to the privileged class. Likewise, she did not introduce herself to the president of Haiti, Stenio Vincent, until she was nearing the end of her field research.[37] She intentionally kept company with a cross-section of Haitian society. She was alternately in the company of black peasants, dark-skinned friends who were upper class according to wealth, and, most perplexingly, a poor white mechanic. Reflecting on her place in Haitian society, Dunham confessed, "I seemed to have wavered or catapulted from mulatto to black, elite to peasant, intellectual to bohemian, in to out, up to down, and tried hard to keep out of trouble but did not succeed."[38]

Dunham focused on studying traditional art forms, but Haitian high society, including its intellectuals, looked down on the tradition of Vodun and were anxious to expunge this "backward" practice from Haitian society to advance the image of a modern and cosmopolitan nation. So she found ways to work around these bourgeois preferences. Recognizing that the elite controlled Haiti's political, economic, and social landscape, she appealed to their own biases. She recalled, "I had a very amusing experience when I first went to the islands, for the Urban society leaders questioned my desire for native research, and needing the moral backing of these leaders, I gave a concert for them and included only numbers which were traditional ballet or aesthetic interpretations. They loved it, and I was given a free hand thereafter to search out my primitives."[39] Dunham no doubt recognized the irony of the situation: she could only achieve access to traditional African dance in Haiti by focusing on European styles that proved her seriousness as a researcher.

Nevertheless, her hard-won access helped establish her as both an anthropological innovator and an envoy for traditional African dance in the United States. Her respect for the culture and her refusal to engage in class inequities with the subjects of her study helped her gain unprecedented knowledge of Haitian peasant society. Immersing herself fully, she became a Vodun initiate and mastered dozens of traditional sacred and secular dances.[40] Via recordings, photographs, and film, she gathered extensive documentation of Haitian, Jamaican, and Martinique dance forms. Photographs of Dunham in the Caribbean reveal what must have seemed like a fantastic oddity at that time—a fair-skinned African American woman anthropologist, sleeves rolled up, at work in a field with other Black women. One can only imagine the impact of such an image on a young African American girl in the mid-1930s, given its enduring power today.[41]

Dunham's research revealed the overlapping edges of African retention across transnational contexts. It formed the understructure of many of her contributions to Black dance and spawned the powerful representations of Black women in her artistic renderings on stage. The levels of resistance are notable: she accessed education that was out of reach of most people, across race and gender; gained the ability to go abroad; conducted anthropological fieldwork; and eventually melded this work into a staged form of sociopolitical performance that contested white and male supremacy.

THE RETURN

Returning to the United States in 1936, Dunham began refining diasporic dance performance but faced the harsh reality of a Chicago still deep in an economic depression. It was impossible for her to immediately turn to Black concert dance as a full-time career or to focus on sharing her dance anthropology research with audiences. Instead, along with the rest of America, she had to concentrate on meeting her basic needs for food and housing. She also needed to sort out several unresolved issues in her life. In 1933, her beloved brother had moved to Boston with Frances Taylor, her best friend and roommate.[42] And Dunham had a husband of her own, Jordis McCoo, to deal with. Years earlier she had hastily married McCoo. As she later said, "to be perfectly honest, I believe I married out of loneliness. . . . [But] when I returned to Chicago from the Caribbean, nothing [in the relationship] had changed, so he gallantly agreed to a divorce."[43] McCoo was a fellow dancer who held a steady job as a postal clerk, and the two remained friends and kept in regular contact through various dancing engagements. But unlike most women of her time, Dunham did not connect her fulfillment to marriage or motherhood. Both would come in time. For the present, she was fixated on dance.

Dunham also had to deliberate on her academic future. Still officially enrolled as an undergraduate at the University of Chicago, she decided to restart her academic studies and earn her anthropology degree. After graduating, she was awarded a grant from the Guggenheim Foundation that would cover tuition for a master's degree at the university. Dunham attended classes in the morning. In the afternoons, she resumed work at the Chicago Public Library, took on odd jobs, and taught classes to make ends meet. She made very little money and later recalled the practical joys of finding inexpensive places to eat, securing credit for a winter coat, and getting dresses from her father's now-defunct dry-cleaning business.[44] And she remained committed to Black dance. In this, she reflected the fortitude and dedication of so many Black artists during the early development of formal Black arts and entertainment. Even when their salaries were low or nonexistent, passion for their art was high.

Success came relatively late for Dunham. She was twenty-eight years old when she gathered a company for the 1937 trip to participate in Edna Guy's New York recital. At her age many experienced dancers were at the height or on the downward slope of their careers. Age mattered particularly for African American women because only very young women typically fit the accepted popular image of a Black female dancer. Lena Horne, for instance, was a mere sixteen when she began dancing at the Cotton Club. Dunham's modern dance contemporaries, such as Pearl Primus, were also much younger than she was.

Certainly, Dunham was attempting to build a life around professional dance. She had founded two dance groups, opened a dance school for youth, performed many times on the stage, and worked as an organizer for the 1933 World's Fair. She had juggled being a full-time student at the University of Chicago with being a full-time dancer and dance instructor. However, the first significant break in her dance career came after the New York recital, when, in 1938, she was hired as a dance director for the Federal Theatre Project (FTP) as well as for the Federal Writers Project. Both units were associated with the Works Progress Administration's (WPA) New Deal arts enterprises.

Dunham put together a ballet script titled *L'Ag'Ya* for the FTP, which was accepted as part of a larger program that included three other works by white choreographers and had the overarching title *Ballet Fedre*. *L'Ag'Ya* illustrated Dunham's aptitude with Afro-European dance fusion, her inclusive approach to composing her troupe, and her skill in integrating the historical realities of the Black experience into her work. The dance's narrative was based on "a tragic love triangle" in a village in late eighteenth-century Martinique, in which the romance between Loulouse and Alcide is thwarted by the ill-intentioned Julot. Although Dunham conceived of *L'Ag'Ya* as a modern dance ballet, it was grounded in Martinique's ag'ya style, a fighting dance similar to African-linked dances like capoeira. The work displayed the range of Dunham's talents as writer, choreographer, director, and star. While it did incorporate European dance styles such as the French-based beguine and mazouk, the influence of African vernacular culture was unmistakable. For example, Dunham honored Martinican folk belief in the Vodun when she chose to have Julot ask the Zombie King for a love charm with which to woo Alcide. Then, at the end of the ballet, Julot murders Loulouse during the ag'ya. The dance scholar Joanna Dee Das has described *L'Ag'Ya* as emblematic of Dunham's "politics of diaspora": that is, the lived connection across communities of African origin that "involves the conscious refashioning of existing cultural forms and . . . the creation of new ones."[45]

The variety of dancers in Dunham's *L'Ag'Ya* troupe was also notable. While the WPA and the FTP were founded with the specific goal of putting people to work during the Depression, Dunham consciously incorporated Black dancers from all walks of life. She recruited not only professional and student dancers but also people "from off the street," such as cooks, typists, maids, and chauffeurs. It took her two weeks of auditioning before she could find a "full complement of fifty." She recalled, "I had always wanted to work with the people—that is, proletariat or lumpen, and this was a golden opportunity."[46] In her view, they "gave the stage the dimension of reality which made the folk myths believable."[47] By choosing this approach to creating a troupe, Dunham linked her onstage work with her offstage political activism and her popular front ideals.

The *L'Ag'Ya* was one of several original, radical performances that Dunham produced through the FTP, and it is now seen as her first dance anthropology production.[48] Her anthropological gaze was embedded in *L'Ag'Ya*, as was her subtle critique of colonialism. The scholar and dancer Vèvè Clark explains: "Dunham's choreography reflects social oppositions existing simultaneously and paradoxically in a society governed at a distance from France and further controlled economically and socially . . . by former plantation families. . . . Dance of the majority population demonstrates the contradictions of New World acculturation."[49] Thus, *L'Ag'Ya* served many purposes and revealed several layers of resistance. Its main objective, as arranged through the WPA, was to employ dozens of Black workers. But Dunham also used it as a platform for considering the impact of oppression and colonialism on the Martinican population and the wider diaspora. Further, she promulgated the richness and cultural value of an African diasporic aesthetic while resisting dominant and degrading Black female imagery and representation. She did this by featuring complex female characters who did not evoke the damaging tropes of mammy or Jezebel.

In *L'Ag'Ya*, Dunham also deliberately used dancers, particularly women, with a range of skin colors and phenotypes. Though some of this variation was happenstance, given her motley collection of out-of-work recruits, it also reflected her conscious rejection of color caste in the staging of Black dance. Any theater- or clubgoer in the mid-1930s would have encountered light-skinned female dancers in almost all Black dance performances, but throughout her career Dunham's troupes featured skin colors that reflected a larger global diversity. She said:

> When I was forming the company, from about 1938 on, the ideal black dancer was light-skinned, somebody who danced at one of the famous whites-only nightclubs, like the Cotton Club. But that was not my ideal. My company was what you might call a "Third World Company" from the beginning. We had Cubans, West Indians, and Latin Americans, and their complexion didn't matter. What mattered was their talent.[50]

Her dancers for *L'Ag'Ya* included artists with whom she had worked before conducting fieldwork in the Caribbean along with newer recruits. The first staging featured the female dancers Carmencita Romero, Lucille Ellis, Patty Bee Yancey, and Roberta McLauren and the male dancers Jordis McCoo and Woody Wilson. Together, they represented African body types in numerous permutations as well as a cross-section of complexions in the global Black community. Not everyone was comfortable with this. But according to her daughter, Marie-Christine Dunham Pratt, "she always took her stance. It was her company."[51]

This diversity, combined with African influences, an intriguing narrative, gorgeous costumes, an outstanding set, innovative choreography, and the troupe's brilliant dancing, inspired both pride and awe in African American audiences. The national Black press covered it extensively. A reporter for the *Chicago Defender* declared, "L'Ag'Ya . . . is the most thrilling theatrical experience one has ever witnessed of Race members, not barring the famous opera, 'Porgy.' Color, drama, enchantment, and superb dancing all contributed to the uproarious bravoes that the audience poured in applause. . . . [It] was directed by Miss Dunham, who dances the lead role with finesse and understanding of the authentic Caribbean Dances."[52] A writer for the *Philadelphia Tribune* noted that Dunham and her company "presented . . . *L'Ag'Ya* with such fire and realism [that] the dancers literally stopped the show and were given an ovation by the overflow crowd."[53] A reviewer for the *Pittsburgh Courier* pointed out that "if one watches closely, one will detect a step or two popular in our American jazz world."[54] *Ballet Fedre* ran for six weeks before ending its triumphant run, and *L'Ag'Ya* became a permanent part of the Dunham repertoire.

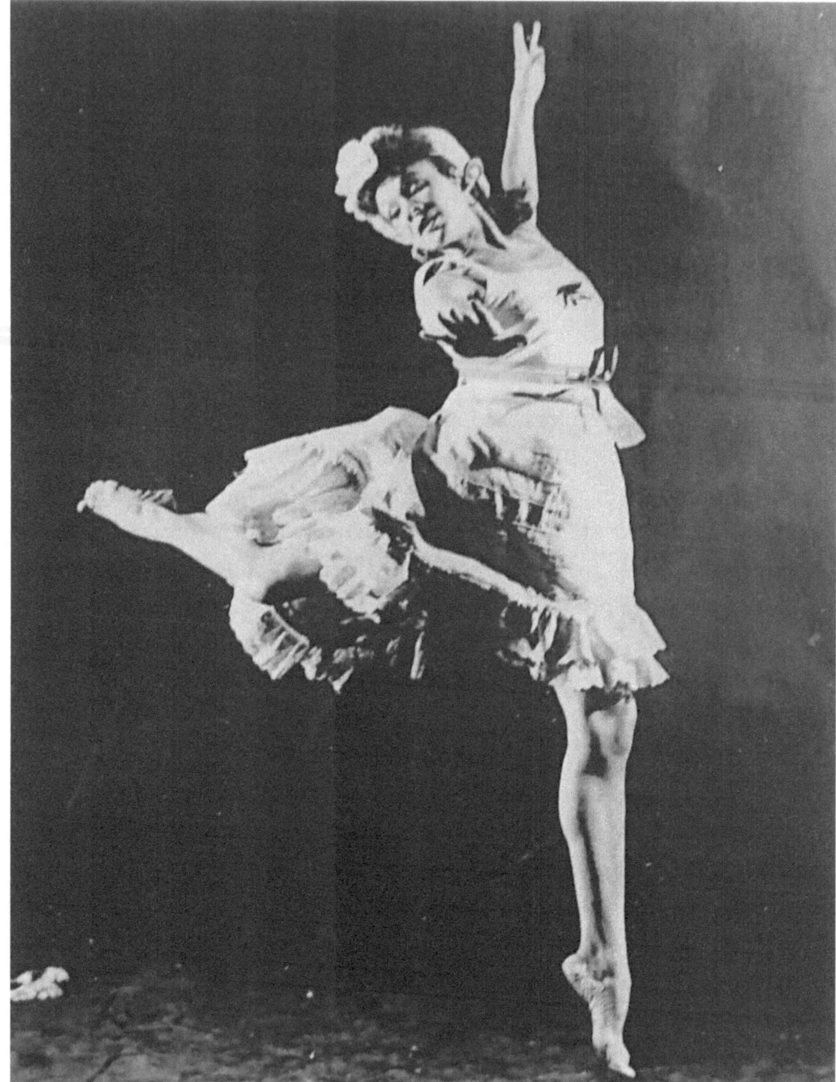

Figure 2. Katherine Dunham dances in *L'Ag'Ya*, c. 1940s. Courtesy of Marie-Christine Dunham Pratt.

The FTP show changed Dunham's life in two major ways. First, it reignited her stalled career and gave it a firm direction within concert dance. In her memoirs, she confessed that "whole new vistas were opening at such a great rate that anthropology receded much of the time into the background, diminished by the stirrings of a desire to create something new and wonderful,

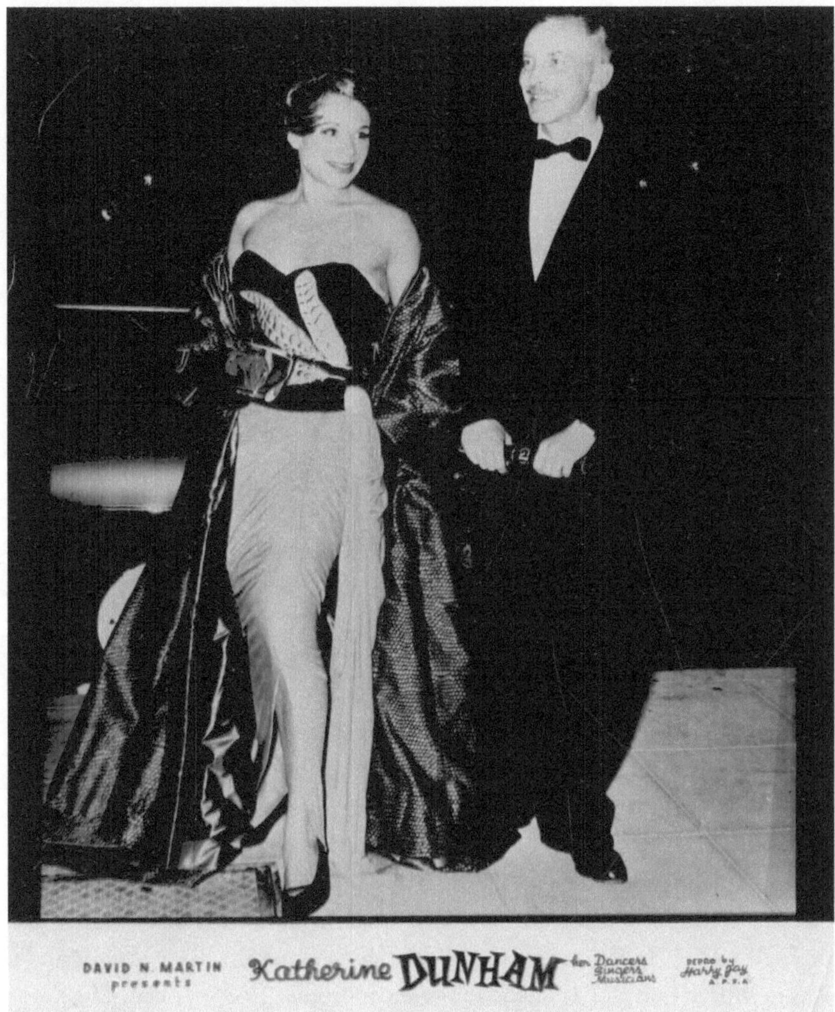

FIGURE 3. Katherine Dunham and John Pratt attend a gala, 1956. Courtesy Special Collections Research Center, Morris Library, Southern Illinois University, Carbondale.

to include me in it, and to make of it something permanent."[55] Second, during work on the show she met John Pratt, who became her company's set and costume designer and eventually her husband.[56] She described their relationship as passionate, loving, stormy—one imbued with extraordinary synergy as romantic and professional partners. They would be together for nearly fifty years. As Dunham created choreography and dance innovations, Pratt created the costumes and sets that were critical to the Dunham concert experience.

She often pointed out that "the Dunham show would not have been the same without his costumes, scenery, and lights. . . . He had quite a vision. . . . It is amazing what he could do as a white man." The daughter they adopted, Marie-Christine, recalled, "My mother, my father were together in love and art."[57] Both were responsible for building the world-renowned company.

Despite the popularity of her work with audiences, Dunham was also dealing with biased and backward-facing reactions to Black dance performance. After *Ballet Fedre* closed, the dancers in her production, including those in her evolving troupe, began rehearsals for other shows in the FTP's Negro Unit, among them *Swing Mikado*, and Dunham was asked to step down from her position. Devastated, she launched a fiery protest. On March 15, 1938, she sent a letter to Harry Hopkins, an administrator for the WPA. In response, he quoted the supervisor of employment in the agency's Chicago branch, who had said that Dunham's work was "highly satisfactory." However, "since she only works with the Negro ballet . . . and these people are rehearsing in the *Mikado* . . . there could be no possible use for Miss Dunham at this time."[58] Undeterred, she continued her battle for reinstatement throughout the summer of 1938. She wrote to the famed educator Mary McLeod Bethune, the head of the National Youth Administration and a member of Franklin D. Roosevelt's Black cabinet. Pleading for reinstatement, she questioned what she believed to be biased practices in the FTP, complaining that "while the other dance groups continue to function and present performances, the Negro group has been dispersed through other activities in the project."[59] She also sent an ardent appeal to Arthur Mitchell, Illinois's first-district congressman. Referring to the productions to which Black dancers had been moved, she pointedly said, "It also enters my mind that these productions are not under Negro supervision, and it seems a little incongruous that with available Negro supervision the main Negro productions so far with the exception of the ballet, have been under White supervision."[60]

The petitions of Dunham and others had repercussions beyond their own specific situations. For instance, they may have affected the career of the playwright Shirley Graham. In reaction to Dunham's plea, Representative Mitchell and several other supporters wrote to Hallie Flannagan, the director of the FTP, who eventually responded that the "Chicago Unit" (that is, the Black division) was planning two productions: *Swing Mikado* and *Little Black Sambo*. Graham was brought on and reimagined Gilbert and Sullivan's

Japanese-themed *Mikado* as a jazz opera.[61] She added the presence of another strong Black woman to the FTP. Graham and Dunham became friends, attending one another's productions whenever possible. While it is not entirely clear if Dunham's protests influenced Graham's employment, in general, artists' combined resistance had a substantial impact, despite New Deal bureaucrats' lack of action. The historian Lauren Rebecca Sklaroff notes that "even while operating within these narrowly proscribed spaces, African American performers promoted a diverse series of racial representations, expanding theatrical roles beyond the confines of conventional racial stereotypes."[62]

The WPA arts programs had created a small opening created for Black artists, but that opening began to shrink in late 1938 after members of the newly formed HUAC started compelling FTC administrators to testify about unproven accusations of communist infiltration. Like other WPA projects, the FTP suffered budget cuts and became a scapegoat for those suspicious of the New Deal's liberal agenda. By 1940, the program had vanished altogether. Meanwhile, Dunham returned to her post at the library, dabbled in her master's studies, and spent much of the late 1930s soliciting venues and sponsors for her newly formed dance company.[63]

She needed employment, but she was also driven to position herself, her diasporic choreography, and her beautiful spectrum of dancers on the popular stage. She could have opted to alter her approach to suit the tropes of Black entertainment of the time. For example, *Amos 'n' Andy*, a touchstone of stereotyped Black representation, dominated the radio airwaves of the 1930s and 1940s; and a plethora of clubs hosted light-skinned chorus dancers in every major city. But both were the antithesis of Dunham's performances, and she passionately wanted to bring her vision of the Dunham Company into the public eye. Her archives include numerous copies of letters that she sent across the country, inquiring into the possibility of performances. Sometimes she received invitations, but mostly she was unsuccessful. She wrote to historically black colleges in the South and to an assortment of organizations and venues. She solicited a friend, Professor Charles Johnson at Fisk University, to see if her troupe could perform at the college's annual folk festival. Her sister-in-law inquired about participating in the Haitian Coffee Fest in Washington, D.C. Dunham's secretary called on Eleanor Roosevelt, whom she felt "might be interested in having [Dunham] dance at some affair at the White House."[64] Tally Beatty, a principal dancer in the Dunham Company, later recalled, "I just think it's amazing that anyone could be so sensational and then be out of work!"[65] But, of course, this was typical for Black American artists and performers throughout the twentieth century.

Under constant financial strain, Dunham and her dancers nonetheless stayed true to her vision—training, taking gigs as they became available, and traveling intermittently. Marie-Christine Pratt said that her mother "always carr[ied] the company on her back."[66] Dale Wasserman, Dunham's future stage director, remembered, "The Dunham Company was characterized by the fact that it was in a constant state of bankruptcy. It could be less bankruptcy or a little more, but the basic situation was always mild or extreme desperation."[67] Yet while more hungry days stood between Dunham and her eventual explosion onto the New York and national stages, the strain did not interrupt her devotion to dance or political activism. For example, she supported the Abraham Lincoln Brigade, a racially integrated volunteer force that fought against fascism in the Spanish Civil War, and used the crisis in Spain as a platform to stage her first overtly political critique, *The Spanish Earth*. Dunham recalled, "I represented the roots of peasant Spain with heels and castanets in a fiery protest . . . [against] the fascist armies of Franco. For years, I refused to appear in Spain as my own private protest."[68] For a time, the company performed this production almost weekly.

Other opportunities arose. Dunham was asked to help choreograph a floundering 1939 Labor Stage Production titled *Pins and Needles*. This production had originally been staged by the International Ladies' Garment Workers Union and had first run in 1936 and 1937. In 1939, it was adapted for Broadway, and Dunham and half of her company were brought in from Chicago. She arranged the number "Bertha, the Sewing Machine, or It's Better With a Union Man."[69] The show's run proved to be profitable and set the Dunham Company on a course that would more visibly transform Black dance.

LE JAZZ HOT

Dunham used her salary from *Pins and Needles* to produce her next show herself. *Tropics* and *Le Jazz Hot: From Harlem to Haiti* premiered in Manhattan at the Windsor Theatre on West 48th Street. Dunham hoped the show's subtitle would emphasize the ancestral line between the dances of Harlem, the hub of Black America; Haiti, a storied capital of the global Black community;

and Africa, the continent of diasporic origin. The second section of *Le Jazz Hot* paid homage to blues-influenced African American juke-joint dance, though Dunham had to struggle to convince the theater owner to allow it. He disliked her embrace of sensual Black vernacular art forms. She persevered.[70]

Le Jazz Hot was Dunham's first program to include a Black Americana suite. She included dances from the prewar era (the shimmy, the Charleston, the black bottom, the cakewalk), a suite of contemporary popular dances (the jitterbug, boogie-woogie), and an infamous staging of the barrelhouse.[71] All honored African American dance and artistry, but the barrelhouse generated the most discussion. The staging was simple. A woman and a man meet in a small juke joint and lose themselves in the barrelhouse dance. They wind their bodies into artistic interpretations of the barrelhouse shimmy that Dunham had first seen in Chicago. During prohibition, she had frequented a barbecue shack that had served moonshine, and it was here that she had first heard and seen the barrelhouse shimmy. She recalled: "I believe the first concepts of the movement of the shimmy came from these after-hours spots; even way back when, as a child, I would see Ethel Waters at the Monogram Variety House with a feather duster tied around her waist, bouncing it back and forth as she described in what manner she would welcome her absconded man when he returned, with the robust side to side twist of the shimmy."[72]

In her choreography of the barrelhouse, Dunham turned her Black feminist anthropological gaze onto urban working-class Black Americans. She was likely not surprised that audiences and reviewers were more enchanted by the concert's "exotic" first section, *Tropics*, which included dances from West Africa, South America, and the Caribbean. Still, she judiciously connected these charming dances to the underappreciated working-class African American dances with which she had grown up. She said, "I was running around getting all these 'exotic' things from the Caribbean and Africa when the real development lay in Harlem and black Americans . . . so I developed more things in jazz."[73] As she explained, "if I could research and present the equivalent from other countries, I could not consider myself a conscientious field anthropologist if I neglected the rich heritage of the American Negro."[74]

The choice to include jazz and blues in her dance performance was a controversial act in 1940. The dominant culture tended to frame the sexual references in these genres as low cultural expression and an affront to Puritan values. But as the Black feminist theorist Hazel Carby has noted, the blues have been a "privileged site" for African American women to express power, sensuality, and sexuality.[75] The stage gave blueswomen not only access to a welcoming audience for such expression but also the opportunity to use public performance as a tool for critiquing American society and the obstacles it constructs for African American women. This is not to say that the stage magically shielded them from greater oppression or discrimination or that all African American women used the stage in this way. But the position of entertainer opened possibilities. Dunham understood the power she could brandish as a performer and, through her blues and jazz pieces in *Le Jazz Hot*, created a privileged site for the unnamed woman in the barrelhouse, a site of freedom that may have eluded those who were constrained by propriety. The inclusion of this character also highlighted Dunham's recognition of African American women's calculated use of layered resistance. Centering this representation as an artist constituted an oppositional act and the manipulation of popular public space to her will. The character is a conduit to freedom through her dance, with her body acting as the harbinger of resistance.

Yet mainstream reviews failed to offer more than a superficial view of the performance. In his article "Dance: A Negro Art," John Martin of the *New York Times* commented, "This is quite in character with the essence of the Negro dance itself. There is nothing pretentious about it; it is not designed to delve into philosophy or psychology but to externalize the impulses of a highspirited, rhythmic, gracious race."[76] Martin identified Dunham's production with an unrefined art that is natural and innate to Black Americans. He saw the African, Black Americana, and Caribbean-based choreography as forms from which better and "more consciously creative and sophisticated" versions of art can be developed. But White Americans like Martin were not alone in adhering to the racial narrative and cultural norms of the time. The essentialist critiques crossed racial lines. Dunham wrote, "I have had to defend on more than one occasion the American section of the program, always in the United States. At one time, it was to a group of 'comrades' who, in the early days in New York, somehow felt this exposé of black culture to be undignified; at another time in San Francisco years later, when a group of militant brothers failed to see the historic value of their own roots."[77]

Inevitably, Dunham also faced criticisms related to the sensual nature of the choreography. Critics were obsessed with her sexuality, which at times they thinly veiled behind the word *exotic*, the most frequent descriptor of her shows. Headlines such as "K. Dunham's Hips Are Sociological," "La

Dunham Comes Back Still Sexy and Sizzling," and "Dunham Makes Learning Alluring" purposely downplayed the artistic and anthropological nature of the productions. Other headlines reveled in innuendo about her "hot" performances: "Katherine Dunham Superb in Dances of Hot Places" and "La Dunham, with 3 New Works, Still Torrid Stuff."[78] Under the gaze of such reviewers, her fearless embrace of sensuality and sexuality lost all complication, and Dunham's battle against a sexualized conception of her art would continue throughout her career.

Despite such misreadings by prominent white and even Black cultural critics, *Le Jazz Hot* generally received rave reviews. It was a meaningful step in the process of recognizing African American dance as a professional art form and demonstrated Dunham's willingness to take political risks within the composition of her concerts. The show, which ran for thirteen consecutive Sundays before it closed, also marked the beginning of one of the Dunham Company's busiest years.

CABIN IN THE SKY, STORMY WEATHER, AND THE AMERICAN RACIAL NARRATIVE

On September 18, 1940, Dunham signed a contract to play her first acting role in a production outside of dance. The play, temporarily named *Little Joe*, would become the smash hit *Cabin in the Sky*, first on Broadway, later as a film. Her role would be the temptress Georgia Brown, and her contract guaranteed a much-needed salary of $400 a week for the 1940–41 season. Originally, Dunham had been the only member of her company to be offered a part in the production, but she insisted that her dancers be hired as well.[79] According to one of them, Lucille Ellis, the play brought the Chicago and New York Dunham dancers into one cohesive unit: "With *Cabin in the Sky*, we all became a full company."[80]

The play tells the story of a dying man who is given six extra months to live to amend his "evil ways," which include gambling, cheating on his wife, and spending his family's hard earned money at a juke joint. Throughout, he is tempted by Lucifer and scolded by "the Lawd's General." The production featured an all-Black cast and included actors who were household names in the Black community, including its star, Ethel Waters, as well as Dooley Wilson and Rex Ingraham. For Dunham and her company, there would be many highs and lows associated with the play.[81]

The renowned choreographer George Balanchine, known as the "ballet maker," was hired to stage, direct, and choreograph the show. He cared deeply about the production and invested his own money in it. Working with Black dancers for the first time, he decided to give them "steps that they could do better than anybody else." His understanding of what he took to be the organic abilities of Black dancers was in line with that of his contemporaries. He insisted, "No one can do hanging, fluent, smooth jumps the way these boys can. . . . There are few dancers in the world whose lack of self-consciousness means more intense and disciplined audience projection, rather than less."[82]

At first, Dunham was asked to assist periodically with choreography. Unfortunately, in the midst of preview performances, the producer, Martin Beck, fired Balanchine because of creative differences. According to one of the dancers, Tally Beatty, "Balanchine was removed from the choreographic scene, and Dunham had to reset all of the dances. And she did reset everything except something called 'The Hell Scene.'" Beatty insisted, "Dunham did all of the choreographing. . . . In the program, Balanchine takes credit for that. But he didn't choreograph it."[83] There is some dispute about this, but in any case Dunham ended up being the principal choreographer on set.[84]

She also took the lead in confronting a script that perpetuated familiar racist tropes and the maligning of Blackness. Initially, she and Pratt had been opposed to accepting any role in the production because it featured a stereotypical ne'er-do-well Black man and portrayed Black women as Jezebels. Eventually, however, Dunham relented and used her influence and choreography to reshape various aspects of the performance. In one scene, her character was supposed to hit Ethel Waters's character Petunia over the head with a beer bottle. As Hazel Scott had done on the set of *The Heat's On*, Dunham refused and threatened to quit, another example of how she took on layered resistance and image control as a joint project. The scene was quickly amended.[85]

Another issue pitted Dunham against the show's producers. In addition to the irritation arising from the ongoing tug of war with the script, they were unhappy about the varied physical appearance of the dancers. They felt that many were too dark in complexion and asked Dunham for replacements. Beatty recalled that they wanted to switch in "all these Lena Horne types. But Dunham did stand up! She did hold her ground. But that didn't deter them. They hired these girls—the Cotton Club girls, just to drape the stage. Every time the Dunham dancers would come on, we had a whole lot of Cotton Club girls, very fair, behind us."[86] Coincidentally, the Cotton Club had recently closed, so there happened to be a bevy of light-skinned female chorus girls out of work. But the idea that these women could stand in for well-trained dancers performing intricate choreography must have been hard for the Dunham troupe to fathom. One can only imagine the incongruity: Dunham's international, multi-complected dancers rimmed with out-of-place near-white chorus girls.

After the Broadway production of *Cabin in the Sky* closed, the Dunham Company toured with the play and ended up in California, where Ethel Waters unexpectedly left the show. Troupe members found themselves stranded on the West Coast without work or sufficient funds to return home. Dunham immediately began booking any engagements she could "to hold it together.[87] Fortunately, Hollywood turned out to be a productive space for her and her dancers. She began her cinematic work in 1941 with a twenty-minute short film for Warner Brothers titled *Carnival of Rhythm* and featuring Brazilian music and dance. But prior to the film's release, Will Hays, the president of the Motion Picture Producers and Distributors of America and the

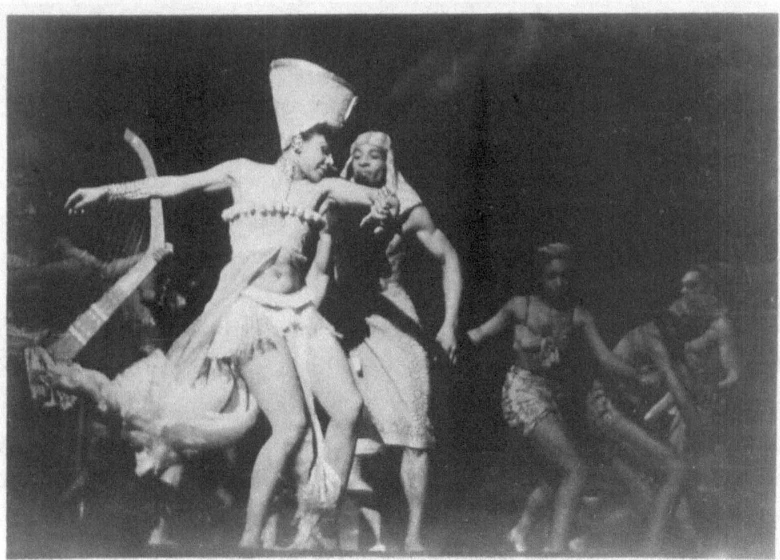

FIGURE 4. Katherine Dunham and her company dance in the *Cabin in the Sky* stage production, 1940. Dunham served as both choreographer and lead dancer. Courtesy of Special Collections Research Center, Morris Library, Southern Illinois University, Carbondale.

creator of the censorship mechanism known as the Hays Code, announced that he "frown[ed] upon the use of Negro actors in parts where they represent Brazilians."[88] During the war, American movie moguls were encouraged to court South American distribution and audiences as part of what was known as the Good Neighbor Policy.[89] As a result, all references to the specific locales of dances and music were removed from the narration, often leaving movie-goers confused about a film's meaning and purpose. Such erasures also dismissed global and diasporic Blackness by ignoring African descent in South America.

Dunham and Claude A. Barnett, the director of the Associated Negro Press (and the son of the journalist Ida B. Wells), exchanged letters about the incident, and they decided to approach Hays and the Brazilian embassy. Barnett explained to Hays, "Negroes of talent have a hard enough time, it would appear, without piling difficulties in their paths." The Brazilian embassy denied any knowledge of the issue: "We never made any representation to the Will Hays office in respect to anything which had to do with racial differences in moving pictures."[90] Hays was unmoved.

To counter the extreme color consciousness that pervaded Hollywood, Dunham chose to prominently highlight the dancer Carmencita Romero in *Carnival of Rhythm*. Because of her relatively dark skin, Romero would never otherwise have been featured in a typical Hollywood production, except in the role of domestic or slave. Recalling such battles, Dunham said plainly, "I know . . . [they] cost me a career in Hollywood."[91] In the case of *Carnival of Rhythm*, the episode revealed the studio's (and Americans') ignorance of race internationally. While no member of Dunham's troupe hailed from multiracial Brazil, all of their complexions were common among its people, including those of the darkest-skinned dancers.

Dunham choreographed and performed in two other films in 1942: *Star Spangled Rhythm* and *Pardon My Sarong*. Then, in 1943, 20th Century–Fox contracted her company to appear in *Stormy Weather*. The film starred Lena Horne, Bill "Bojangles" Robinson, and a who's-who cast of prominent Black entertainers, including Cab Calloway, Fats Waller, Dooley Wilson, Ada Brown, and the Nicholas Brothers. The plot of *Stormy Weather* centered around a backstage revue held together by a thin boy-meets-girl-loses-girl-gets-girl-back narrative. Its main focus was pure entertainment; but like *Cabin in the Sky*, it was not always successful in avoiding stereotypes and negative constructions.

Dunham made serious interventions in that regard. Her opportunity came when she was asked to choreograph a dance sequence during the syncopated bridge of the famous title song. The scene opens on stage, with Lena Horne singing at a window in a sitting room. Outside, rain pours, accompanied by lightning and claps of thunder. In the middle of the song, the camera swoops out to focus on Dunham and her dancers, who stand on the avenue beneath an elevated train. In the writers' original vision, the dancers would perform a well-known popular dance in street clothes, but Dunham insisted instead on an ethereal modern dance sequence melding African and Caribbean movements, ballet, and Black Americana, one set on an architectural stage in formal theatrical costumes.[92]

Before filming, she wrote to her friend Yvonne Wood, a costumer at 20th Century–Fox: "I would like something else for the Stormy Weather sequence if we use it—something earthier and still with more movement."[93] In the end, her choreography and costume choices transformed the original minstrel-like tropes into a Black modernist moment within the film. According to the scholar Shane Vogel, "coming after earlier scenes of tap dancing, cakewalking, and vaudeville acrobatics, Dunham's performance marks a choreographic contradiction within the film between the history of stereotyped minstrel dance and the emergence of [the] modern Negro." In his view, "Dunham's kinesthetic rewriting of 'Stormy Weather' situates the song and its racial inscription within a diasporic rather than a national horizon."[94]

In 1943, both Black and white audiences across the nation watched and enjoyed *Cabin in the Sky* and *Stormy Weather*. Thanks to Dunham, the films gave Americans a glimpse of Black modernity. Her choreography and scene interpretation would foreshadow the modernist musicals of the 1950s, in which dancers such as Gene Kelly and Cyd Charisse incorporated dance sequences that relied on abstract interpretation. For instance, a vignette in the lauded *Singin' in the Rain* (1952) echoes Dunham's modern fantasy: on a sparse set, Charisse, dressed in a white chiffon dress with a billowing yards-long scarf, beautifully performs a modern dance–ballet fusion with Kelly.[95]

SOLDIERING AGAINST RACIAL OPPRESSION

By the early 1940s, the war and America's racial caste system were having profound personal and professional impacts on Dunham and her troupe. After America became officially involved in the war, her husband, John Pratt, was "order[ed] to report for induction" on July 9, 1943, just twelve days before the release of *Stormy Weather*.[96] His departure meant that Dunham now had to oversee set design and costuming as well as manage the company's myriad affairs, including personnel, travel, choreography, and rehearsals.

The segregated armed forces were a difficult place to be if one were a liberal leftist from the North or a white man married to an African American woman, and Pratt was both. After reaching Fort Eustis in Virginia, he wrote to Dunham, "I came in with a bunch of toughies from Little Sicily in Chicago and find thousands of 'crackers' here."[97] While Pratt's specific views about the war are not completely articulated, he was certainly aware of the contradictions inherent in fighting a war for democracy while representing a deeply and often violently divided America. In a letter to Pratt, his friend Louis reflected that conundrum:

> Doesn't it strike one as odd that freedom for this and freedom for that far away is worth killing and dying for, but working and being creative for freedom right here at home only gets bullets? . . . Frankly, until there is complete freedom for over twelve millions of colored people, I'm deaf and blind to all of the hullabaloo elsewhere. O yes, I'm for a world freed from the mad fool Hitler and the like but he's only the scab of a social cancer.[98]

While traveling, the Dunham Company, like most Black performers and athletes in the Jim Crow era, repeatedly felt the sting of inequality and segregation.[99] Members were routinely humiliated when trying to find accommodations, rehearsal space, and transportation. Their stage director, Dale Wasserman, recalled that the company often needed to book sleeping cars on trains, and whites regularly complained that "the niggers" had sleeping accommodations while they did not. Many of these complainers were soldiers who had supposedly been fighting for freedom and democracy abroad. More trouble met them in the cities where they were scheduled to perform. Tommy Gomez, a long-time Dunham dancer, recalled that an "advance man would go to the black area or to one of the black churches and ask the minister to ask members of the congregation to house us. . . . We went through the problems of racial prejudice all the time, from the very beginning of the company." Another troupe member, Lucille Ellis, said that the dancers sometimes had to use "whorehouses" as accommodations.[100]

Company members recognized that conditions in the North were not much better than those in the South, despite northern cities' liberal reputations. According to Carmencita Romero, they encountered the most racism and the strictest segregation in California. In one instance, she and three other dancers were able to procure housing for the company only by pretending they were part of an international dance troupe. The dancers spoke in front of the lodging staff in French or Spanish, a ruse that worked because hotels were willing to accept international travelers, though not Black Americans. Dunham herself was sometimes, but not always, able to use her influence to avoid the indecent accommodations to which her dancers were subjected.[101]

Racial discrimination was not limited to the United States. While traveling in South America in 1950, Dunham and Pratt attempted to book a room at a Brazilian hotel and were told, "It was against hotel policy to accept Negroes." After the couple pointed out that the singer Marian Anderson had a reservation at the same hotel, the management chose to cancel Anderson's reservation rather than change their racist policy. Dunham and Pratt had to find alternative lodging, but Dunham published a protest in several newspapers and magazines and sued the hotel for "redress for the humiliation suffered."[102] Over time, she would file several lawsuits against landlords and realty companies that employed discriminatory practices. Layered resistance was always necessary for survival.

Dunham's personal papers reveal the nonstop racial discrimination that she and her company encountered during these years. After reading one of her protests in the press, an admirer named Alexander Sterne wrote to her in solidarity. Lamenting the discrimination that the company had faced in New York hotels, he said, "It indicates, at least to me, that we are very far from putting into practice the ideals expressed in the Four Freedoms."[103] In another letter, a friend told her about confronting bigots on a bus who had been deriding the Dunham show. In 1943, Dunham wrote to her stepmother, Annette Dunham, "[The Waldorf Astoria] refused my reservation on Tuesday, November 30."[104] In Cincinnati, she was asked to leave the Netherlands Plaza Hotel after complaints from the American Federation of Labor Leaders, who were holding their conference there and threatening to move it elsewhere. When management arrived at her room, she said she would jump out the window if they evicted her. She then called on her friend Harry Bridges, the president of the International Longshoreman's and Warehouseman's Union, to negotiate with the hotel. He was successful. Unfazed by the confrontation, Dunham, at the close of her stay, made a reservation for another activist performer, Paul Robeson, who was coming to the city. Thanks to her dramatic public reaction, the Netherlands made no further attempt to block Black performers from booking accommodations at the hotel.[105]

Dunham consciously combined her successful onstage remaking of Black dance and image with her offstage politics. She was well aware of the financial and career costs of her activism, but this did not daunt her. The Dunham Company refused to stage productions for segregated audiences and played below the Mason-Dixon line only in exceptional circumstances. On one remarkable night in Kentucky, Dunham courageously held to her convictions. The company discovered too late that an appearance before a Louisville theater had not been desegregated, though the management had promised to do so. The performance before the cheering crowd went on, but afterward Dunham delivered more than the audience had bargained for:

> At the close of the show, Dunham stepped out and announced, there comes a time when every human being must protest in order to retain human dignity. I must protest because I have discovered that your management will not allow people like you to sit next to people like us. I hope that time and . . . this war for tolerance and democracy, which I am sure we will win, will change some of these things— perhaps we can return.[106]

In an interview, Marie-Christine Pratt, recalled her mother's pride in this protest.[107]

Dunham's direct activism, such as her refusal to play to segregated audiences, has not received as much attention as it deserves. Nor has her participation in progressive organizations. During the war years, Black performers and artists in the public eye often served as the popular face of activism. Dunham lent her name and assistance to many causes, including the American Conference for Racial and National Unity and the Abraham Lincoln School in Chicago. She accepted posts as vice chair of the Dance Committee for the National Council of American-Soviet Friendship and as vice president of the Negro Actors Guild.[108] She appeared at the 1945 Negro Freedom Rally at Madison Square Garden, organized by Robeson and the boxer and actor Canada Lee, and at a rally for Russian war relief.[109] She attended countless benefits and fundraisers. She supported Benjamin Davis, the first Black communist elected to the New York city council. A complete packet of his campaign materials has been preserved in her archives, which may indicate that her involvement more than casual. Association with these and similar organizations were why many of Dunham's contemporaries, including Lee, Robeson, and Hazel Scott, were called before HUAC or investigated by the FBI. Dunham, too, was eventually targeted.

SOUTHLAND

Dunham's greatest career risk involved the staging of *Southland*, her ballet Americana—a historic performance that almost didn't take place. Commissioned by the Symphony of Chile, the production premiered in Santiago in January 1951.[110] The Dunham troupe performed the exquisitely choreographed and costumed piece, but Dunham herself did not appear on stage.

Southland is a riveting tale about the lynching of an innocent man in the American South, and Dunham wrote the scenario after reading about an actual case. As was usual in many real-life lynchings, the Black man in the ballet is falsely accused of the rape of a white woman. Although the woman has in fact been assaulted by her white lover, she instead identifies a Black assailant.

Southland faced obstacles from its inception. The first came internally from the dancers. On their world tour, they had been temporarily insulated from stark American racism. Now, in rehearsals with this new controversial piece, many felt that it was unnecessarily creating a racially charged atmosphere within the troupe.[111] Julie Robinson Belafonte, the wife of the singer Harry Belafonte, was playing the lead. A white Jewish woman, she had begun studying with Dunham as a sixteen-year-old student and had graduated to instructor before formally joining the troupe. By the early 1950s, she had been with the company for several years. Although the troupe had previously featured a few white dancers at different periods, Belafonte was its first white veteran.[112] She recalled the hostility that arose in the other dancers when she spoke the one word of dialogue throughout the piece: "Nigger!" Other dancers exclaimed, "Do you hear the way she says 'Nigga?' Nobody would say it that way if they didn't really mean it."[113] The show's disquieting themes were carving a rift in the usually tight-knit group.

The company also faced other difficulties during the show's run, most of which had nothing to do with the diversity of the cast or internal racial tension. The fact that the show was being staged in Chile was at the root of much of the trouble. At a period of intense antagonism between the Soviet Union and America, the U.S. government viewed Chile as friendly to communism, and Dunham's public association with the country was embarrassing. She knew that the production's staging was a career risk and wrote to a friend at home inquiring about the media response. He responded, "No news or reports here on 'Southland' yet. As you may know, this country is proudly publicizing the fact that in 1952, for the first recorded full year, there was not a lynching."[114] The U.S. government suppressed all reviews of the show, both nationally and abroad. Even Chilean newspapers, which depended on America for newsprint, did not print reviews. Now in the grip of the Cold War, the United States could not afford publicity about the racist characterizations in *Southland*. It had no intention of acknowledging the violence perpetuated against Black Americans.

Yet Dunham defiantly restaged the piece in Paris, ignoring the dancers' discomfort and the State Department's repression.[115] This action would cost her dearly, as J. Edgar Hoover, the head of the FBI, began taking a personal interest in "undermining her career."[116] The troupe's much-needed governmental subsidy, a common necessity for international traveling companies of its stature, was swiftly canceled.[117] As late as 1967, the FBI was still describing Dunham as a risk to send internationally to represent the United States.[118] Her troupe never again reached the level of notoriety it had achieved before the staging of *Southland*. However, the show's fallout by no means marked the end of Dunham's resistance to oppression or her contributions to the world.

In 1956, after touring more than seventy countries, Katherine Dunham's company performed its final show at the Apollo Theater in Harlem, marking the end of a significant era in Black concert dance and leaving a lasting legacy for future generations of dancers and activists.[119] In subsequent years, Dunham continued creating and educating. She choreographed a landmark production of Giuseppe Verdi's *Aida*, performed in 1964 and 1966 at the Metropolitan Opera House, and she spoke before the Senate about the importance of dance and dance education. The National Endowment for the Arts was established based on the testimony of Dunham and other artists.[120] Her pioneering work in anthropology expanded the discipline to include dance anthropology as a field of study. Dunham was the first Black dancer to have her style codified, and today the Dunham technique is still taught in isolation from other dance forms, centering on Black women's bodies, image, and movement. Yet her relentless engagement with layered resistance reached beyond her transformation of both dance and anthropology. It included cultural, political, and social protest as she confronted racism, called for desegregation, pushed for gender parity, and reoriented the popular image of Black women.

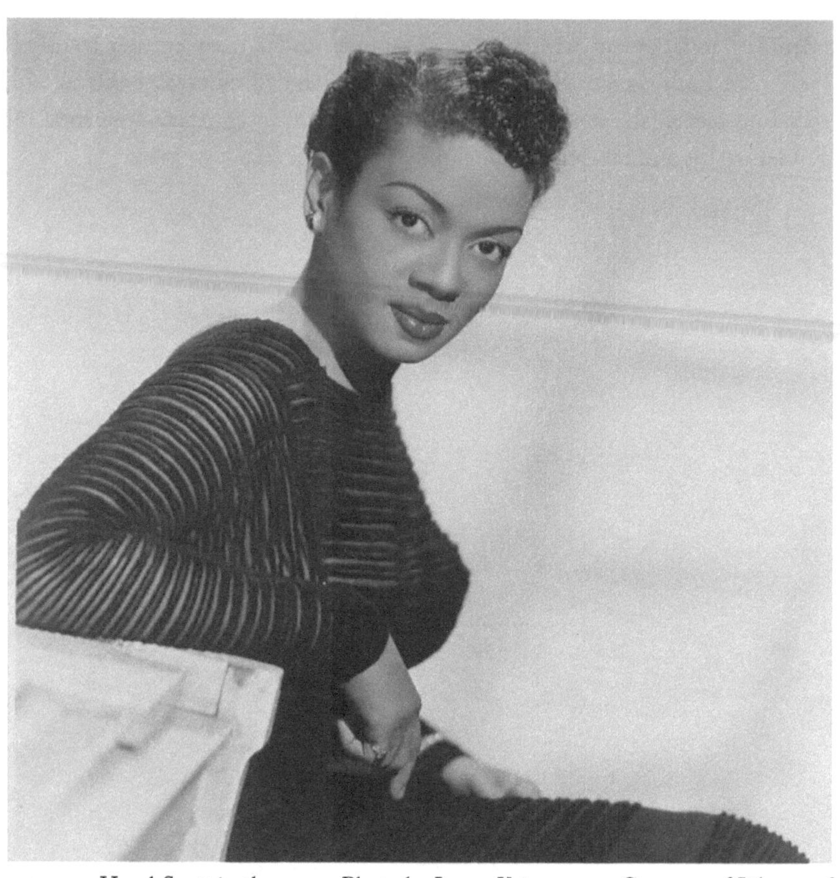

FIGURE 5. Hazel Scott in the 1940s. Photo by James Kriegsmann. Courtesy of Library of Congress, Washington, D.C.

CHAPTER 2

"Colored Performers Represent Their People"

Hazel Scott and Popular and Private Protest

Little girl
Dreaming of a baby grand piano . . .
To confound even Hazel Scott
Who might be passing[1]

—Langston Hughes, "To Be Somebody"

In June 1924, Hazel Scott announced to all who would listen that today was her birthday and she was four years old. She was aboard a ship leaving Port of Spain, Trinidad, the island nation from which her family hailed and where she had been born. With her mother and grandmother, she was embarking on a journey to begin life anew in New York. Bragging to the captain that she could play the piano, little Miss Scott, surrounded by onlookers, began tapping out popular Trinidadian calypsos on the keyboard. By the time her worried mother discovered her, she had entranced a crowd of passengers.

Hazel's grandmother was already familiar with her granddaughter's talent. At age two and a half, the child had climbed onto a piano stool and played a hymn perfectly by ear. Her gift was amazing but not entirely surprising, given that her mother, Alma Scott, was a classically trained pianist who had studied and taught for most of her life. By age three, young Hazel had learned to read, demonstrated perfect pitch, and debuted in public as a pianist.[2] By the time she arrived in New York, she was well known as a child prodigy in Trinidad. Eventually, as a pianist and actress, Scott would become the aspirational subject of a Langston Hughes poem. She would grace Broadway stages, appear in Hollywood films, and play jazz sets with the likes of Art Tatum, Lil Hardin, and Charlie Parker. But even as a child she was establishing herself as a star attraction, showing a knack for accessing and manipulating popular public spaces. As Hughes's poem so eloquently states, Scott was pushing herself "to be somebody," to make some room "at the top" for Black women.

Though Scott's activism has often been overlooked, she consciously and skillfully used her positioning, image, and representation as weapons to subvert the oppressive racial and gendered narratives of her time. Her stage, film, and television personae and performances stood in stark contrast to the common images of African American women in popular culture. Her son, Adam Clayton Powell III, said of his mother, "As long as I can remember, she would talk about . . . how Black people, Black women especially, had to be dignified and had to really be models for everyone else. I think that she found it so totally unacceptable that there was no room in her universe to compromise on this."[3] While Scott's understanding of the duties of public Blackness relied on respectability politics, it also revealed her view of Black people as worthy of citizenship, humanity, and dignity in a world in which their humane treatment was violently challenged.

It is no coincidence that Scott was at the height of her fame during World War II, years when African Americans were hesitantly hopeful about some level of national transformation following the war. This was particularly true of women. The feminist scholar Maureen Honey argues that "for all its racial barriers and limited opportunities for real economic change, . . . World War II provided an empowering political base for African American women. . . . The war against racism . . . furnished [them] with models of pride and resistance."[4] Before and after the war years, Scott positioned herself at the forefront of the battle over Black female representation, becoming a conduit and symbol of Black pride and resistance. Between 1938 and 1957, she intentionally created an onstage and film persona that represented affirmative, self-defined, and self-generated African American women. Like the other women discussed in this book, she merged her onstage artistic resistance with offstage political and social activism. Her emigration from Trinidad gave America a rare nationally recognized Black woman star and activist.

"I AM IN THE PRESENCE OF A GENIUS"

The seeds for a life of resistance were sown during Scott's unusual childhood and adolescence. Her family background was typical of the transnational identities created via the transatlantic slave trade and the African diaspora. Her mother, Alma Long, was the daughter of Afro-Venezuelans who had immigrated to Trinidad by way of a ten-mile ferry ride. She was a sought-after debutante and a talented classical pianist.[5] Scott's father, R. Thomas Scott, was born and raised in Scotland, where his Yoruban Nigerian ancestors had been brought during enslavement. He was educated in England, where he became an English professor. After moving to Trinidad, he worked as a government architect, designing several "official buildings" and becoming a "man of considerable importance [o]n the island."[6] He saw that his daughter had the best musical education available.

The Scotts' lineage, income, education, and status suggest that they belonged to the island's bourgeois class.[7] Thus, their position in the class hierarchy should have been somewhat protected. In the early twentieth century, the average Trinidadian worked as a farm laborer, earning as little as 35 cents per day in the booming sugar and cocoa industries. While Thomas Scott was educating the island's male elite at Saint Mary's College, more than 43 percent of the island's population remained illiterate.[8] But he himself was the cause of his family's unexpected struggle to survive. After several years of marriage, Thomas Scott left his family in 1923 to seek his fortune in the United States. Unlike many Caribbean emigrants at the time, he did not send money back to support his wife and daughter but chose to begin another life without them.[9] His departure forced Alma Scott to work at a variety of jobs and descend in class status.

It is not entirely clear why a man of Thomas Scott's standing and elite occupation would have chosen to move to the United States. One biographical account suggests that he moved to take a job as a professor at Fisk University, but there is insufficient proof to verify this claim.[10] he likely moved to the United States to chase the dreams that most other immigrants had. Men and women from all classes were lured by the promise of opportunity and increased access to wealth. These same aspirations motivated Alma Scott to follow him. Like many, her destination was Harlem, a Black enclave in northern Manhattan.[11] There, the Scotts lived with a host of relatives as they made their way in the new city. They settled with several family members in a brownstone on 118th Street. Alma Scott worked as a domestic and took on odd jobs to keep her family afloat.

In 1924, the neighborhood was poised on the brink of a renaissance that would attract Black intellectuals and artists from around the globe.[12] The historian Arthur P. Davis writes:

> Harlem in the 1920s was a delightful place. . . . [It] was then still a relatively new settlement for Negroes, and the grime and the deterioration that came with subsequent years of poverty and job discrimination and frustration had not blighted the black city, . . . a city of black intellectuals and artists, of peasants just up from the south, of West Indians and Africans, of Negroes of all kinds and all classes.[13]

Harlem in these years had a strong southern and Caribbean overlay and was burgeoning with artistic creativity and notions of Black modernity. Yet the excitements of Black Harlem's cultural renaissance belied rising poverty, disenfranchisement, and labor exploitation. More than half of the Black men in Harlem earned $23 a week or less, at a time when the cost of living required a minimum of $33. Most married Black women worked outside the home, and approximately 80 percent of all Black women in Harlem were employed in domestic service. Lack of access to quality healthcare and education led to higher-than-average death rates as well as rising delinquency and crime. Never due to a lack of hard work, much of the poverty that racked Harlem was caused by exorbitant rents, restricted access to well-paid employment, and blatant discrimination.[14] For most residents, Harlem was a mixed blessing: it was an urbane Black northern space that delivered freedom in a myriad of ways yet was anchored in paucity. Black intellectuals, Black businesses, Black gangsters, and a significant Black cultural movement blossomed in tandem. This was the version of Harlem that four-year-old Hazel Scott encountered with her family, and it had a great influence on the exceptional person she would become.

In New York, Scott continued to develop her musical talent and began to showcase it in the community. At age five, she debuted at the Town Hall performance space in Manhattan. At eight, she auditioned for Paul Wagner, a renowned professor of music at Juilliard. Afterward, he reportedly laid his hand on her head and said, "I am in the presence of a genius." He agreed to teach her privately, as she was far too young to attend Juilliard. By early adolescence, Scott had transitioned from private student to professional musician. In 1933, she was officially introduced to the Harlem community at a recital at the Alhambra Ballroom. A poster for the event shows her sitting on a piano stool, alongside the caption "Little Miss Hazel Scott, Child Wonder Pianist."[15] Her star was ascending rapidly.

"THEY WANT TO MAKE A LITTLE LADY OUT OF ME"

Although Thomas Scott was estranged from his family, he did occasionally come to Alma and Hazel's home to take his daughter on excursions. The racial binary embedded at all levels of American society had quickly dashed his dreams and aspirations. According to one of his daughter's biographers, his "sense of dignity constantly conflicted with American race prejudice."[16] Unable to secure a job in which he could display his academic prowess, Scott was "reduced to odd jobs" and "fell into a deep depression." Yet in the years before he became ill, he instilled a great sense of racial pride in his daughter, which heightened after he became enthralled with Marcus Garvey's United Negro Improvement Association.[17] He would sometimes bring along his impressionable daughter to association meetings. Meanwhile, Alma Scott, eager to stop relying on domestic service and odd jobs to support her family, taught herself how to play the tenor saxophone and began playing gigs with various bands.[18]

For Hazel, her father's struggles with racism and her mother's ingenuity and hard work must have imparted sobering lessons. In their lives, she saw the devastating impact of racial oppression on Black Americans. Yet through her mother's gigs and contacts, she glimpsed a community of capable Black women who functioned in nontraditional occupations. Their versions of Black womanhood were very different from those perpetuated by mainstream attitudes. Rejecting the dominant gender narrative, these women spurned the rigid boundaries imposed by the politics of respectability. They saw themselves as both respectable and empowered to redefine gendered norms. As she grew into womanhood, Hazel Scott found models for her own choices within this dynamic subculture of Black women musicians. [19] These women employed traditional vehicles of resistance in new ways, borrowing from those historically adopted by Black women as they survived slavery, racism, colonialism, and segregation. They constructed their own criteria for resistance and appropriate representation. In this way, they were similar to many of the women that Scott would encounter later in her career.[20]

Alma Scott built professional relationships and friendships with a host of women who worked against and outside the dominant gender narrative. Among them was Valaida Snow, who led an all-women band with which Alma Scott briefly toured. Snow was best known as a trumpet player but was proficient on several instruments and could also sing and dance. She was the definition of a one-woman show. Her practice was to pull together her own groups between bouts of touring with other bands domestically and abroad.[21] Alma Scott toured longest with the piano player and bandleader Lil Hardin, who eventually married Louis Armstrong.[22] According to the jazz historian Linda Dahl, "in her long and many-sided career, [Hardin] provided inspiration and often playing opportunities for other aspiring jazzwomen, and her piano style defied the myth of the timid, lukewarm female touch." Hardin said of her own playing, "I hit the piano so loud and hard, they all turned around to look at me."[23]

After disbanding the Harlem Harlicans, a Black all-women band, Hardin formed a mostly male band but kept Alma Scott on the tenor sax. The sight of a beautiful woman with a "strong way of playing" sometimes upset male audience members, who undoubtedly felt threatened by her presence in this traditionally male-dominated space. Their harassment was so incessant that Scott developed one-liners to combat their insults. When a man complained, "Lady, you play that thing just like a man," she would retort, "Mister, you carry your children just like a lady!"[24]

In the jazz and swing world, women were often limited to being vocalists. It was easier to attach sexuality to singers than it was to female instrumentalists, who tended to be more aggressive in their performance and were less easily framed as sex objects. Women instrumentalists were seen as freaks, especially those who played instruments that had been coded as masculine, such as drums, trumpets, and saxophones."[25] The urge to ridicule such women was exacerbated at the intersection of racism and segregation. Yet Alma Scott, like many other Black woman instrumentalists, was not deterred. Instead, her occupation of this musical space became a form of resistance to endemic patriarchy, sexism, and racism.

Another influence in Hazel Scott's life was her mother's friend Billie Holiday, who became her own mentor and confidant. Scott recalled, "She always protected me. She had a very fierce protectiveness where I was concerned." After a show that Scott gave very early in her career, Holiday chased the young performer down the street and through several subway cars to scold her and bring her back to her mother. Apparently, Scott had lied about her age, pretending to be eighteen to impress an older male musician. Scott said that Holiday was always attentive to other female musicians: "God help you if you sang out of tune, but if you had something going, she was very interested and willing to help you."[26] In fact, it was Holiday who secured Scott the gig at Café Society that job jumpstarted her career.[27]

From such unorthodox women, Scott learned and assimilated a range of tools for her life as both a musician and a woman.[28] Yet none compared to the influence of her mother. Alma Scott took an unconventional approach to raising her daughter. For example, she did not teach her to cook, fearing that Hazel would burn her hands on the stove and end her promising career as a pianist.[29] Speaking of her mother, Scott said, "She was cool and level-headed. When I stumbled or bumped my toe, she was right there saying, 'Forget it. Move on.' And when she found me getting carried away with myself, she was on hand to tug my coat. As a result, I kept my feet firmly on the ground. I still have them there."[30] When the fourteen-year-old began bucking at the notion of being groomed exclusively for classical concert halls, her mother allowed her to play with the band. She seemed to understand her daughter's reasoning: "I can't stay home with people who are not in the business—they want to make a little lady out of me."[31] Alma and Hazel understood that other family members did not share their vision of womanhood. Yet it is also clear from Scott's descriptions of her mother that the women in this subculture of Black female musicians were assertive, outspoken, and clear-eyed, attributes that were not traditionally acceptable within the dominant gender narrative but were valued within the African American community as key components of layered resistance. In the writings of the scholar and activist Angela Davis, they are identified as Black feminist traits.[32]

In 1935, Hazel Scott performed her first professional solo, playing on a bill with the Count Basie Orchestra at the Roseland Ballroom.[33] She recalled her excitement: "The Basie band! Sixteen men. When they walked off the stand, I went on."[34] In 1936, she won a competitive radio audition sponsored by the Mutual Broadcasting System and was awarded a six-month radio contract in which she was charged with "sustaining programs with the added privilege of announcing her own numbers."[35] Sustaining programmers were supported by monthly subscribers instead of corporate sponsors, and Scott's success on air was evidence of her popularity.

Scott played at various venues regularly—among them the Yacht Club on 52nd Street, where she served as the between-set pianist. Scott recalled that the show's star, Frances Faye, would habitually listen to Scott's performances, "and whenever I'd start something—one of the tunes of the day—the busboy would come over and whisper, 'You can't play that number. Ms. Faye does it in the show.'" Frustrated, Scott muttered to herself, "Let's see if Miss Faye does this in the show—and I started jazzing the Bach Inventions." By making this move to "swing the classics," she expanded her place in the spotlight. "Jazzing the classics was self-preservation," she explained.[36] Yet she wasn't wholly happy with the move. She said, "I know lots of people have good reasons why it's all right to swing the classics, but—well, I wish I didn't do it. . . . I just can't help it. . . . My stuff is hybrid. I'm not grim enough for the classics. As for swing—well, I'm not sufficiently aboriginal."[37]

Twenty years later, during the height of the Black Arts movement, the poet Amiri Baraka (then known as Leroi Jones) wrote dismissively about Scott's playing style in his book *Blues People*, deriding "the shabbiness, even embarrassment of Scott's playing 'boogie-woogie' before thousands of middle-class white music lovers."[38] Like many of his generation, he was rejecting the artistic expressions and aesthetics of former generations as not radical enough. Yet it is clear that Scott had made a lasting impression on the young poet. She had positioned herself to be seen and remembered: by him, by others in the audience, by the national press. This was an achievement for any Black musician of the day, particularly for a woman. Her decision to swing the classics made Hazel Scott a household name in the Black community and among segments of the white community nationwide. It also allowed her to position herself in the center of a popular public space and shift it. Despite her immense talent as a classical pianist, she might never have become a celebrated musician or have appeared in newspapers or on film without this hybrid style. America was not willing to accept a famous Black woman classical pianist. Yet she managed to survive as a member of the small group of professional Black female musicians who earned a reputation and a living.

Philippa Schuyler, a younger contemporary of Scott's, did embark on a career as a classical pianist. She began playing professionally at the age of six.

By all accounts, she, too, was a prodigy: with an IQ of 185, she learned to read at two and played the piano like an adult master. A contemporary recalled:

> [Schuyler] cast a long shadow across the early years of those of us who chose to fritter away our Harlem childhoods playing games instead of reading philosophy and taking to the concert stage. In the 1930s, '40s, and '50s, hers was a household name, unusual enough that all the syllables, to many a young ear, seemed to run together; she was "Fillupaskyler," and that meant child prodigy.[39]

Schuyler became a draw on the concert stage, and at first her performances were well attended. But her popularity as a classical pianist was short-lived, ultimately because she was treated as a peculiarity rather than as a bona fide talent, which she surely was. For Black American classical pianists, both male and female, success remained elusive.[40]

Jazz was a more accessible route for Black male musicians. But for a woman, breaking onto the scene as a jazz instrumentalist was only slightly easier than doing so on the classical stage. Even if she could gain entrée, she had to prove herself continuously. The challenge of building a substantial career seemed nearly insurmountable, and Hazel Scott had few role models. One, however, did make a strong impression. Mary Lou Williams, the most respected female jazz pianist of the twentieth century, was yet another child prodigy. Born in 1910, she was ten years older than Scott, and her childhood contrasted sharply with that of the much younger and more privileged Schuyler. Williams grew up in Pittsburgh's East Liberty neighborhood and at age six began playing the piano to help support her family. Her mother, a migrant from Atlanta, earned a hardscrabble living as a domestic, and Williams had a rough and violent childhood. She left home early and began touring with bands at the age of fourteen. At fifteen, she was playing with Duke Ellington's early group, the Washingtonians. By nineteen, she was a key arranger and performer with Andy Kirk's famous band, the Twelve Clouds of Joy.[41]

Williams was respected by men and women players alike and was honorably treated as "one of the boys" in jazz circles. In "A Great Day in Harlem," Art Kane's well-known photograph of jazz legends, Williams is one of only three women among the fifty-seven assembled musicians. Two of the three, Williams and Marian McPartland, were pianists; the third, Maxine Sullivan, was a singer.[42] Williams set the standard for women instrumentalists and symbolized the possibilities for Black women in jazz. She did not stoop to musical gimmickry or sell herself via her looks. She was dark-skinned, reserved, and deadly serious. Although she was beautiful, she did not choose to emphasize this characteristic in her performance, and that choice did not seem to impact her popularity—a highly unusual feat for women in music. In the late 1930s, Scott idolized Williams and kept her picture on the wall of her room. And in later years, the two would become the closest of friends.

"THE WRONG PLACE FOR THE RIGHT PEOPLE"

In 1938, Scott's popularity as a "swinger of classics" soared. She played first with her own short-lived fourteen-piece band and was invited to perform at the exclusive Le Mirage in downtown Manhattan, the first Black performer to integrate the club's entertainment. She became a regular on the *Fun Club* radio show and quickly earned the moniker "the mistress of Swing" in the media.[43] At age eighteen, she was featured in the Broadway production *Sing Out the News*, bringing down the house with her rendition of "Franklin D. Roosevelt Jones."[44] That appearance was instrumental in landing her an extended engagement at Barney Josephson's nightclub Café Society. In 1939, after the managers were left without entertainment on a busy election day, Billie Holiday, who had headlined there, suggested Scott as a fill-in.[45] She accepted a three-week gig that went on to last for six years. Still only in her late teens, she was already a seasoned entertainment veteran, yet her run at Café Society would prove to be pivotal in her personal and professional life, just as it would be in Lena Horne's.

Josephson, formerly a New Jersey shoe salesman, had opened Café Society just a year earlier. As a Jewish liberal, he wanted to create a space unlike the rigidly segregated atmosphere of most New York nightclubs. He hired staff and musicians of all races and, controversially, catered to customers of all races and classes. The political cabarets of Eastern Europe served as his inspiration for the club, whose slogan was "the wrong place for the right people."[46] Café Society became a downtown hub for radical left politics. Helen Lawrenson, the celebrated leftist editor of *Vanity Fair*, later claimed that it had been opened explicitly to raise money for the Communist Party USA, by order of Earl Browder, the party's general secretary. "Jazz and politics were what it was all about," she wrote. Lawrenson, who acted as hostess and co-collaborator with Josephson during the earliest stages of the club's development, was a self-identified fellow traveler of the party. As she noted, the Depression had created an ideal environment for this kind of activist political gathering place: "The politics of hunger bred left-leaning radicalism, it raised the prospect of interracial workers' alliances . . . because poverty [or the threat of poverty] stalked black and white alike."[47]

On any given night, a patron might encounter a table of communists next to a table of socialists and mingle with early civil rights activists and others who considered themselves to be part of the Black freedom movement or the popular or cultural fronts.[48] Thus, the owners, the artists, and some of the club's patrons were under constant FBI surveillance and were regularly questioned and harassed.[49] The bureau tracked the movements at Café Society so closely that, by 1944, when Scott had to elicit help from the FBI due to a string of threatening telegrams, agents already seemed to have an extensive dossier on many of the people involved. Scott's connection to Café Society and its activism was one of the reasons her name eventually appeared on HUAC's blacklist. But she was not the only left-leaning celebrity who frequented the club. The actors Lucille Ball, Desi Arnaz, Fredi Washington, and Henry Fonda were regulars, as was the dancer Bill Robinson and the future congressman Franklin D. Roosevelt Jr. Listeners in any corner of the 210-seat venue could overhear conversations about politics, alternative philosophies, and injustice, and nineteen-year-old Scott soaked up the atmosphere.[50] Along the way, she struck up lifelong friendships with Paul Robeson and other activists, performed at countless fundraisers for radical and progressive causes, and grew even more staunchly committed to activism. She needed little prodding: she was already well aware of the economic and racial inequities that concerned the radical community.

Even without its leftist leanings, Café Society would have drawn packed houses, thanks to the high quality of its entertainment. In addition to Scott, numerous top-notch acts overlapped at the club during the era. Billie Holiday headlined there exclusively for two consecutive years, and the vocalists Lena Horne and Josh White, the dancer Pearl Primus, the comedian Jimmy Savo, and the pianists Mary Lou Williams and Art Tatum also performed.[51] Katherine Dunham made occasional appearances with her dance troupe. A young singer named Sarah Vaughn got her start there.

According to the historian Mark Naison, the Communist Party made purposeful efforts to embrace Black culture during the 1930s. Young American-born communists were "convinced that Afro American music represented the keystone of an American musical culture that was 'democratic' in spirit and form." They were especially interested "in black musical idioms that were commercially successful—swing and hot jazz." Via these popular forms, "some communists saw a unique opportunity, in identifying with this music, to dramatize the Afro-American contribution to American culture and the cultural benefits of interracial cooperation."[52] Café Society's goal was to illuminate these contributions; and for gifted African American performers, the opportunity to earn a steady living by singing or playing was compelling. Beyond a paycheck, they also understood the cultural and social significance of Black music as the foundation of popular nonsecular American music and social dance. Long underappreciated and unrecognized, they were now receiving the recognition they deserved. Moreover, as the dance historians Sondra Lomax and George Jackson note, "African American artists of many genres . . . [were] focused on the possibilities of broadening American democracy to include Blacks."[53]

Within this collection of extraordinary talent, Scott, confident and enchanting, became the star attraction of a sophisticated club crowd. But yet another opportunity transformed her into a genuine celebrity. RCA-Victor invited her to participate, with five other musicians, in a jam session that the musician and producer Leonard Feather would record on wax. All four of the songs they recorded—"Mighty Like the Blues," "Calling All Bars," "Why Didn't William Tell?," and "You Gave Me the Go-By"—were his compositions. The records sold well, and Feather became a champion of Scott's career. In 1940, RCA-Victor signed her to a hefty six-album deal. Musicians and enthusiasts were impressed, and the saxophonist Coleman Hawkins hired Scott to write arrangements for his new band. In 1939 and 1941, Barney Josephson featured Scott as the main attraction, along with the other regulars at Café Society, in a series of Carnegie Hall concerts with the theme "Spirituals to Swing."[54]

Black newspapers followed Scott's every move, and the white press also took notice of her rise. Reporters tracked her appearances, charity work, and activism as well as her salary and possessions. She became such a draw at Café Society that Josephson increased her salary from an initial $40 per week to a whopping $1,500, an unheard-of figure for a Black woman performer in the 1940s. It was also notable, given that Josephson had a reputation for underpaying his artists. In June 1940, Scott appeared on the cover of the NAACP's magazine *Crisis* and was also featured in *Vogue*. In May 1941, she premiered a show at the New York University's School of Education, where she was crowned the first Black "Queen of Senior Prom." A few days later, she performed in a newly organized program series for the Harlem Cultural Society. She was in astonishing demand among Black and white patrons alike. Her popularity was so intense that a Hazel Scott/Café Society association was formed, lasting from 1939 to 1943.[55]

"SOME THOUGHT HER ARROGANT, OTHERS KNEW THAT SHE SIMPLY DEMANDED RESPECT"

Night after night, in every performance, Scott offered her audiences an alternative to the light-skinned, curly-haired, black beauties who pervaded the national music scene. Though she was not dark-skinned, she was brown in appearance and had cropped hair. Her popularity during her heyday was primarily based on her musicianship, but it was secured by a carefully crafted image of African American glamour and pride that challenged negative conceptions of Black women.

Scott was always concerned about the persona she projected to both white and Black audiences. Many observers describe her as confident, poised, and sophisticated.[56] Gene Caldwell, a Harlem resident during this era, often watched Scott perform at the Apollo Theater and recalled the artist's impact on her as a young girl:

> She was a beautiful woman and talented. The Black community really supported her. . . . Little girls have dreams about what they want to do [and] I thought, gee, maybe I could play the piano like Hazel Scott. I used to sit on the side of the Apollo where the piano was, so I could see her hands. I was fascinated with her hands. . . . She was always a lady. She always played the piano. She always played herself.[57]

The Black community offered some safety, but Scott's concerns about image and representation in front of white audiences were justified. Every contribution made by Black activists, artists, and performers was viewed through a racialized and chauvinistic lens. For instance, in a 1944 issue of the *Partisan Review*, the cultural critic James Agee published an egregiously racist critique of Black popular artists, targeting several celebrities, including Paul Robeson and Duke Ellington, but saving the thrust of his critique for Scott. He accused her of "being Niggery" and selling herself to audiences by engaging in the "exploitation of her bust and armpits" and expressing "grimaces of creative mock-orgasm." Regarding her musicianship, he wrote, "She plays the kind of jazz that one could probably pick up through a correspondence school" and "which any mediocre elementary piano teacher would slap her silly for."[58] Agee's critique of Scott's abilities as a pianist and entertainer reached far beyond the pale. His response to her image, persona, and musicianship was visceral and violent. He attacked every aspect of her performance and appearance, and his article is peppered with racialized and gendered insults. Yet he was not alone in such excoriations. His critiques were emblematic of the extreme reaction that some whites had to Scott's dignified presentation and layers of resistance.

The African American community reacted to Scott's popular image much differently. In January 1945, *The School Review* published an article by the researcher Rebecca Evans Carroll titled "Relation of Social Environment to the Moral Ideology and Personal Aspirations of Negro Boys and Girls." The article documented her study to "determine the relation of the socioeconomic status of boys and girls in a Negro community." It was designed to illuminate their conception of right and wrong and identify "their ideas of the person they would most like to resemble."[59] One section asked girls and boys (most were about age thirteen) to describe their "ideal self." The majority of girls identified, first, Hazel Scott and, second, Lena Horne as a "glamorous adult." The boys overwhelmingly chose the boxer Joe Louis.[60] Although the children were given a minimal selection of famous African Americans from which to choose, their decisions emphasized the most revered national figures. By showcasing national Blackness with pride, glamour, and prestige, these children had placed themselves in the modern historical moment.

African American resistance to negative constructions was an essential component of the Black struggle during the World War II era. A key layer of Scott's opposition centered on her affirmation of the professional performance of African American womanhood, her conscious focus on Black dignity and pride, and her off-stage activism. In a 1944 description of one of Scott's performances at the Café Society Uptown (the club's second venue, which opened in 1940), a reporter from *Baltimore's Afro American* wrote about her influence on the pervading atmosphere:

> The difference between Café Society Uptown and most other night-clubs is similar to the difference between chess and blackjack. Miss Scott contributes to this atmosphere. Men look at her and pant, but

> they are polite about it. . . . Watch Miss Scott flitter down the aisle to
> the piano. White spectators lean out to talk to her, but she maneuvers
> away and sits at the piano. All the lights are dim. Her round, brown
> face and sensuous shoulders are illuminated only by a spotlight. She
> plays three or four numbers. As soon as a number is over, she floats
> through the café, which she calls a "room," and gets upstairs to her
> dressing room.[61]

Patrons took Scott's accessibility for granted, but she would not capitulate. Controlling access to her person was yet another layer of her resistance. Never one to sit and mingle with the sometimes-raucous crowds at the clubs, she preferred the privacy of her dressing room. She explained to an interviewer, "I am not kidding when I say I don't like nightclubs. People go to them to get drunk and show other people they're having a good time."[62] This avoidance is not surprising, given Scott's understanding of the way in which African American women, since enslavement, had been positioned as wanton objects of sexual desire. Sexualization had become entrenched in society's view of African American womanhood. As a result, according to the historian Darlene Clark Hine, "resistance to sexual exploitation . . . had major political and economic implications."[63]

Scott recognized her predicament as a Black woman in the entertainment industry, recalling that audience members and managers sometimes "mistook her sensuality for promiscuity." As with Dunham, newspaper coverage of Scott too often focused on her physical attributes instead of her talents. Earl Wilson of the *New York Post* exclaimed, "In a strapless evening gown, she makes most sweater girls look underfed." An article in *Time* referred to her as the "hot classicist." The white media insisted on highlighting her color and her sex appeal. In *Collier's*, Luther Davis wrote, "On the stage appeared a lovely colored girl of an even twenty years, a dusky beauty with large flirtatious eyes, a pouting mouth."[64] Racist expectations combined with homophobic norms meant that Scott's rejection of male advances placed her in a double-bind: "Everyone wants to sleep with you. If you don't, you've got problems. When you brush off the bosses and geniuses in the front office, you automatically become a lesbian. If you do go along with these idiots, you're a bum. Name it and take your choice."[65]

There is no doubt that both Black and White women, in all occupations, could have told stories like these. However, being an African American woman artist added complications. Like many before her, Scott walked a fine line as an entertainer. At times, she embraced her sexuality and sex appeal in an effort to advance and secure her career. At others, she rejected it in an effort to be taken seriously by the entertainment industry and the larger society. Though she was characterized as a sex symbol in the media, intimate descriptions of her personal life do not reveal any overemphasis on sex or sexuality. The media was never privy to the totality of Scott.

As Hine writes, in this atmosphere, a "culture of dissemblance" was a necessary survival mechanism for Black women. Due to their historical experiences of rape, sexual exploitation, and oppression, they needed to develop skills "that created the appearance of openness and disclosure but actually shielded the truth of their inner lives and selves from their oppressors."[66] If we see Scott as operating from within this culture, then we should interpret her sensual, celebrity persona as merely a small part of her complete and authentic self. Part of her success as an entertainer relied on the audience's perception of her as open, engaging, and approachable, no matter what her inner feelings might be at the moment. The reporter Roy Coverley picked up on the duality of Scott's existence when he wondered, "What kind of person is she inside? This is hard to say. She is definitely an enigma." He continued:

> She is extremely pleasant to meet when you can manage to meet her, which is not too easy. She rather avoids the crowd, and though she is grateful for the admiration of people she shows diffidence in mixing with them. . . . She does not talk much but, when moved to talk, can talk of things that you never thought she had the slightest knowledge of, like philosophy. When among her friends and not in the public eye, she likes to be treated as a friend and not as *the* Hazel Scott.[67]

Because Scott was working in an integrated and privileged liberal space, she was, at times, able to be more transparent than many other Black women performers were. Offstage, she could retire to her dressing room, but during her performances she was less accommodating. Leonard Feather recalled, "The bright-eyed jubilance with which she performed could freeze in an instant; nobody who ever saw her will forget her habit of stopping suddenly, transfixing any noisemaker with an icy glare and waiting for total silence before she resumed. Some thought her arrogant; others knew that she simply demanded respect."[68] In such moments, the audience was certainly privy to her inner feelings.

Scott was notably able to use the culture of dissemblance as both a shield and a dagger. She engaged in the practice to keep her inner self safe but also as a means of denying access to her full persona, if she so desired. Her contribution to image and representation, on her own terms, was striking in an era when Black performers suffered countless indignities and careers were often short-lived. She rose to the top of the entertainment industry while also refusing to compromise her dignity.

"COLORED PERFORMERS REPRESENT THEIR PEOPLE"

Scott came to the attention of Hollywood in 1941, when she was asked to test for the film *Panama Hattie* and Orson Welles selected her to play the role of Lil Hardin Armstrong in a movie that would trace the history of jazz. Neither project materialized, but by 1942 other directors were in hot pursuit. Scott appeared first in *Something to Shout About*, and she was subsequently offered parts in two other films that year: *I Dood It* and *Tropicana*. In successive years, starting in 1943, she appeared in *The Heat's On*, *Broadway Rhythm*, and *Rhapsody in Blue*. Scott's preexisting popularity, as well as her skill as a pianist and a showwoman, made her stand out among the handful of Black actresses in Hollywood. Barney Josephson, who acted as her manager, drew up a contract template specifying that she would appear only as herself in movies, prohibiting misrepresentations of her skin color and other degrading representations: "You cannot change her color, nor make her darker or lighter than she is. She would play the piano and sing, but not as a maid in somebody else's house. You cannot put a bandana on her head, nor an apron on her body. You cannot present her in any way that would be a bad reflection upon her people; if you do she won't work."[69]

The wording of the contract anticipated Hollywood's many tactics for perpetuating negative representations of African Americans in movies of the era. American audiences needed to be able to identify actors as obviously Black or white. Black actors were treated as a static commodity: either very dark in complexion or light enough to pass for white. Though Lena Horne, as a light-skinned woman, was offered a larger variety of roles than darker-skinned woman were, the Black press often referred to her as "the copper-colored girl," and she faced casting difficulties. Color photos reveal that her actual skin tone was bronze-hued, but black-and-white film and early movie cameras failed to capture accurate complexion gradients, and stage makeup was designed for white skin.

Scott's prohibition against appearing in bandanas or aprons may have seemed curious to white actors but was completely understandable to African American performers, even among those who willingly donned them. Most of the few opportunities for Black actors involved portraying servants. Scott explained, "I've turned down four singing maid roles in movies during the past year or so. . . . There are plenty of white performers who can play maids' roles and then step into a penthouse or a school classroom. Colored performers represent their people."[70] Even when she appeared in films that distorted the image of African Americans, she believed that, by appearing as herself—a poised, talented, and successful woman who demanded respect from whites—she was advancing the economic, cultural, and political advancement of African Americans, particularly women.

For instance, in *I Dood It*, Scott and Horne were featured as peers and professionals. At the beginning of a short scene, three white producers eagerly await the performers' arrival. First, Scott strides into the audition wearing a full-length white fur with an elegant black sequined gown. She rushes onto the stage, and then Horne enters the scene in similarly elegant attire. Together they perform the song "Jericho." The scene features a collection of secondary singers and musicians attired in tuxedos and beautiful dresses. Although the scene was so short that it could be cut from the film when it was shown in the South, it treats the Black actors, particularly Scott and Horne, with respect, and their characters are imbued with some measure of dignity.[71]

Horne and Scott were also allowed to shine in 1943's *Broadway Rhythm*, a backstage musical, though, again, their parts were not integral to the loose narrative. For the most part, they dress in fashionable costumes in the film and are treated as illustrious performers. However, in one unfortunate scene in "The Jungle Room," Horne is outfitted in a sparse, exotic costume that shows her midriff. Conga players and dancers back her as she sings "Brazilian Boogie." In Scott's scene, the pianist plays herself, as stipulated in her contract. Bejeweled and wearing an evening gown, she performs a boogie-inspired version of Frédéric Chopin's "Minute Waltz."[72] For African American women who believed they were on the cusp of a new American equality, such a vision must have felt like a symbol of the coming world.

There was a chasm between the efforts and activism of actresses such as Horne and Scott and the realities of Hollywood in the 1930s and 1940s. The depictions of life as seen in the movies had little relation to the physical space of Hollywood's studio lots and high-end residential neighborhoods, where segregation and racial inequality were still at work. The industry's wartime aspirations to exhibit some semblance of American unity across lines of race and class stood in stark contrast to the nation's legacy of racial separation and oppression. When Red baiting ascended in the late 1940s, the leftists among Hollywood's producers, directors, actors, and writers were among the first communities to be investigated and prosecuted, in large part because of their potential impact on interracialism.

Scott saw this contradiction firsthand in her next studio film, *The Heat's On*. In her first scene, an elaborately staged musical number, she is seated at a black piano, wearing a black gown studded with white accents. She belts out the song "The Black Keys and the White Keys."[73] After a solo by a horn-playing puppeteer, the camera pans back to Scott, now seated between two grand pianos, one black and one white. She plays the melody with a hand on each instrument.

This song, composed by Jay Gorney, Henry Myers, and Edward Eliscu, was one of many musical numbers of the era to be heavily influenced by popular front ideology. The lyrics' subtext transparently refers to interracialism and unity, both popular front objectives. By featuring a groundbreaking African American woman pianist playing a tune that advocated for equality and eschewed racialized, stereotyped constructions, the scene was very close to the limits of Hollywood progressivism. And at least one of the song's composers paid the price. In the early 1950s, Gorney, also the writer of the well-known Depression-era song "Brother, Can You Spare a Dime?," was blacklisted for radical activity.[74]

Scott's next scene in *The Heat's On* was more problematic. "The Caisson Number" was intended to appeal to African American patriotism and acknowledge Black citizens' contributions to the war effort. But as I discussed in the introduction to this book, it included debasing representations of African American women. In the original conception, actors, dressed as soldiers, and actresses, playing their sweethearts and dressed as maids, dance to a syncopated version of "The Caisson Song." A few older Black women are dressed in mammy-like attire, and a stray dog is thrown in for good measure.

This was Hollywood's vision of Black urban spaces. After blowing up in anger, Scott asked the choreographer David Lichine, "Have you ever seen any Negroes other than your own domestic servants?" With this question, she highlighted the legacy of American segregation and racial inequality that complicated every Hollywood production. Movie sets were dominated by whites who had little to no interaction with African Americans and harbored the same racial attitudes as most of the rest of their white American contemporaries did. Scott refused to perform in the scene until the costuming was adjusted. She recalled, "Until my fight at Columbia, no Black person had ever dared oppose the establishment. You either kept your mouth shut and took the roles you got or remained out of work."[75] In the end, the film's producers gave in to her demands in order to continue production, but the uproar short-circuited Scott's film career. She would shoot only one more, *Rhapsody in Blue*, as required by contractual obligation.

In later years, Scott identified *Rhapsody in Blue* as her favorite film role, and there is much to like.[76] The film is a biopic of the composer George Gershwin and is set in Paris. In her scene, the camera opens with Scott at the piano singing "The Man I Love." When the actor Robert Alda (playing Gershwin) appears, Scott introduces him to the crowd in French before returning to her performance. Dressed in a white satin gown and dripping in diamonds, she is portrayed as glamorous and worldly, a musician worthy of playing for the renowned composer. The Black community responded favorably. During the making of the movie, the *Afro American* announced, "Miss Scott will recreate the character of a colored pianist who inspired [Gershwin] one afternoon while strolling the streets of Paris. . . . So Miss Scott will be both seen and heard when the great feature is finished and released." Phil Carter, a reporter at the *Chicago Defender*, was impressed, dubbing her "Queen once more in Warner's *Rhapsody in Blue*." [77] He reflected, "It is doubtful that anyone who has followed films over the years can remember when a Negro artist has been permitted to display her cultural abilities as does the glamorous Hazel in *Rhapsody in Blue*."[78]

The film is unusual in that Scott's scene appears to be an integral part of the narrative. In it, her playing is interspersed with Gershwin's conversation. He sits at a table where he will meet his love interest, and her music is audible in the background, even when she is not visible. It would have been difficult to cut Scott out of the scene for southern movie audiences, as Gershwin's romantic meeting plays an essential role in the film. Whether intentional or not, this made the scene extraordinary for the time. Most scenes featuring

Black performers were continuous segments that could be easily added or removed and held no significance in the film's sequencing.

Unsurprisingly, the South had an adverse reaction to the film; and regardless of the impact on its integrity, Scott's appearance was edited for southern audiences. The image of a worldly and poised Scott was far too alarming. The Memphis Board of Censors was among those that removed her from the film. The same year, they also pulled a scene from *The Sailor Takes a Wife*, in which Robert Walker, the white hero, tips his hat to Rochester, a popular Black actor. The film *Brewster's Millions* was banned altogether because the Black character "moved through the film on easy terms with the white principals." Southern cities that did screen *Rhapsody in Blue* and other films featuring more affirmative portrayals of African Americans did so in segregated theaters. In 1945, Scott herself encountered Jim Crow face to face when she attempted to see the movie at a theater in Washington, D.C. Although the nation was at the height of the war for democracy abroad, its capital continued its practice of segregating theaters. The star was turned away at the door.[79]

Unfortunately, roles like Scott's in *Rhapsody in Blue* were not a reality for most African American women in Hollywood during or after the war. Long after Scott took her stand against "dirty Hoover aprons," Black women were continuing to fight negative depictions of African American womanhood. In 1946, Billie Holiday was cast in her only feature film, *New Orleans*. She described the making of the movie: "I'd fought my whole life to keep from being somebody's damn maid. And after making more than a million bucks and establishing myself as a singer who had some taste and self respect, it was a real drag to go to Hollywood and end up as a make believe maid."[80] Her experience reinforced the worst fears of African American women performers who had been "discovered" by Hollywood.

Throughout her career, Holiday was maligned in the press and harassed by the government. She did sometimes deploy her art as resistance, as seen in her performance of the song "Strange Fruit." Still, she was bemused by the way in which Hollywood had manipulated her image. Her experience in *New Orleans* confirmed that the small amount of Black female pride that had filtered into films during the war was a mirage. Clearly the conflict had not been the panacea for American inequality that many African Americans had hoped it would be. Holiday's casting in this film was a reversal of the gains that Scott and Horne had made.[81] Scott, too, came to see the impact of this reversal on her life after the war.

"A NEW KIND OF NEGRO COUPLE"

Scott allowed one audience member to see her in totality: Adam Clayton Powell Jr., the much-loved Harlem congressman, whom she would marry in 1945. Like many who watched her, he was captivated by her beauty, intelligence, and dignified stage persona. Known as a playboy, he nonetheless developed a genuine admiration and respect for Scott. Powell was Harlem royalty, the son of Adam Clayton Powell Sr., pastor of the century old Abyssinian Baptist Church, and Mattie Powell, a devoted wife and esteemed community member. Their son grew up roaming the church's hallways and the streets of Harlem. He attended prestigious Townsend Harris High School and Colgate University. A rebellious young man, Powell surprised his parents by announcing that he would follow in his father's footsteps and enter the ministry. By 1937, he had succeeded his father as acting pastor and was a busy community leader. In 1941, he was elected to the New York city council, becoming the first African American to hold a seat. [82]

Powell and Scott became friends through their political work and Powell's regular visits to Café Society. By this time, the offstage, protest-based layer of Scott's resistance had begun to crystallize, and Powell's rising political star and Scott's skyrocketing popularity gave them something in common: invitations to make appearances and lend their names to various causes. Another commonality was their involvement, like most of their peers, in the Double Victory campaign, which focused on victory abroad over fascism and victory domestically over racism.[83] Their involvement in this campaign clarified their shared aspiration to break down barriers of discrimination and segregation. Scott also worked with the People's Council, a lobbying organization that Powell had formed to combat racism. They were often on the same bill at Double Victory fundraisers, rallies, and political events. It was at one of these rallies that Powell made an unscheduled announcement of his candidacy for Congress. In an impassioned speech before 20,000 people, he condemned America's treatment of African Americans and proclaimed to the captivated crowd, "American fascism marks the wolf of Ku Klux Klan hypocrisy behind the sheep's clothing of pseudo patriotism." His answer to this hypocrisy was to encourage Black protest. Powell's unexpected announcement effectively stole the congressional nomination from A. Philip Randolph, who had been unable to speak at the rally due to time constraints.[84]

For African Americans, few leaders symbolized the new face of Black America more than Adam Clayton Powell Jr. By now, he had given up his seat as councilman, where his early activism in the "Don't Buy Where You Can't Work" campaign had revealed him to be an unrelenting and radical advocate for Harlem residents. That campaign had begun as an effort to force white Harlem businesses to hire Black employees. Although it had been initiated by a broad coalition of Black organizations, not by Powell himself, it nevertheless helped propel him into the national spotlight. In 1942, he founded the *People's Voice* newspaper, which covered local, national, and world events and featured a host of well-known writers, intellectuals, and artists as columnists and subjects. Fredi Washington was the theatrical editor and Marvel Cooke an assistant managing editor. The paper was a conduit for Powell's activism and his ego, but it also published hard-hitting stories and did not hide its communist affiliations, making it a unique and unusually radical space among newspapers, whether Black or mainstream.[85]

Powell was outspoken, brave, and flamboyant. Worse, he was a relentless advocate for African American rights. He was the embodiment of what white society feared in Black protest, and this drew the unwanted attention of J. Edgar Hoover, the director of the FBI, who requested intelligence on him even before he was elected to Congress. The FBI saw him as such a serious threat to the status quo that it kept a dossier on him for more than thirty years. During World War I, the government and its agencies had placed Marcus Garvey under surveillance, with the goal of destroying his political power and organization. They hoped to do the same with Powell. But despite their efforts, he kept his seat, becoming an excellent politician and representative and helping to pass more than fifty bills between 1961 and 1966.[86]

His marriage to Scott only aided his career. Yet they were an unlikely match for several reasons. Powell was a minister, while Scott was a secular star in the entertainment world. Powell came from a light-skinned family that was part of the Black bourgeoisie, while Scott had been raised by single working immigrant mother in a crowded Harlem brownstone. Powell was also a married man. He had been with his first wife, the actress Isabel Washington, a sister of Fredi Washington, for thirteen years when he fell in love with Scott.[87]

Regardless of these differences, friends and family soon saw that Powell and Scott's relationship was not simply friendship. Scott said, "He was turned on to me first, and I ran. Much to my regret, I have to admit that I ran from him." She recalled, "He took his time. First, the gifts. Nothing elaborate: a book; a photograph; the loan of a silk scarf that I kept. His ring; his handkerchief, his favorite poetry." The romance slowly grew. As Powell later revealed later to an interviewer for *Ebony*, "our courtship was compounded of visits to Café Society, dinners at Reubens, luncheons at '21,' liberal quantities of floral perfume and hours of intense discussion of such varied topics as philosophy, politics, boogie-woogie, and war."[88] His intentions were serious. Before winning his election, he told a friend, "I'm going to marry that girl—but first I'm going to Congress! No one is ever going to call me Mr. Hazel Scott!"[89]

The affair scandalized Harlem circles. Aside from their shock at the blaring sin of adultery, the color-struck, churchgoing Harlem bourgeoisie felt that the brown-skinned performer from Trinidad was unworthy of a man of Powell's stature and hue. Scott remembered, "Oh, there was a great deal said by others about him marrying a brown skinned woman and a nightclub performer. But Adam had married his first wife because he loved her, not because she was fair, and he married me for the same reason."[90] Most onlookers, however, preferred the light-skinned Isabel, whom they saw as a far more appropriate match.

According to Powell, his first marriage was already under strain before he and Scott began their affair.[91] As he was leaving for the Capitol, Powell coldly informed Isabel that their marriage was over and set a date to marry Scott, telling his first wife that he would be bringing Scott to Washington as Mrs. Powell. Devastated, Isabel rightfully felt betrayed and shared her scorn with the press. Many readers agreed with her, seeing Scott's "other woman" behavior as shameful, not what a "good woman" would do. Yet Scott remained defiant. Unfazed by the pressure to conform to traditional expectations, she told inquirers that she was happy to be marrying someone as distinguished as Powell.

The Scott-Powell wedding was the affair of the 1945 summer season, making the cover of the widely circulated Harlem-based *Amsterdam News*. The headline, quoting Powell, read, "At Long Last, the Woman I Love."[92] A reporter described the scene outside the reception at Café Society: "Three thousand guests organized in a single column by twenty-five cops slowly filed into the nightclub, where they gawked at the famous bride and groom." He called it "the biggest, boldest and most talked about wedding. . . . It took precedent over Yolanda Dubois's marriage to Countee Cullen in 1929 and topped by a big margin the daughter of Mme. A'Lelia Walker's $15,000 wedding."[93]

Beyond all the sensationalism surrounding their love affair, the marriage brought together two people with deep political concerns about the second-class status of African Americans. It also cemented Scott's status as a leading African American star and race woman. According to the historian Donald Bogle, "[as] the second wife of fiery politico Adam Clayton Powell II, she represented half of a new kind of Negro couple: educated, cultured, political, outspoken; a modern woman who didn't brook fools easily."[94] Deeply in love, Powell often expressed his admiration for his wife. "Her mind is brilliant," he declared. Marveling at her quest for knowledge, he said, "She is never anywhere without a book by her side, usually the heavy, challenging, demanding type."[95] The Powells were the picture of Black upper-class modernity and wielded considerable political, economic, and social power. They purchased an expensive property in Harlem, had a house built on Long Island, and owned a home in Washington, D.C. They vacationed globally; spearheaded campaigns; were involved in court cases fighting for equal rights, housing, and jobs in New York; and were regularly featured in the national Black and white press as a model Black couple.

Scott gave birth to a son, Adam Clayton Powell III, a year into their marriage, but this did not slow her down. Many women, including entertainers, automatically stopped working outside the home after getting married. Scott continued performing but also made time to be a mother. Her son, known in the family as Skipper, fondly remembers how his parents worked to construct a life for him that was as normal as possible. At the end of each week, his mother would fly home overnight so as to spend every weekend day and as many other days as possible with her family.[96] Despite their hectic schedule, both parents created family rituals for their son. Like other families, they went to the movies and attended church. Because Scott was out of town for most of the week, the weekends became the center of their unusual life. In an interview in *Ebony*, she said, "Saturdays is what we call our family day. We make it a point to be at home. . . . We take Skipper to the show and sit through millions of cartoons." Family dinners, walks, and reading occupied their downtime.[97] Adam Clayton Powell III especially looked forward to the family's customary Sunday stroll down Eighth Avenue.[98]

Come Monday, however, both parents would be off to their jobs. Against the gender expectations of her time, she was convinced that women should honor their own personal interests: "I believe . . . that every woman should have some interest, some preoccupation outside of her home and husband.

She should spend an hour or two on something every week—and I don't mean bridge either. She has to get outside herself, has to do something if she doesn't want to become narrow."[99] Yet as she would discover, resisting the heavy expectations of motherhood and wifehood was a hard task.

Powell and Scott were strong personalities; and by the time they married, both had already developed fully formed opinions of the world. What drew them together would eventually tear them apart. Despite the public image they created, fissures developed early in their marriage. Scott was twenty-five years old when they wed. In the 1940s, most women of her age would have been married for several years. And although many Black women worked outside the home, most still expected the man to be the primary breadwinner. But Scott was a veteran performer who was used to earning her own money. She had been forced to grow up quickly, navigating nightclubs, musicians, unions, and the stage in order to support her family. In contrast, Powell was thirty-seven years old, a divorced man, well educated, and a community legend with considerable influence. He felt he had the right to demand changes in Scott's approach to her career. He wanted her to stop all appearances at nightclubs, retire from Café Society, and begin a touring as a concert pianist.

Scott recalled, "Adam had been adamant that no nightclub work was to be permitted. Although I had given one or two isolated concerts, I had never taken on a full-scale concert tour with all its rigors. He insisted that as a concert artist, no one could find fault with his choice of me as a wife. He declared that all of my classical training was wasted if I did not concertize." He also stepped in to manage her career and took charge of her financial holdings: "As if it were yesterday, I can recall the phone conversation with Adam leaning over my shoulder as I talked with the representative of the Shuberts. A brand new musical was being mounted. . . . It was a marvelous opportunity and would have meant the continuation of a bright career. Instead, I refused the offer. At Adam's insistence, I declared that it would have been too confining for a newly married lady."[100]

At first, Scott gave in to Powell's patriarchal control, but her nontraditional attitudes toward womanhood and her desire for freedom guaranteed failure. Jealously, infidelity, and violence also began marring their relationship. Divorce rumors arose early in their tempestuous marriage.[101] Still, for more than a decade, they stayed together. In her memoir, Scott wrote of arguments and brutal physical altercations in which she was on the losing end.[102] Her shock was deepened by Powell's numerous affairs. His infidelities were public knowledge, and Scott regularly discovered them for herself. She later mused, "It has long been a matter of some perplexity, why men, seeing women like myself at the top of their professions, are driven to pursue, win, and wed these women, only to attempt to pull down, desecrate, and destroy us."[103] Though there was genuine love between them, the power couple who so enamored the press was partly a mirage, and their unstable marriage would never become the fulfillment that Scott had hoped for. Luckily, the constant travel demanded by their careers kept them apart most of the time, and they remained a powerful team in the fight for social change.[104]

"I AM READY TO FIGHT NOW, NOT FOR MYSELF ALONE, BUT FOR MY RACE"

It might seem easy to connect Scott's social and political activism solely to her marriage to Powell, and the histories that focus on Powell do position her in this way. Yet in his biography of his father, Adam Clayton Powell III emphasizes the need for research on his mother and her political and social work. For that reason, his discussion of her in that book is intentionally minimal, and he has expressed pleasure at new research on her life and career.

Overt political work was an organic layer of Scott's resistance. Like the activist celebrities Paul Robeson and Langston Hughes, her schedule was packed with political appearances. She was deeply connected to the freedom rallies held in New York in the mid- and late 1940s. One of the largest, held in 1945 at Madison Square Garden, featured Scott, Robeson, Canada Lee, Kenneth Spencer, Pearl Primus, and Josh White in a revue titled *Carry On, America*, co-written by Hughes.[105] Along with the People's Committee and the Women's Action Committee, she was a primary organizer of a June 1947 rally to protest HUAC. Here and at many similar events, her most significant contribution was as a performer. At one point, she played the piano for four or five benefit concerts each week. She also lent formal and informal support to a variety of other issues, including Trinidadian independence and women's causes. In addition to her talent, Scott regularly contributed financially to causes. For instance, she donated a large sum of money to Benjamin Davis's controversial campaign to become the first Black communist member of New York's city council.[106]

Like many people, Scott hoped the war would reduce discrimination and racial segregation in America, so she performed for American GIs whenever

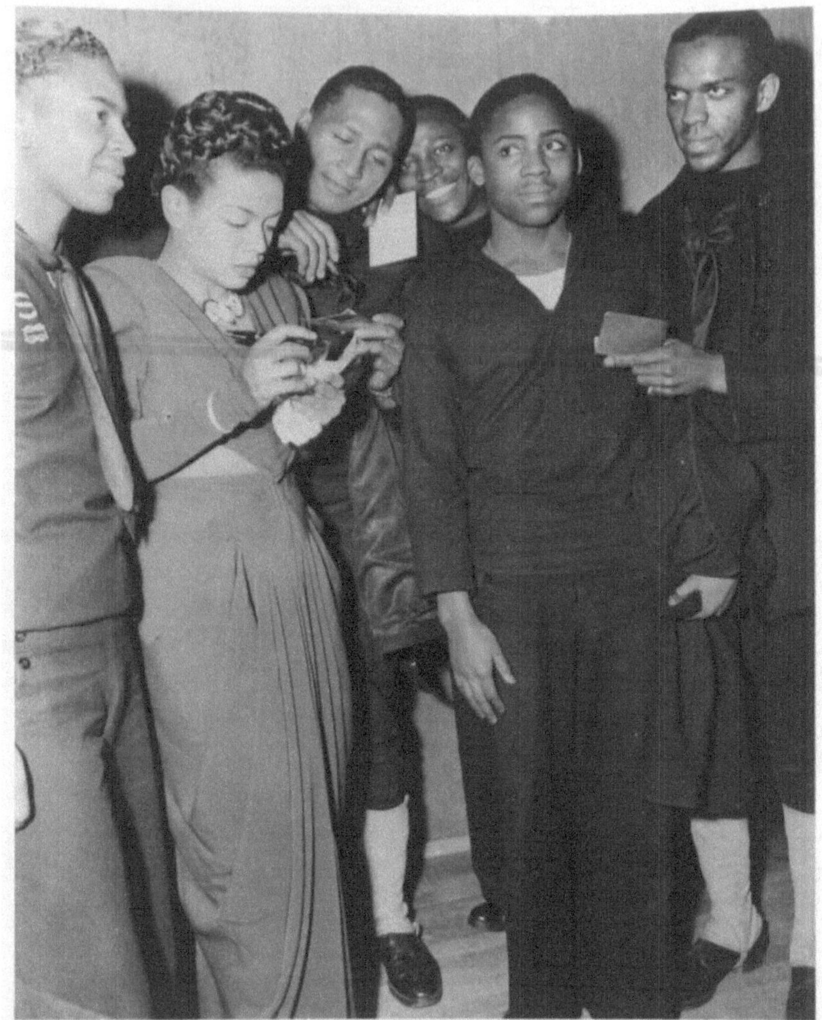

FIGURE 6. Hazel Scott signs autographs for Black servicemen at the Great Lakes Naval Training Station, December 1943. Courtesy of the Naval History and Heritage Command, Washington, DC.

an opportunity arose. She played at more than 1,000 shows for servicemen and belonged to more than a dozen war-related organizations. She even volunteered to perform for Black and white troops recovering in infectious disease wards, both in America and abroad, a risk that many other performers avoided.[107] Yet as she toured the country, her expectations for racial change in American life soon diminished.

After the Powells arrived in Washington, they were slowly invited into the beltway's intimate circles of power. Yet at first there was hesitation: Powell's swagger and self-confidence were repugnant to white powerbrokers, and the lingering air of scandal around his marriage kept the Black elite at arm's length. Scott herself had little interest in pursuing a social life in Washington, and Powell's primary focus was on breaking down the walls of discrimination and inequality for Black people. He had a tremendous ego, which could work to both his credit and detriment, but it did allow him to thrive without social acceptance in D.C.

Scott experienced many slights in the segregated city, but one in particular led to the couple's first major engagement with American racial injustice. Despite Scott's service to the war effort, the Daughters of the American Revolution (DAR) would not permit her to perform at Constitution Hall because she was African American. In response to that smear, she and Powell embarked on a full-throated media attack, castigating the DAR, First Lady Bess Truman (who had accepted an invitation to a tea with the DAR following the incident), and President Harry Truman himself. In interviews, Powell derided Mrs. Truman as "the Last Lady" because of her refusal to distance herself from the DAR and condemn its racism.[108] For Powell, this media attention was a convenient and politically expedient way to gain power in Washington. But for Scott, it was an affront to her humanity. She announced to the press that she would tour the country to fight "DARism." She added, "I know I won't be alone. . . . Many persons of that stamp will come along with me." She worked with the People's Council, whose goal was to "carry on campaigns for enlightenment against prejudice," to arrange a concert at Carnegie Hall. Scott told the press, "Every nickel that I earn at my Carnegie Hall concert . . . will go to the People's Council Fund. I am ready to fight now, not for myself alone, but for all my race. Since V-J Day, three Negroes have been lynched in this democracy."[109] With this pronouncement, Scott began one of her many tours to battle segregation and discrimination.

In integrated New York, her encounters with segregation had been limited. At Café Society, her main gig, the crowds had always been mixed. But incidents like the *Rhapsody in Blue* screening and the DAR's rejection made it clear she would have trouble elsewhere. So at the outset of her first nationwide tour, Scott added wording to her performance contract, declaring that she would not play to segregated audiences.[110] Her message was clear: if white segregationists wanted to see her, they would have to sit in a mixed audience or stay home.

Scott may have been able to keep her own audiences from being segregated. However, she still had to deal with the irreparable racial divide marking America and to make tactical use of her layered resistance. She remembered, "I played packed houses everywhere, even in St. Louis, where I was refused hotel rooms and not because of overcrowding. I finally got rooms with a private family." She noted that "other mid-west cities were more polite simply because I was Hazel Scott. In fact, they told me so."[111] When her car broke down in Boonoville, Missouri, the staff at Holt's Café said, "You'll have to eat in the kitchen." Scott retorted, "I'm sorry, but I don't eat in kitchens!" The "stony-faced waitress" then explained that her party could order takeout but would be unable to wait at the counter for it. Defiantly, Scott placed her order and refused to move. The waitress, with little choice, finally relented and allowed her to wait. When a reporter asked if she had identified herself to the café staff, Scott said, "I don't want any special privileges. There are 13,000,000 Hazel Scotts in America. They just don't play the piano!" She also spoke to the press about the racial discrimination she experienced in Topeka and Kansas City during her tour.[112] Yet in some ways Scott was fortunate. In 1940, the actress and singer Nina Mae McKinney ended up in the hospital after asking a soda fountain clerk in Lake City, Florida, for a cup of coffee. His response was to hit her with a "heavy club."[113]

During a 1948 tour in Texas, Scott refused to appear before a segregated crowd of 7,000 people at the University of Texas at Austin. The promoters had previously assured her that the booking would be integrated and that all attendees would be "sitting on the same level in the orchestra." But as Scott readied herself to perform, staff laid a red carpet down the center aisle, separating white attendees from Black attendees. She asked, "What justification can anyone have who comes to hear me and then objects to sitting next to another Negro?" The reaction in Texas was swift and unpleasant: Scott "was carried out of town by the sheriffs." Marian Anderson performed in the same venue later that year, much to the chagrin of the Black press and many Black Texans. who urged her to follow Scott's example.[114]

In 1950, Scott caused a stir at the University of North Carolina at Chapel Hill, where she had scheduled several performances. Following the first one, she learned that seating for African Americans had been limited to a small balcony section. She refused to play again until the school relented and allowed the audience to be integrated. An infuriated student wrote to the school's newspaper, the *Daily Tarheel*: "I am a native of this state, and I did not enter this tax-supported institution to have tolerance shoved down my throat. . . . Is it not indeed possible that a minority might persecute a majority on occasion?" But Scott dismissed such responses. She said, "I am proud of the fact that I am the first colored artist to refuse to play to segregated audiences. . . . I can do no less than refuse to be a silent partner of Jim Crow.[115] Scott was instrumental in desegregating, at least for a night, several venues. At her shows many Americans experienced their first ever mixed-race performance. Her tours were a one-woman fight for civil rights.

In February 1950, Scott was stranded on a train in Washington State that had been halted by heavy snowfall for three days. She and a friend got off the train and went into a diner in Pasco to order a meal. At the time Scott was suffering from a high fever, but this mattered little to the waitstaff, who promptly informed her that "colored" people were not served there. When Scott complained to the local police, the officer asked, "Are you going to get out of here, or am I going to have to run you in for disturbing the peace?" Scott did not eat dinner that night. On her arrival in Spokane, she declared, "I want the following three things in the following order: a bath, a hot drink, a lawyer." She called her husband that night, and together they swiftly filed a $50,000 lawsuit against the restaurant owners. On April 20, an article in the Spokane-based *Spokesman Review* announced, "A federal court jury awarded $250 in damages, yesterday, to New York concert pianist Hazel Scott, after deliberating more than sixteen hours."[116]

The story spread nationwide. In his column in the *Chicago Defender*, Langston Hughes condemned the incident and the American practice of segregation: "After those fine speeches the politicians made last November . . . now Hazel Scott can't get a bowl of soup in Pasco, Washington, U.S.A., because she is a brown girl, not white. If that is democracy, it's not a good brand." Though he pointed out that no one should have to be famous to be served, "when a Hazel Scott is refused service, it highlights the absurdity of American racial custom."[117] Scott's monetary award was not significant, but the case did bankrupt the restaurant owners and set a precedent in the state of Washington that eventually led to the 1953 Public Accommodations Act, bringing an end to statewide desegregation.[118]

Scott risked her professional reputation and livelihood each time she refused to perform at an engagement or took legal action against segregation.

These battles were not up for compromise. They were natural and critical layers in her contesting of race and gender inequality.

FADE TO BLACK

In 1948, 14,000 people squeezed into New York City's Lewisohn Stadium to see Scott perform with the New York Philharmonic Symphony Orchestra in her first appearance as a soloist. Her concert tours had spread her fame to a whole new segment of the nation. Along with her films, her nightclub appearances, and her political work, they had made her one of the most recognized Black performers of her day. She had raised her public profile to rare heights for a Black woman of her era, rivaling and initially even surpassing Lena Horne's.[119]

In 1950, at the zenith of her career, the DuMont Television Network offered Scott her own show. *The Hazel Scott Show* was the first television show to be hosted by an African American and to feature musical entertainment performed primarily by its host. It premiered a full six years before Nat King Cole's variety show, which is often mistakenly identified as the first Black-led show. But her victory over the new medium of television was short-lived: "Ultimately, the candor that had made Hazel Scott such a distinctive personality also helped to curtail her television career."[120]

Scott's layered resistance took many forms during the war and postwar years. But her popularity made her activism highly visible to the rising anti-radical, anticommunist crusaders who were sweeping the nation. No Black activist escaped the government's eye during the era of Red baiting. A month after her show premiered, Scott's name appeared in *Red Channels: The Report of Communist Influence in Radio and Television*, a special issue of the journal *Counterattack*, founded by former FBI agents with conservative backers.[121] Such publications, with their obsessive focus on communist infiltration, were peculiar to the early Cold War era. The *Red Channels* approach was to list the names of accused celebrities along with the organizations they were associated with. It included no testimonies, explanations, or interviews—in short, no proof. There were ten organizations listed beneath Scott's name, including the Committee to Elect Benjamin Davis and the National Negro Congress.

In an effort to defend her name and save her career, Scott volunteered to be interrogated by HUAC.[122] Although her son was very young at the time, he was deeply affected by the events that unfolded.

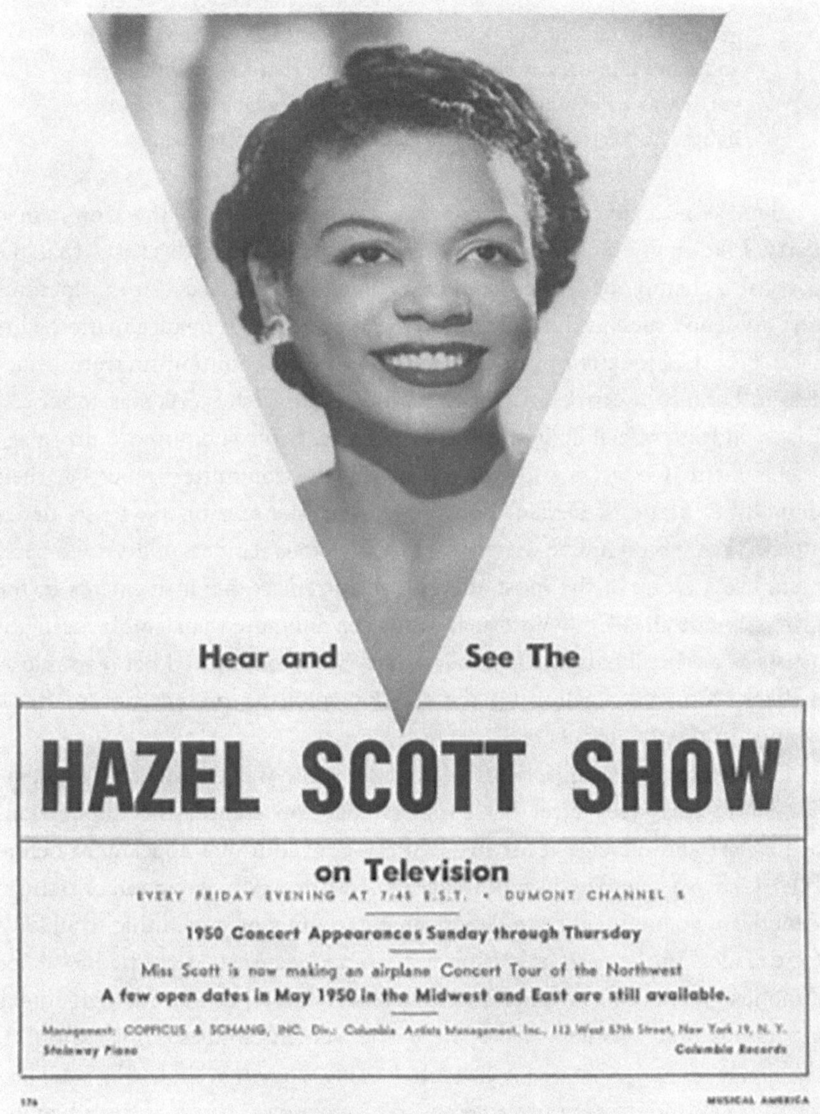

FIGURE 7. An advertisement for *The Hazel Scott Show*, 1950. It was the first television show to be hosted by an African American. Collection of the author.

I remember as a—I must have been five years old at the time . . . my father thought she was absolutely out of her mind to go before the committee. He said, "You can't win. No one wins by going before HUAC." And she said, "I want to go and clear my name. And who are you to say that I shouldn't do something which is right?" He was getting into all kinds of political trouble for the Powell amendment and other things, early civil rights legislation that he was writing. So yes, it was a defining moment, but a moment which was not taken lightly. And certainly, she wasn't unaware of what could happen.[123]

There is no evidence that Scott was ever a member of the Communist Party. Like many of her contemporaries, she did ally with causes that the party also championed. She also traveled in circles that had a strong communist influence, such as the Café Society crowd. But such nuance mattered little to HUAC. Her attempts to distance herself from communism were unsuccessful because the true goal of the anticommunist hysteria was to repress Black and interracial activism. In her defense, Scott submitted a fifty-page statement to Congress and testified before the committee, rebutting their dubious accusations. Defiant but also shaken, she said of the artists under attack, "We should not be written off by the vicious slanders of little and petty men. We are one of the most effective and irreplaceable instruments in the grim struggle ahead."[124] With such words she did more than simply highlight artists as a critical part of the public estate. She promulgated her own role as a Black woman struggling for the self-constructed representation of Black women in the public sphere.

Despite strong ratings, Scott's television show was canceled on September 29, 1950, a week after her congressional appearance. The implications of her on- and offstage resistance had crystallized in her appearance before HUAC. Scott's sudden disappearance erased a powerful depiction of African American womanhood from American entertainment, a void that would last for decades. In the early television era, women were not permitted to shape American media consumption and representations, especially not high-toned, glamorous Black women. According to the women's studies scholar Carol A. Stabile, Scott and other outspoken left-leaning women in the media were targeted because they were perceived as too influential: "None of these women represented proper American womanhood in the eyes of anti-communists."[125] They had dared to step out of their boxes.

Like the careers of other performers on the blacklist, Scott's would never be the same. Vilified in the papers, with her marriage crumbling, she toured Europe and moved to France, where she lived for a decade. She supported the American civil rights movement from abroad by making her home a respite for visiting Black artists and performers. She participated with the writer James Baldwin and others in a demonstration in support of the March on Washington. In the late 1960s, she eventually returned to the States but was unable to ever fully salvage her career.[126]

The renowned pianist went from being one of the most lauded Black women entertainers of the 1940s to a virtual unknown. By the time she returned, people had forgotten her contribution to the long freedom movement. Some accused her and her generation of being Uncle Toms. Her response to the 1960s radicals was direct: "I have a deep and abiding resentment for the so-called 'new Negro.' . . . I think he is late in arriving. . . . I'd like to know where you were 25 years ago when I put myself out of work, when I was called . . . a Communist, a radical, a professional Black lady, and an apologist for my race. I was told I waved my color like a banner."[127]

Scott's layered resistance was early, public, and unapologetic. Her pioneering refusals to play degrading film roles and perform to segregated audiences were only the most visible aspects of her opposition.[128] By merging offstage racial and gender justice activism with her onstage struggle for laudable images of African American women, she entered the pantheon of Black intellectuals, activists, performers, and artists who undertook Black struggle. She used her career to further Black advancement and quell oppression, and her uncompromising life was a model of Black feminist resistance.

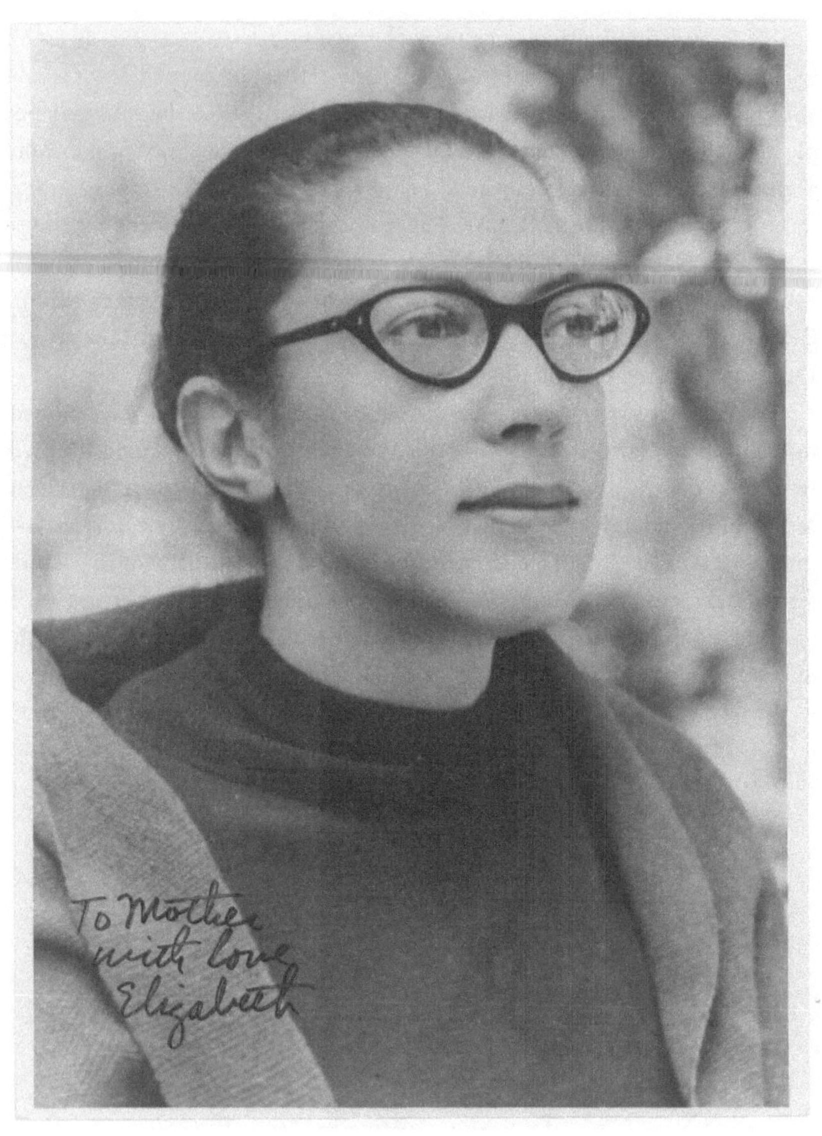

FIGURE 8. Elizabeth Catlett in the 1940s. Courtesy of Amistad Research Center, New Orleans.

CHAPTER 3

"I Did Black Women Because They Had to Be Done"

Elizabeth Catlett in Resistance and Representation

In 1946, Elizabeth Catlett left the United States for Mexico, exhausted by teaching and hoping to refocus on her art. She was desperately trying to complete a series of pieces for a Rosenwald Fellowship she had won a year earlier. Catlett had long been captivated by Mexico's revolutionary artists, whose goal was not to please the critics of high art but to create intellectually and physically accessible art for the masses, such as prints and murals.[1] They employed their art to support the community as well as to serve as political protest. This approach was familiar to her from her creative and political work in Black American artistic hubs such as Chicago and New York. The marriage of radical Black and Mexican art was an easy one; and she hoped that, in Mexico, she could soak up energy, build fellowship with like-minded artists, and complete her series.

Catlett's stay in Mexico extended and deepened her work in the struggle for justice. She would marry, have children, and make a life in Mexico for the next sixty years, all while creating works that, as she insisted, "spoke for both of my peoples "—Black Americans and Mexicans.[2] Because of this immersion, the connections among transnational freedom struggles became especially clear to her. Countless Black intellectuals, activists, and artists spent years abroad, intentionally escaping American racism and repression. Catlett, however, was one of very few radical activists who experienced government-sponsored exile. From her home in Mexico, she not only stayed in conversation with Black freedom struggles but also fully supported them with her artistic and political statements. Her brilliant artistic output in the 1960s and 1970s spoke urgently on behalf of Black people, helping to shape both the civil rights and the Black power movements and becoming, in the words of the art historian Kellie Jones, "part of the [Black] art-historical narrative."[3] Those lauded works include *Homage to My Young Black Sisters* (1968), *Malcolm X Speaks for Us* (1969), *Target* (1970), and *Political Prisoner* (1971).

This chapter focuses on Catlett's life up to 1948, the year when most discussions of her artistic production begin. She left the United States at the onset of the second Red Scare, which also chased Hazel Scott out of the country and impeded the careers of Lena Horne and Katherine Dunham. So what shaped her as a radical artist and activist before she was exiled from the country of her birth?

EARLY CATLETT: ART, EDUCATION, AND ACTIVISM

Alice Elizabeth Catlett was born in Washington, D.C., in 1915. She said of her parents, John Catlett and Mary Carson Catlett: "My mother met my father, and they married. They had two boys . . . and a girl, and then my father died, and I was born."[4] Her father never knew that his wife was pregnant with their youngest child. Both parents were well educated. John had been a professor of mathematics at Tuskegee Institute and taught mathematics in the public school system after moving to Washington. He was also a musician and a wood carver. Mary had trained as a teacher at Scotia Seminary in North Carolina, near her family's hometown.[5]

After John's death, Mary struggled to make use of her college degree in the provincial, racist, and patriarchal D.C. job market. To support her family, she was forced to work as a domestic and as a coat clerk until friends could help her land a job as a truant officer for the city's public schools. Catlett's biographer Samella Lewis points out that Mary's struggle against gender and race expectations was her daughter's first exposure to injustice.[6] For Elizabeth, Mary was a model of determined Black womanhood and the layered resistance it necessarily employs for survival. Mary Catlett's labor as a domestic and a truant officer likely also exposed young Elizabeth to the experiences of the Black working class. Yet despite her own hardships, Mary encouraged her daughter's desire to be an artist. "My mother would buy me paints and crayons," Catlett recalled.[7] This kind of support was exceptional among members of the city's Black middle-class. The pursuit of fine art as a career was highly unusual for an African American woman in the early twentieth century. Most parents pushed their children toward a professional career such as teacher, lawyer, or doctor and encouraged women who could afford it to be homemakers. The pressure of respectability politics was very real.[8]

Growing up in a segregated city, Catlett cultivated a keen sense of justice. As a teenager, she was already a serious activist: "When I was in high school, I was always very radical. . . . I remember . . . standing in front of the Supreme Court building in Washington with a noose around my neck protesting lynching. . . . All I remember is that the police took us away."[9] After graduation, she continued to confront social injustice, this time in her education in the arts. After taking the entrance exam for the Carnegie Institute of Technology (now Carnegie Mellon University), she arrived in Pittsburgh to attend a required two-week summer preparatory course. Her work was admired, and she excelled. But near the end of the course, she overheard two teachers discussing her work: "It's too bad she's a Negro, isn't it?" Such racial attitudes only deepened Catlett's resolve: "That was my first experience with that kind of thing. I began to fight it wherever I found it."[10] Clearly she had no future at the Carnegie Institute. Frustrated with her harsh racialized treatment and barred from attendance, she explored other options.

Catlett ended up studying painting at Howard University. At the time, it was the only historically Black university in the country that housed an art department, which had been established in 1921. There Catlett worked under a number of well-known Black artists. She recalled, "At Howard, there was James Porter and Lois Jones. I started out with Lois Jones. She wanted to make me a commercial artist, so I switched to [James] Wells."[11] Jones had likely encouraged Catlett to become a commercial artist due to the racist and sexist climate within the fine art world, a fact that made Catlett's ultimate success that much more astounding. Her choice to focus on painting was also spurred by her discovery of the Mexican muralists and Porter's own masterful works: "[The teachers at Howard] showed me some paintings by Mexican artists and that's why I decided to . . . go to Mexico." This marked the beginning of her interest in the activist art and artists who would profoundly impact her life.[12]

After graduating in 1935, Catlett went south to North Carolina because "my mom told me they needed an art teacher in Durham" and there were few open teaching positions in D.C. She taught for two years in the Durham public schools. Involving herself in local political activism, she, along with other Black teachers and the lawyer Thurgood Marshall, unsuccessfully rallied for equal pay.[13] Catlett did not enjoy teaching, which left her little time to pursue her own art. So she enrolled in the graduate program at the University of Iowa to study with the painter Grant Wood: "I went there because of him, and it was only $7 a semester."[14] At Iowa her focus shifted from painting to sculpture. Because Grant encouraged students to make art from "what they knew best," Catlett took Black women as her theme.[15]

On Iowa's segregated campus, the few African American students scattered among the different majors formed close bonds, and Catlett made lifelong friends, among them Charles Stallings, a future dean of faculty at Bowie State College, and Margaret Walker, who became a well-known poet and novelist.[16] Walker entered the master's program in creative writing as Catlett was beginning her second and final year. Black students could not live on campus due to racial restrictions, so they stayed off campus in houses that hosted Black students, which were divided into "girl" houses or housing for men. This created an automatic community of Black women students, and Walker and Catlett became roommates.[17]

Catlett was the first student to graduate from Iowa with a master's degree in fine arts, yet from the beginning she struggled against racial and gender discrimination. Initially, the chair of the art department had encouraged her to apply for a master of arts degree, as some in the university did not want to bestow the first fine arts degree on an African American woman. Not only did white men dominate the fine arts, but sculpture was a nearly sacred space for them. Catlett said, "No other field is [as] closed to those who are not white and male as is the visual arts. After I decided to be an artist, the first thing I had to believe was that I, a black woman, could penetrate the art scene, and that, further, I could do so without sacrificing one iota of my blackness or my femaleness or my humanity."[18]

Catlett's 1940 thesis exhibition demonstrated this belief. It centered on a limestone sculpture titled *Negro Mother and Child*, a sign that even in her earliest artistic productions she was in conversation with gender, race, motherhood, and injustice.[19] In her thesis, Catlett wrote that creating "a composition of two figures, one smaller than the other, so interlaced as to be expressive of maternity, and so compact as to be suitable to stone, seemed quite a desirable problem." *Negro Mother and Child* is significant in the way in which it centers Black women and seeks to claim sacrosanct space for them within fine art. Calling upon the trope of the madonna and child, the piece offers an image of

Black women that forces viewers to acknowledge their humanity. Rather than a thin representation of Black womanhood, it is a multidimensional portrayal that evokes emotion and demands quiet respect. The pair look real enough to rise from the pedestal. Catlett later said, "The implications of motherhood, especially Negro motherhood, are quite important to me, as I am a Negro as well as a woman."[20] Not only does the sculpture reveal the pair's astounding beauty, but it also pushes the viewer to recognize how slavery, racial violence, and inhumanity have habitually worked to separate the organically interlocked mother and child.

Catlett's *Negro Mother and Child* was awarded first prize in sculpture at the 1940 Exhibition of the Art of the American Negro in Chicago, an event organized by Alain Locke.[21] In his introductory address, Locke praised the evolution of Black art and artists: "More and more, you will notice in their canvases the sober realism which goes beneath the jazzy, superficial show of things . . . to the deeper truths of life, . . . for today's beauty must not be pretty with sentiment but solid and dignified with truth. . . . In doing so, [they] can teach us to see ourselves, not necessarily as others see us, but as we should be seen."[22] Locke had been steeped in the robust artistic legacy of the Harlem Renaissance, yet he acknowledged the popular front's rising influence on Black art in radical Chicago. Focusing on "sober realism" and the "deeper truths of life," he pinpointed art's political functions within the larger social movements in America.

A young Katherine Dunham also performed at this event; and as Dunham did, Catlett responded to Locke's call for Black artists to create art that would help African Americans "be seen." Her winning sculpture reflected Black art's transition and renewed purpose, marking the centering of African American women in her work and her commitment to art as a vocation. Other artists were doing the same. A year earlier, Augusta Savage had presented her commissioned sculpture, *Lift Every Voice and Sing*, at the 1939 World's Fair in New York City. She was the only African American woman to be so honored, and her piece was displayed in the prestigious contemporary arts pavilion. The exhibition's theme was "The American Negro's Contribution to Music," and Savage's sculpture depicted a sixteen-foot-tall harp in the shape of an outstretched Black arm. The bodies of a Black choir formed each harp string, and in front of them a kneeling man held a sign reading "Lift Every Voice and Sing,"[23] Like Catlett, Savage combated the common belief that Black women had made little mark on the American historical narrative, either socially, politically, or culturally. Instead, she positioned them as equal contributors to cultural and social production, doing so in this work by alternating female forms with male forms. In the 1920s and 1930s, her unwavering dedication to her craft brought well-deserved exposure to her art, no small accomplishment for a Black woman during the Depression. Although the exhibit at the World's Fair was temporary, it nonetheless allowed Savage to successfully hijack and manipulate American public space.

Black women who devoted their lives to art radically risked their economic and mental security; and like so many other African American women artists throughout history, Savage paid a heavy price, despite her brief burst of fame. Due to the time pressures of her commission work for the fair, she lost her job as director of the Harlem Community Arts Center, a blow that ultimately ended her artistic career. In addition, because of time and budget constraints, Savage had been forced to cast her World's Fair piece in plaster and paint it to create the appearance of bronze. As a result, her silver medal–winning sculpture was thrown away at the close of the fair.[24] The short saga of *Lift Every Voice and Sing* reveals not only the national importance of Black women's artistic production and their resistance through art but also the harsh, uneven treatment they received from the public and the fine art community. Like Savage, Catlett would face similar trials and occasional triumphs in the battle against racist and sexist oppression in the art world.

The art historian Lisa Farrington describes those challenges:

> A persistent theme in the art of African-American women has been the configuration of their own image without racial or gender stereotypes. Prompted by an unwelcome inheritance of axiomatic portrayals that falsely defined them as lustful, loathsome, and inferior, many women artists of color have chosen to counteract these perversions by portraying themselves with dignity, honesty, and insight. Others have challenged the status quo by doggedly pursuing artistic careers despite prejudices that excluded them from the realm of the artist.[25]

Farrington notes that, historically, Black women artists and the representations they created were treated with apathy at best—more often, with violent disdain. Yet by challenging dominant images, they added a significant layer to Black cultural resistance and American visual culture, a powerful site for disrupting racist and sexist centers of power.[26] Black women tended to more easily find a place in the performance arts, which were seen as acceptable outlets for them. In contrast, they were often barred whole-sale from visual forms. Yet in the years around World War II, Black women such as Catlett who positioned themselves as visual artists took ownership of images and representations that had a lasting impact on the American and international popular imagination. They challenged dominant white aesthetic standards and emphasized issues that plagued the African American community.

After graduating from Iowa, Catlett undertook a short stint teaching at Prairie View College in Texas before joining the faculty of Dillard University in New Orleans. As chair of the art department, she taught drawing, painting, and printmaking. The latter included linoleum cuts and silkscreen, both easily accessible to interested community members. While in New Orleans, Catlett waged pitched battles against segregation. For example, she challenged African Americans' lack of access to cultural spaces. Blacks were not allowed to enter entire neighborhoods of the city, and it was no accident that institutions of culture, such as museums, were located exclusively in white-only areas. When a large Picasso exhibit came to the Delgado Museum, which sat within a segregated park, Catlett defiantly circumvented the system.[27] On a day the museum was closed to the public, she made arrangements for her classes to visit and had them bused directly to the steps of the institution. This allowed all 160 students to enter the museum without setting foot in the park grounds. Because of segregation, none of these students had been to an art museum before.[28] Catlett recalled, "Well, . . . they didn't say the museum was prejudiced, I mean separated . . . so we saw the whole museum."[29] For students in Jim Crow New Orleans, it was a marvel.

This visit to the Delgado exposed Catlett's working- and middle-class students to historical and contemporary art that had previously been denied to them and thus allowed them to position themselves within a national and international context. According to the scholar Christina Heatherton, who later interviewed several of these students, Catlett's act of resistance became widely known in New Orleans and affected students "for generations."[30] The incident captured several key themes of her life, art, and work. First, it inserted Blackness and Black bodies into a racially policed cultural space—an ironic situation, given that some of Picasso's most celebrated works were heavily influenced by African art.[31] Second, it demonstrated Catlett's layered resistance in action. Finally, it showed how her political resistance to oppression was becoming increasingly entwined with her cultural resistance.

Because of her outspokenness and her approach to art, Catlett never completely fit in with the more conformist middle-class staff at Dillard. The artist Samella Lewis, who had been one of the students transformed by the trip to the segregated museum, recalled that Catlett was the first professor to introduce nude models into her drawing class, a shock to the school's conservative southern administration.[32] Her predecessor, the painter Vernon Winslow, had been fired simply for placing the painting of a female nude in plain view. Catlett involved herself in protests against police brutality and segregation in public transportation and stood apart from her colleagues in her choice of living space and neighborhood: "People didn't want to come to my house. . . . I lived in the French Quarter. I had a little house, and I went down the alley to the back door and went in. I never used the front door or the front room because there was an area of prostitutes. People would ring my bell. I didn't answer it." Across the street, a prostitute ran her business from the stoop and waited for customers to come by. Catlett was undisturbed: "She didn't bother me." In addition to prostitutes in the neighborhood, there was a man who lived across her back courtyard who regularly beat his wife: "She would run to the patio screaming, and we would all run to the window to see what was going on. I can remember it clearly."[33] The ease with which Catlett blended into this working-class neighborhood was undoubtedly linked to her urge to be an artist of the people as well as to her Black feminist nature.

Catlett spent the summer of 1941 studying in Chicago, where she joined the South Side Community Arts Center (SSCAC) and became good friends with one of its founders, the artist Margaret Burroughs. The SSCAC had been, in part, inspired by Augusta Savage and was modeled after the Harlem Community Arts Center, one of the many centers that had opened around the country during the Depression. Savage was among the first speakers to be invited to speak in the new space.[34] Sponsored in part by the WPA's Community Art Centers Project, the SSCAC was a community hub and played an important role in Chicago's radical Black art and politics for decades. According to the scholar Bill Mullen, "arguably no black cultural institution better documents both the mid-century absorption and revision of 1930s American cultural and political radicalism into black public space."[35]

In Chicago, Catlett was surrounded by radical ideas and radical people. Their impact was more than artistic and political; they also expanded her worldview.[36] Though she had been involved in many Black academic and artistic circles, the SSCAC and its allied spaces were the most progressive she had yet encountered. Many artists and intellectuals were attracted to the center, including the cartoonist Jackie Ormes. Most members also belonged to local and national Black organizations, such as the National Negro Congress, and some were members of the Communist Party.[37] Though Catlett often denied that she'd ever joined the party (for obvious reasons of persecution), she did, in later years, discuss her serious involvement with it in Chicago.[38] But the SSCAC was more than a locus of radical agitation. More important, it granted the Black South Side community access to art and hosted now legendary artists who rooted their creations in the community's image. In work from that era, one can see the influence of Mexican and populist Black New York arts collectives that Catlett would later be part of.

Burroughs and Catlett must have connected instantly, for their work had a similar focus on Black women and Black humanity. Burroughs said, "Elizabeth came to Chicago to go to the Art Institute to take some summer courses and was looking for a place to stay. Somebody told her that I had a studio and some extra space. She called me and came to stay in my coach house."[39] The two would become lifelong friends. Catlett studied ceramics at the institute, lithography at the SSCAC, and returned to sculpture in a small studio in Burroughs's garage.[40]

Burroughs played another important role in Catlett's life: she introduced her to Charles White, a brilliant painter known for his social realist paintings and murals. The two began a relationship and fell in love. The rapport between Catlett and White made sense. Their political and social temperaments were similar, as was their history. His childhood on Chicago's South Side bore resemblances to Catlett's as a Black Washingtonian. Initially self-taught, White began painting in his youth and later studied at the School of the Art Institute of Chicago after earning a rare scholarship. Like Catlett's work, his emphasized African American identity and struggles and showcased the Black proletariat. Each also fused art with resistance work. White's political activism was bolstered by his membership in the Art and Crafts Guild alongside the dancer Katherine Dunham, the artists Charles Sebree and Eldzier Cortor, and the writers Gwendolyn Brooks and Richard Wright.[41] With those of many other Chicago artists, White's protests had forced the Illinois WPA to extend visual art opportunities to African American artists in the city, and the SSCAC was the result.[42]

NEW YORK, THE BLACK LEFT, AND TRANSFORMATION

Romance aside, Catlett was greatly affected by her time in Chicago: "It was a very fulfilling summer. I felt that I had done the right thing to go to Iowa and then to get a job at Dillard. I felt that I was progressing."[43] In 1942, six months after leaving the city, Catlett and White were married.[44] That same year, Catlett left her position at Dillard to concentrate on her art and personal life. She was now twenty-seven years old, increasingly radical, and increasingly focused on dignifying the Black female image. For an African American woman of the era, her life was bold, intrepid, and unconventional. She had earned both a bachelor's and a master's degree and had served as a professor at an esteemed university while cultivating a career as a fine artist. She had not prioritized motherhood, marriage, or her professional vocation. She did all this in the aftermath of the Great Depression, in a country in which Black women were disproportionately employed as domestic or agricultural workers.

Catlett's evolution as an artist focusing on social justice had been hastened by her experience in Chicago's politically driven arts collective, and her decision now to move to New York gave her even more tools of resistance. On arriving in the city, Catlett and White folded themselves into the Black left. She recalled: "From New Orleans, I went to New York—Mecca. Soon after I arrived, I met many, many Black artists. I had occasions to meet and talk with writer Langston Hughes, actor Paul Robeson, journalist Gwendolyn Bennett, and numerous other individuals who were involved in the activist and creative expressions of Harlem."[45] This who's who of artist-activists used their work to uplift Black life and combat broad social inequality. Catlett said, "There were many Black visual artists working there at that time: Charles Alston, Jacob and Gwen Lawrence, Norman Lewis, Ernie Crichlow, and so many others who were beginning to make important contributions to art and education."[46] She and White sublet an apartment that a friend had vacated at 409 Edgecomb Avenue, a storied building in Harlem. Hughes and the journalist Marvel Cooke were their neighbors.[47] At one time or another, the building was also home to the boxer Joe Louis, the labor unionist A. Philip Randolph, and many other members of Harlem's Black elite.

Living and working in Harlem further radicalized Catlett, expanding her understanding of internationalism and struggle.[48] The neighborhood was becoming a unique Black international space, thanks to the enormous number of immigrants and migrants who had relocated there. Between 1910 and

1930, New York's Black population had grown from approximately 30,000 to more than 100,000, and most resided in Harlem.[49] Many Black residents had worked to re-create their home communities within Harlem's boundaries. Yet even though the cultures of the Black diaspora were distinct, they also shared similarities and influenced each other in this cosmopolitan space. Such diasporic exposure became central to Catlett's personal development as an artist-activist who would live a transnational life.

The Black artistic class in Harlem was closely knit. As an example: Catlett and White became good friends with the stage and screen actor Kenneth Spencer and his wife, Dorothy. In 1943, Spencer would appear in *Cabin in the Sky* alongside Lena Horne and Ethel Waters. His baritone was so strong that he sometimes served as an understudy for Paul Robeson. The Spencers, White, and Catlett were regulars at Café Society, and Catlett later laughed over her memories of the integrated club: "They had two [cafés]. When they ran out of liquor at one, they would run over to the other one to get some."[50] This suggests that Catlett was a patron when Hazel Scott was the club's star attraction, as the second site had been opened expressly to cater to Scott's large following. It is a delight to imagine the two women practicing their particular forms of layered resistance in this shared theoretical and literal location. During her visits to the club, Catlett became acquainted with many other artists, including Josh White.[51] She must have often encountered Robeson, who was a regular at Café Society, as they shared acquaintances and friends.

But in 1943, the couple's social life with these progressive artist-activists was cut short. After the Rosenwald Fund awarded White a $2,000 grant, the two set out for the South so that White could paint the southern Black working class. Originally, he had hoped to paint in Mexico, but he was not allowed to travel outside of the country during the war. Instead, he created a mural at Hampton Institute, a historically Black college that had been founded in 1868. Titled *The Contribution of the Negro to Democracy in America*, it is a transhistorical tapestry of African Americans who helped shape the United States and a narrative of their tumultuous experience. Measuring twelve by seventeen feet, it includes figures such as Frederick Douglass, Denmark Vesey, Sojourner Truth, Booker T. Washington, Harriet Tubman, and Marian Anderson as well as enslaved African Americans in chains. The mural illustrates the epic tale of African American history, resistance, and contribution. What is also significant is the way in which it reveals both a passion for Black freedom fighters and the suffering of everyday Black folks. It is distinctly a Charles White work, featuring enlarged hands, which was his signature style.[52]

White was twenty-five years old at this time, and Catlett was twenty-eight. They shared specific subjects in their art even as they were developing their individuality. For instance, Catlett, bringing the Black female subject to the fore, would go on to create several artistic iterations of Harriet Tubman and Sojourner Truth during her career, including the linocuts *Harriet Tubman* (1953–54) and *Harriet* (1975).[53] She provided these women with solo space, not only so that they could be admired but also to remind viewers of their tremendous contributions.

After White completed the mural, the couple returned to New York City, hoping to continue their work there. But in 1944, White was drafted into the army, where he contracted tuberculosis. After being released from the military, he underwent a long convalescence, shuffling between upstate New York and Washington, D.C., staying at the home of Catlett's mother. In the meantime, Catlett found an apartment in Greenwich Village, which she planned to share with Margaret Walker until White could return.[54]

While still in Harlem, Catlett and White had begun working at the George Washington Carver School. In his absence, she continued there, becoming a valued staff member. Congressman Adam Clayton Powell Jr. and the writer Max Yergen had recently founded the socialist institution, and the actor Canada Lee, the councilman Ben Davis, and the educator Melva Price served on its board. Run by the activist and writer Gwendolyn Bennett, the school had a forthright mission: to be "a People's institute, a school to develop thinking citizens who can take their rightful place in the modern world, an aid to understanding the People's War and the role of the Negro in it, a guide to a postwar world of peace, freedom, and equality for everyone, and, finally, an educational and social center belonging to the people of Harlem."[55] Its primary goal was to provide education, of all sorts, to impoverished and working-class Black residents. It also attracted some white and middle-class students. In its first term alone, the school drew 157 students.[56] The school's curriculum reflected the founders' concerns: art, radical leftist ideology, the struggle for racial justice, and Black internationalism. Overlapping and interlocking political ideologies, social groups, and immigrant communities of color made it a unique and inimitable learning space.

The school's Marxist framework included practical as well as theoretical classes, and the instructors represented the best of progressive leadership in the arts, politics, literature, and the sciences. Courses included "Modern Dance," taught by Pearl Primus, and "The Negro in Latin America," taught by Jesús Colón.[57] However, Catlett's course, titled simply "How to Make a Dress," was the most sought after. It was so popular that the school added an advanced course for those who wanted more instruction.[58] The course fit the practical needs of Harlem residents, but Catlett extended it beyond dressmaking, often chatting with her eager students about politics. When one student was in a hurry to go get a newspaper, she asked, "Do you know what the people who write the papers think about you?"[59] In her sculpture courses, she also slipped in radical topics for discussion.

For Catlett, art had always been a tool of liberation and resistance to oppression. Nonetheless, to this point she had viewed the world primarily through a middle-class lens and had adhered to many of those assumptions. So her work at the Carver School "was a turning point, artistically, and in my life," teaching her much about diverse Black cultures and the struggles of the poor and disenfranchised. For instance, "my experience was that all the Black women in Harlem were always buying dark clothes because they could wear them longer than light clothes. They didn't show the dirt. . . . [The women in class] always brought [in] dark colors like navy blue and brown and black. I started out with red and pink. We had a fashion show."[60] Until this point, "I had never been around so many poor people," and these encounters with her working-class students changed her approach to art.[61] She became ever more convinced that art should be accessible to the masses and should strive to portray their humanity. She later said, "The experience [at the Carver School] made me conscious about who I should do art about, which is Black people, because all the art in New Orleans, Chicago, even Harlem was about white people." Catlett also reconsidered her medium: "I wanted to work with poor people, so I started doing prints."[62] As she had discovered during her stint at Dillard University, printmaking was inexpensive art form accessible to the community.

At Carver, Catlett discovered that her working-class students were eager to consume a wide variety of the arts. On one scorching day, 350 of them huddled together to listen to a Juilliard professor deliver a lecture and share a recording of Dimitri Shostakovich's *Seventh Symphony*. Though the symphony was more than an hour long, the students refused to take a break for cooler air and a cold drink. Their commitment was a revelation for Catlett.[63]

The school's progressivism made it a political target. Still, it continued to attract hundreds of students, despite, or because of, its radical reputation.[64]

Catlett served as its chief fundraiser and informal co-director and performed secretarial duties such as mimeographing. She often had twelve-hour work days, on top of her long commute. She said, "I had to be there by nine in the morning, which was terrible. I would get out about nine at night, usually hungry, and I lived in the Village, which is a long way from Harlem. I would stop off in the Italian Restaurant, and I would eat a pizza"—an affordable food, given her low salary. Her son, Francisco Mora Catlett, later recalled speaking with a former student of his mother's at the Carver School: "She doesn't know how [Catlett] did it all."[65]

Catlett was deeply immersed in political and social activism beyond the Carver School. She was the head of the Russian War Relief Fund in Harlem and served on (and illustrated for) the arts committee of the National Negro Congress. She taught ceramics at the Marxist-based Jefferson School.[66] But her teaching and activist schedule took a toll on her artistic production. Moreover, even in her husband's absence, she was viewed in relation to him and considered the lesser part of a greater whole. While her talent was admired, she was seen as the wife of a great artist instead of a major artist in her own right. According to Catlett, this view matched White's own masculinist preference for how they were framed as a couple.[67] A 1942 article in the *Amsterdam News* about their art endeavors yoked them as "Mr. & Mrs. Charles White," which, while a normalized way of addressing married women, emphasized his success and minimized hers. Such slights, among other issues, gradually widened a rift in their marriage.[68]

A young Frida Kahlo, who was married to Diego Rivera, received similar treatment in early U.S. press coverage. A headline in the *Detroit News* declared, "Wife of the Master Mural Painter Gleefully Dabbles in Works of Art." The article went on to assert: "In Detroit, she paints only because time hangs heavily upon her hands during the long hours while her husband is at work on the court." Though Rivera was a more famous artist at the time, the sexist proclamation belittled Kahlo's ability—an ironic choice, considering that, in time, she would become better known internationally than he was.[69]

In 1945, Catlett won her own Rosenwald Fellowship for a proposed series of prints, sculptures, and paintings that would express the beauty, struggles, and contributions of "the Negro woman." Inspiration for the idea had come partly from her work at the Carver School: "Suddenly I wanted to draw these people, these women, who were to me so strong and so wonderful, and from whom I was learning a lot."[70] By now, her chosen subject matter (Black women and the working class), the mediums in which she worked (those that were accessible across class), her political involvements, and the nontraditional and radical ways in which she lived her life as a Black woman and artist in the mid-twentieth century were revealing themselves as layers of her cultural and political resistance.

Yet her decision to continue teaching at the school was a mistake. She was unable to create within her highly demanding schedule. So when her fellowship was renewed in 1946, Catlett decided to travel to Mexico to work on her art. Initially, she and White went together. Though their marriage was failing, they both admired the populist artists and art of Mexico, and increasing political pressures in the United States convinced them that now was the time to go. They became part of an informal exodus. During and after World War II, many African American artists took up residence in France, England, Germany, and elsewhere. In their book on the history of African American art, Romare Bearden and Harry Henderson later mourned, "No one knows exactly how many of these artists there are, but their absence represents a cultural loss to the United States."[71]

Mexico may seem to be an unusual locale for a Black woman artist to produce art in the mid-1940s. In that era, men had more privilege and freedom of movement, whereas women were often anchored by gendered expectations, domesticity, motherhood, and economic limitations. The Black women artists who did manage to travel mostly went to Europe. Yet the scholar Stacy Morgan points out that Black radical creatives in the United States saw Mexican artists such as Diego Rivera and David Alfaro Siqueiros as models and comrades. They were drawn to Mexico because they were "interest[ed] in producing work that was at once both representatively American *and* emblematic of ethnically distinctive black cultural traditions."[72] The Black American artists Hale Woodruff and John Wilson and the writers Langston Hughes and Richard Wright all studied and produced in Mexico during the 1930s and 1940s.[73] According to the scholar Rebecca M. Schreiber, the work they made there "articulated a decidedly critical transnational aesthetic through its fusion of representational techniques, multiple audiences, and thematic transpositions."[74]

Many political, social, artistic, and historical ties bind the experiences of Black Americans and Mexicans. Nearly 95 percent of those enslaved on the African continent during the transatlantic slave trade were transported to Central and South America or the Caribbean, so descendants of the Black diaspora in the western hemisphere are still more likely to be residents of these areas than of the United States. During the Mexican-American War (1846–48), the Black population of Mexico was so significant that some major Mexican newspapers "wonder[ed] whether a victorious United States would enslave African-descended Mexicans."[75] Historically, Mexican people and African Americans had both been exploited by vicious western capitalist labor systems, and each had engaged in rebellions, small and large, against their European colonial masters.

In solidarity with other oppressed countries and established communities, many people of color around the world practiced what the historian Paul Ortiz calls "emancipatory internationalism." That is, they linked freedom struggles in the United States, Latin America, the Caribbean, Africa, Europe, and elsewhere in a combined "vision of human rights."[76] This international framework came to the fore at the close of the Haitian Revolution (1791–1804) and later during the Mexican Revolution (1910–1917), which began partly because of the high numbers of enslaved African Americans who fled to Mexican territory and the greed of enslavers who hoped to extend their cruel business by annexing Mexican lands.[77] Over the course of her long career, Catlett would point to this shared political and social history again and again in her artwork and interviews.

In the 1950s and '60s, more than fifty African nations threw off their colonial chains and gained independence, triggering great celebration among Black people around the world. But in earlier decades, Black radicals drew inspiration from across the Americas. Mexico was a primary site due to its proximity to the United States and its relatively recent populist revolution, which had ended in 1920. In the period between 1920 and 1950, a wide array of scholars attempted to reconstitute the contours of the Black diaspora; and in the 1940s, several prominent anthropologists and scholars, including Melville Herskovits and W. E. B. Du Bois, founded a short-lived international association in Mexico City to coordinate research on the diaspora.[78] In articles published in the two issues of their journal, *Afroamerica*, they concluded that West African cultural retention abounded in North, Central, and South America as well as the Caribbean.[79] Catlett came to see these adjoining sites of diaspora as vital to liberation, and she brought an element of diaspora with her as well. Her biographer Melanie Anne Herzog writes, "[She] . . . carried with her a 'core' of African-Americaness," one that was further shaped by her womanhood.[80]

According to the scholars Tiffany Ruby Patterson and Robin Kelley, "diaspora is both a process and a condition." They explain, "As a process it is constantly being remade through movement, migration, and travel, as well as imagined through thought, cultural production, and political struggle. Yet, as a condition, it is directly tied to the process by which it is being made and remade."[81] By traveling to Mexico, and eventually moving there permanently and living there for fifty years, Catlett's presence, with all of its "African-Americanness," remade the Black diaspora and re-created Black womanhood in the United States and abroad. She carried her Black feminist layered resistance transnationally, remaking it as well.

Even if Catlett had not chosen to leave New York, her days in the city's Black progressive art scene were numbered. As the war drew to a close, any creative labor even remotely connected to populism, socialism, or communism was quickly associated with anti-Americanism. During the Depression and the war years, many in the United States had been able to flirt with populist ideology in the midst of capitalism's devastation. U.S. war allies included the Soviet Union and China, both communist nations. Joseph Stalin was marketed in America as "Uncle Joe" and celebrated as *Time*'s "Man of the Year" in both 1939 and 1942.[82]

But the Cold War between the United States and the Soviet Union began in 1945, almost as soon as the last battle of World War II was fought. This turn of events was disastrous for many Americans but particularly for Black activist artists who used their mediums to uncover injustice and promote social equity. Scores lost their livelihoods because of blacklisting, including access to commissions, grants, fellowships, gigs, and patronage. Whether they were actually communists in affiliation mattered little.

The Carver School was targeted, supposedly because of its radical agenda and Marxist associations but more likely because of its work with the Black laboring class in Harlem. In 1943, six prominent white members of its board of directors quit, accusing the institution of being under "too much under communist control."[83] Those remaining on the board were distressed, blaming the resignations on "the vicious campaign of Red-baiting intended to discredit the school and the community leadership which supports it."[84] But eventually such attacks put an end to the school and those like it across the country.

Heightened political anxiety dovetailed with a growing tendency to condemn social realist art, a form that dominated African American work, which deliberately focused on critical figurative portrayals of social and political concerns. By the late 1940s, the rise of abstract expressionism was supplanting social realism, and many Black artists felt they were not welcome into those domains, which aimed to return art to the white elite and away from the cross-racial masses. Still, a few Black artists, such as Beauford Delaney and Norman Lewis, did turn to abstraction during this time. Perhaps their interest was heightened by the attitudes of African Americans who were returning from war and seeking assimilation, which they saw as a path to civil rights. It was also true that Black artists wanted the freedom to express themselves in any way they saw fit.

Meanwhile, for Catlett, the move to Mexico was life changing. That year she returned to the United States briefly, to divorce White and hold a solo show at the Barnett-Aden Gallery in Washington, D.C. In 1947, she married fellow revolutionary artist Francisco Mora, with whom she would have three sons. Her marriage and her art prompted her to make her move to Mexico permanent, but by the early 1950s the U.S. government was directly targeting her and for decades refused to allow her back into the country of her birth.[85]

Undeterred, Catlett remained steadfast in her art. She continued to create politically charged social realism and found a home among kindred spirits in the artists' circles in Mexico, including the Taller de Gráfica Popular, which was active between 1937 and 2010. This cooperative space for collaborative art production centered on community-accessible art forms such as murals, printmaking, and lithography. Its prolific prints were internationally recognized as a benchmark in political art during the thirties and forties. The Taller de Gráfica Popular was dedicated to art that would raise political consciousness and elevate awareness of the plight of disempowered communities in Mexico and internationally. In 1938, it had been one of the first presses to publish anti-Nazi posters, demonstrating a commitment to anti-fascism and social justice well before many countries, including the United States, moved to condemn the atrocities in Germany.[86]

As an African American woman, Catlett saw these Mexican artists as comrades in the struggle to use art as a tool of liberation. She was one of the first women to join the collective and continued her involvement for more than twenty years.[87] She would use the studio to produce representations of both African American and Mexican people that emphasized their linked struggles, humanity, and beauty. She also stayed in conversation with Black American and Black international movements through the incredible artwork she created in Mexico.

I AM THE NEGRO WOMAN

Schreiber writes that the Taller de Gráfica Popular greatly influenced Catlett's "approach to the process of production as well as the form and content of her work."[88] It helped her become the artist that the world would come to know and allowed her to make an enormous imprint on representations of African American women in fine art, even from abroad. Her 1946 work, known collectively as *The Negro Woman Series*, was an early but pivotal example of the way in which she brought together the Black woman as subject, her expanded technique, and her political consciousness.[89] The series narrates Black women's history of oppression and their demand for human rights and Black equality, sentiments she expressed again and again throughout her career. It also presaged the main concerns of the Black liberation movements to come. The series highlights her commitment to art as an instrument for ending oppression and her Black feminist understanding of Black women's positioning and form.

In *The Negro Woman Series*, Catlett reveals the future and the past. She traces her roots and Black identity to Africa and recognizes the imprint of slavery and injustice. In my interview with her, she put it plainly: "I am Black because my great-great-grandmother was kidnapped on the beach at Madagascar and was brought to the United States as a slave. Both of my mother's parents and my father's mother were slaves."[90] As an artist, and through this series, she located the Black woman as forged simultaneously from history and the present.

When she made the series, Catlett risked opportunities for further funding; American institutional support from galleries, buyers, and patrons; and her own citizenship. Via the pieces, she was sharply critiquing the harsh experiences of Black American women while showing them in their full humanity. Her layered resistance was striking and salient, both politically and artistically. While other artists were pivoting to apolitical art, she was immersing herself in the exact opposite.

The Negro Woman Series consists of fifteen linocuts. To create each, Catlett cut an image into inexpensive linoleum tile, inked it, and pressed it onto paper. Together, the linocuts depict the unembellished contemporary conditions and struggles of Black women in the United States. They are intense, stark, and full of movement. Catlett's approach was purposely spare, and the prints do not evoke comfort. The images are accompanied by straightforward text that leaves little room for political interpretation. Catlett said of the series: "I was trying to present Negro women . . . as what their lives really were, really are. . . . I wanted to do something that has to do with all of us. That's what gave me some direction in art. . . . I decided that I was gonna work with the problems of black women, . . . was gonna try to make people see them as beautiful, dignified, strong people instead of, as Ralph Ellison says, invisible."[91]

Print 1, "I am the Negro woman," reveals the closely cropped face of a woman who looks away from the viewer and is partly in shadow. The harsh style of the etching speaks to struggle, dignity, and survival.

Print 2, "I have always worked hard in America," is a circle of images in which the same woman does various back-breaking tasks. The repetition calls to mind "The Bronx Slave Market," a 1935 exposé series in *The Crisis* by the journalist Marvel Cooke and the activist Ella Baker, who went undercover to detail the exploitation of domestics in New York City, including sexual harassment and abuse, wage theft, and overwork.[92]

The next two linocuts continue the theme of labor. Print 3, "In the fields," depicts a woman holding a hoe and wearing a large straw hat. Her small frame house is visible in the distance, beyond rows of crops. Print 4, "In other folks homes," is a gorgeous waist-up portrait of a domestic holding a broom.

With Print 5, "I have given the world my song," Catlett shifted her focus to the cultural contributions of African American women. In it, a Black woman with a guitar sits on a stool and looks reflectively at the floor. A faint background illustration reveals a Ku Klux Klan figure beating a young Black man, and a tombstone suggests the racial violence that might have led the woman to have the blues. The guitar player may have been a nod to Sister Rosetta Tharpe, a gospel and popular singer who has sometimes been called the mother of rhythm and blues. Catlett undoubtedly knew her 1944 hit, "Down by the Riverside."[93]

The next few linocuts celebrate historical figures. Print 6, "Sojourner Truth, I fought for the rights of women as well as Negroes," shows Truth standing at a lectern. She raises one hand into the air and rests the other on the Bible. Her countenance is serious, and she gazes directly at the viewer as if to demand respect and acknowledgment.

Print 7, "Harriet Tubman, I helped hundreds to freedom," is one of the most reproduced pieces in the series. Fierce and determined, Tubman stretches out her arm, pointing a line of enslaved people toward freedom.

Print 8, "In Phillis Wheatley I proved intellectual equality in the midst of slavery," Wheatley, the first known African American woman poet, sits

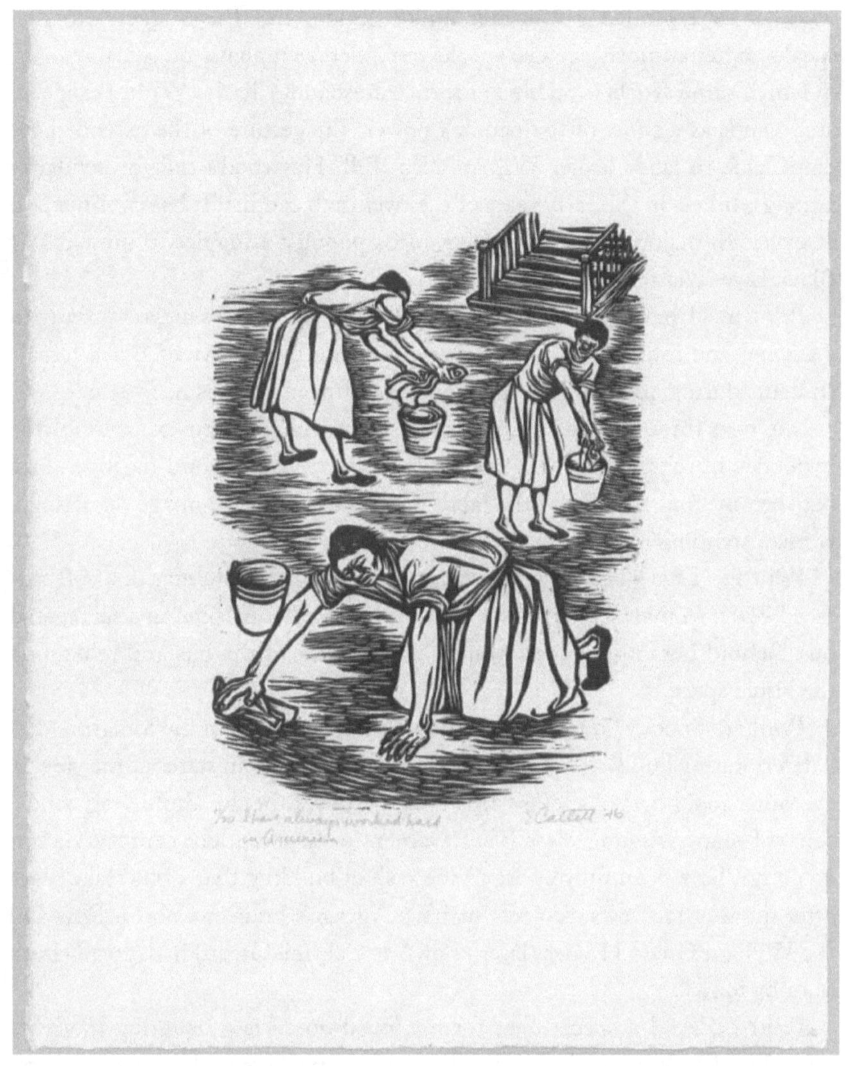

FIGURE 9. Elizabeth Catlett, "I have always worked hard in America," 1946. Collection of the Smithsonian National Museum of African American History and Culture, Gift of Winifred Hervey, © 2020 Catlett Mora Family Trust. Licensed by VAGA at Artists Rights Society (ARS), New York.

in profile at a desk, writing, as shackled women slaves appear in the background. Over the course of her career, Catlett created several other renderings of Wheatley, including a life-sized bronze bust in 1973.[94]

Print 9, "My role has been important in the struggle to organize the unorganized," depicts a central female figure who stands in the middle of a circle with her fist extended as four men huddle around her. The exaggerated hand speaks to her authority. It also speaks to Catlett's emphasis on social realism, in which some artists (notably her former husband, Charles White) exaggerated hands as a show of the people's power. The gesture of the extended fist dates back to labor leader William "Big Bill" Haywood's call for solidarity among workers in the early years of the twentieth century. It has continued to resurface in major movements, from 1930s populist struggles to present-day Black Lives Matter protests.[95]

Print 10, "I have studied in increasing numbers," shows a classroom with a teacher and four seated students, emphasizing the resolve of Black female students during an era of intense racism, sexism, and classism.

The next three linocuts are particularly arresting in their exposure of the hypocrisy of segregation and Jim Crow. Print 11, "My reward has been bars between me and the rest of the land," is a closely cropped image depicting a woman standing behind a barbed-wire fence.

Print 12, "I have special reservations," is a rough-cut etching of a solemn-faced Black woman seated just behind the "colored only" sign on a segregated bus. Behind her, other Black women fill the back of the bus and remaining the visual space.[96]

Print 13, "Special houses," shows two women standing in the foreground as a deteriorating building looms behind them. One woman stares at the viewer; the other looks away listlessly. This image exposes the dreadful living conditions of many working-class Black women in the twentieth century. Catlett could not have been fully aware of the rash of building that would take place after the war. However, projects such as Chicago's Frances Cabrini Row and the William Green Homes (later known as Cabrini-Green) had already been built by 1942.[97]

Print 14, "And a special fear for my loved ones," is a haunting image of a lynched Black man lying at the feet of his attackers with a noose around his neck. It is easy to imagine him as a son or younger brother, and the print points to the fears internalized by Black mothers. Anti-lynching had been one of Catlett's crusades since high school.

Print 15, "My right is a future of equality with other Americans," is the closely cropped image of a woman's face looking upward, perhaps toward the heavens, perhaps simply holding her head high. In either case, the print suggests hope for the future, a contrast with print 1, in which the same woman looks pensive and melancholy.

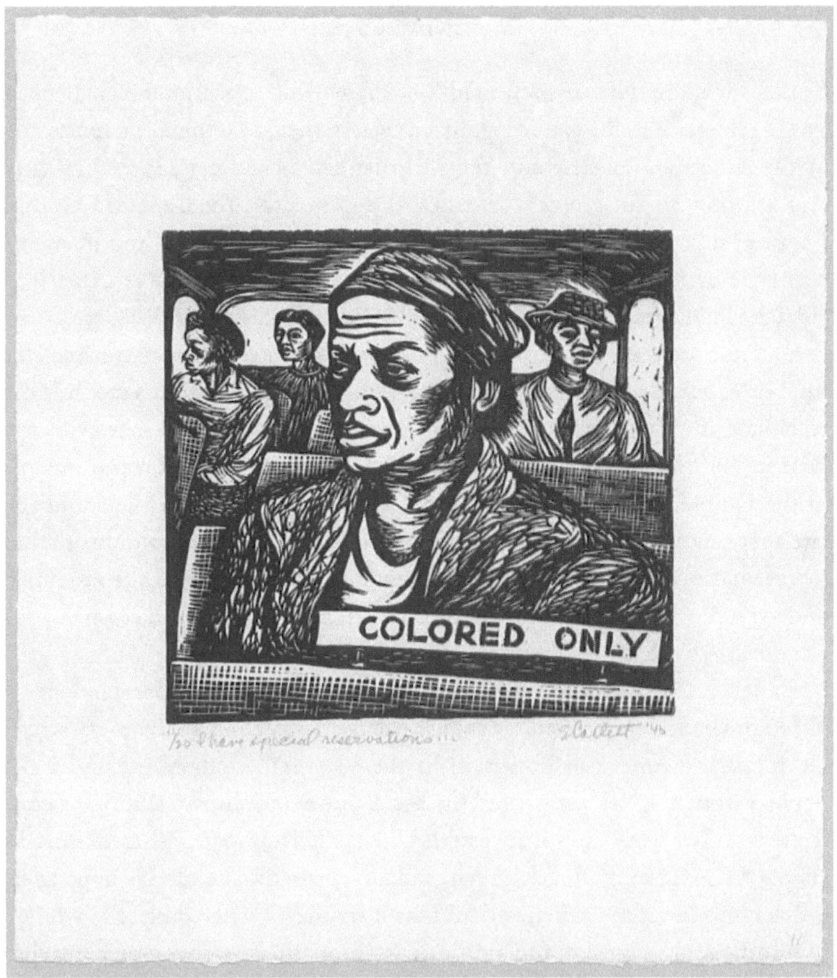

FIGURE 10. Elizabeth Catlett, "I have special reservations," 1946. Collection of the Smithsonian National Museum of African American History and Culture, Gift of Winifred Hervey, © 2020 Catlett Mora Family Trust. Licensed by VAGA at Artists Rights Society (ARS), New York.

Each part of Catlett's linocut narrative was salient in the mid-1940s, yet none has lost its significance today. Like her layered resistance, the power of the series is rooted in her ability to convey multiple meanings and messages within a single act or image. By looking at the collection as a whole, the viewer recognizes the connections and interlocking oppressions as well as the women's pride and endurance.

LEGACIES

Catlett's work in the 1940s reflected Black American concerns and challenges, and it gained international recognition, even in the face of ongoing repression by the American government. Yet the artist-activists in her adopted country also fell prey to antiradical forces. By the mid-1950s, the Taller de Gráfica Popular had been designated a communist-front organization, and its members were barred from the United States. Even though she was an American citizen, Catlett was unable to return to her home country for decades.

Catlett's focus on the working class, women's struggles, and accessible cultural production made her art particularly relevant during the 1940s. But her reach and imprint continued to expand in later years. Despite her exile, she kept in continuous dialogue with African American liberation movements in the United States. Though her art had its most significant impact in the late 1960s and 1970s, her work in the 1940s laid important groundwork. her representations of working-class Black women during that decade redefined understandings of the beautiful and conveyed Black agency and dignity. They were peerless.

Catlett often said, "I did Black women because they needed to be done."[98] Through her art and layered resistance, she participated in nearly every struggle for Black American liberation in the twentieth century, including the popular front, the civil rights, and the Black power movements. During a conference on her work at Northwestern University in 1970, she shared remarks via phone, exclaiming, "I have been, and am currently, and always hope to be a Black revolutionary artist, and all that it implies!"[99] Incredibly, she worked in printmaking, painting, and sculpture for more than seventy years, until her death in 2012. Her art and activism continue to speak to and for Black women, rendering them fully visible and human.

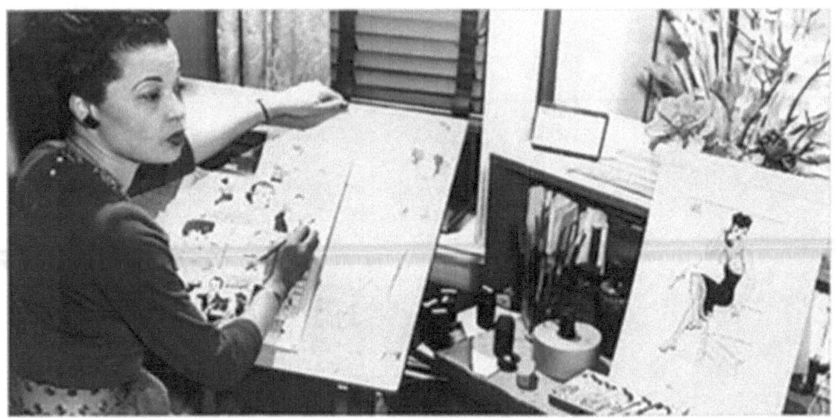

FIGURE 11. Jackie Ormes sits at her drafting desk in her apartment, 1956. From Nancy Goldstein, *Jackie Ormes, The First African American Woman Cartoonist* (Ann Arbor: University of Michigan Press, 2019), vi.

CHAPTER 4

Framing/Claiming Black Womanhood and Outing Injustice

Jackie Ormes Illustrates Layered Resistance

In his June 1948 column for the *Chicago Defender*, the writer Langston Hughes published a short list of things he would long for on a desert island. "I would miss . . . Jackie Ormes's cute drawings," he mused.[1] This reflects the status she had earned in the Black press and Black popular culture. By the early 1950s, her comic strips were reaching millions weekly. She had also created one of the first mass-marketed Black dolls, modeled after the character Patty-Jo in her widely circulated *Patty-Jo 'n' Ginger* strip.

Today Ormes remains the longest-running, most frequently syndicated Black woman cartoonist. Beyond acknowledging the cuteness of her drawings, Hughes surely noted the social and political agency that she assigned Black women in her cartoons as well as the boldness and danger of her resistance. During her career, Ormes created four comic strips centered on African American women: *Torchy Brown in "Dixie in Harlem"* (1937–38), *Candy* (1945), *Patty-Jo 'n' Ginger* (1945–56), and *Torchy in Heartbeats* (1950–54). Her comics are not simply vehicles for easy laughs; they are powerful Black feminist radical clapbacks and pointed societal interrogations. They offer an unvarnished critique of American life and inequity at midcentury via the voices and bodies of Black female characters.

Black comics allowed Ormes to undertake political work that would have been far more difficult in other artistic or journalistic formats. Decades later, she told an interviewer, "Me, I was always fighting battles, I was antiwar—I was anti everything that's smelly!"[2] Her radicalism came through clearly in the funny pages of the Black press. Thus, like the other women in this book, Ormes combined political activism with activist artistry to create layers of resistance to inequity, marginalization, racism, sexism, and white hegemonic representation.

Film such as newsreels and animated shorts and print such as newspapers and magazines formed the popular media landscape of the mid-1930s, 1940s, and 1950s. The imagery of the fine art world was an entirely separate sphere. Regardless, in the hands of white creators, every popular and fine art genre had become a site for assaulting Blackness. In their case, African American women rarely appeared in white mainstream comic strips; but when they did, the images were degrading. The one-panel strip *Mammy's Lil' Lamb*, which dated back to 1911 and featured a Black mother and her little girl, was one of the few that *presented* African American women as central characters. Although their rendering was far less offensive than others that would follow, the strip nonetheless taps into familiar mammy and pickaninny tropes.[3] Although Black female characters occasionally appeared as the sidekicks or girlfriends of Black male characters, as in *Amos 'n' Andy* during the 1920s and early 1930s, they were more commonly depicted as servants.

Comics were a bastion of white male Americana. The women who appeared in the funny pages were largely white, drawn by men, and reflective of the white male gaze. This is apparent in the most popular strip of the early twentieth century, *Blondie*, a one-dimensional construction that embodied white male desire. Blondie began her career in comics as a dizzy gold digger with the body of a pinup but was later toned down to a sexy yet wise housewife who was the epitome of domestic success and virtuous white womanhood.[4] African American women had a different role within the white male imagination. Like Blondie, some were sexualized yet subservient, but most received further degradation. In all configurations, they were stripped of respectability, agency, and intelligence. The representations and images in film and print were troubling, not only because of their wholesale inaccuracy but also because they denied Black women membership in the modern world.

A trip to the movies was an hours-long event that encompassed a newsreel, several animated short films, and two feature films. The choice of shorter pieces often depended on which main features were being shown. Film scholars have explored the stereotyped constructions of Black women via the mammy, tragic mulatto, and Jezebel figures who abounded in full-length movies during this period. However, the imagery that moviegoers encountered at the start of the theater experience has been less thoroughly studied, and those shorts were a significant site for the misrepresentation of Black womanhood.[5] Most newsreels did not portray any images of Black women or their accomplishments. In contrast, animated shorts had an unusually high number of Black representations as compared to those in other media. Between 1931 and 1938, 32 percent of the characters in animated shorts were Black, probably because shorts of the period heavily relied on racial, ethnic, and gender stereotypes as comic relief.[6] It is not clear how many of those characters were Black women. However, they did appear regularly in the shorts and received the same stereotypical treatment as they did in film. In fact, their representation in the shorts was arguably worse.

A moviegoer who attended a 1934 screening of *The Imitation of Life* may have begun the evening by watching a newsreel on the progress of President Roosevelt's recently enacted New Deal and the communist struggle in China, followed by an animated short or two from a film series starring Bosko the Talk-Ink Kid. The Bosko character was one of several animated acts in a new Warner Brothers cartoon series called *Looney Tunes*. Bosko had been drawn to mimic a blackface minstrel, with a large white mouth, round eyes, and jet-black skin. He spoke in a poor imitation of Black English, and his features were so exaggerated that they made him look inhuman. One reviewer described him as a monkey.[7] During this period, Bosko was such a prominent character in the *Looney Tunes* arsenal that his original closing line, "That's all, folks," became the signature ending for all *Looney Tunes* cartoons. In the shorts, he almost always appears with his girlfriend, Honey, who shares his exaggerated features and is identified as female by a single thin braid sticking straight up on her head tied with an enormous ribbon. Honey is mischievous, has a high, silly voice, and breaks out into popular song in almost every episode. These traits are frequently associated with early adolescent Black female film characters, such as Farina in the *Our Gang* films (a series later known as *The Little Rascals*), which were shown in theaters between the mid-1920s and the mid-1940s.[8] Bosko and Honey engaged in countless antics during their nationwide run from 1929 to 1938. A minimal amount of tweaking on the animator's part would have easily transformed them into Mickey and Minnie Mouse, who first appeared in 1928 and became the animated apex of Americana in the twentieth century.

The formula for a great animated cartoon was comedy and the exaggeration of human nature. In the hands of white male creators, this formula easily lent itself to caricatures of African Americans. Later animated shorts included Black female characters such as Mammy Two Shoes, a disembodied Black domestic who appeared in *Tom 'n' Jerry* cartoons. Except for one episode, animators drew her solely from the torso down, focusing on her breasts and disregarding her face. Mandy, also a domestic, was a blackface caricature who occasionally appeared in the long-running *Little Lulu* comic strip and film shorts.[9] Among her other duties in the strip, she serves as a nanny. In all of Mandy's scenes, her dark, portly, tall frame is juxtaposed with tiny Lulu's body for comedic effect. She appears to be nearly a giant.

But Jackie Ormes challenged such representations. In their layered resistance, her groundbreaking strips contested both deleterious image constructions and sociopolitical repression. In many ways, their outlook and authenticity stemmed from her own experiences. Her art was a close imitation of her life.

GO "CHOP IT UP": FROM PITTSBURGH TO TORCHY

Jackie Ormes was born Zelda Mavin Jackson in Pittsburgh, Pennsylvania, in 1911. She was the younger of William Winfield Jackson and Mary Brown Jackson's two daughters. According to the 1910 census, the Jacksons were newly married and living in Pittsburgh with Mary's parents.[10] William's World War I draft registration card identifies his occupation as printer. Records also show that he owned an outdoor theater that screened silent movies. Given that the majority of Blacks in Pittsburgh worked as maids, laundresses, coachmen, and custodians, these businesses placed the Jacksons solidly in the Black middle class.[11] Unlike less fortunate Black families, they were able to live on the earnings of a single breadwinner while Mary Jackson labored as a housewife.

As a young child, Ormes had an idyllic life, but tragedy befell when she was eight years old and her father died in a car accident. This event changed the family's fortunes. Ormes and her sister, Delores, temporarily boarded with an aunt and uncle while their mother looked for work. She eventually found employment as head housekeeper for a wealthy white woman. But the job and the separation from her children lasted less for than a year. In 1918, Mary Jackson married Porter M. Simmons, and the new family moved to Monongahela, a small integrated suburb seventeen miles outside of Pittsburgh. Unlike her first husband's family, who had come from the South, the Simmons family had lived in western Pennsylvania long before Emancipation.

In fact, they were among Monongahela's pioneer settlers.[12] Ormes recalled her years there with fondness: "[It] was like suburbia: spread out, and simple. Nothing momentous ever happened there. Nobody had much, but we were OK. We grew up around music–nice sounds!–and no bad language and no violence. So, we thought the world would be a pretty nice place to go chop up. I was ready for it, honey!"[13]

Nicknamed "Jackie," young Zelda had plenty of talent for "chopping up" the world. She had been drawing since she could hold a pencil. She was a true natural artist: paper and pen were her constant companions, and she made lifelike carvings from bars of soap. As a teenager, she drew for the Monongahela High School yearbook, in time becoming its art editor. Those intricate illustrations showcased her attention to detail as well as her emerging personal artistic style. Ormes also had plenty of moxie, and she wasn't afraid to go after what she wanted, even at a young age. In 1930, when she was seventeen years old, she wrote to Robert L. Vann, the publisher of the *Pittsburgh Courier*, asking for a job: "I guess I said something funny in it. He said, 'Write us another letter.' I wrote another letter. He said, 'How would you like to go to a boxing match?' This was my first assignment." Ormes was excited, even though (or perhaps because) this was an odd assignment for a young woman. But "I couldn't go by myself. I was just a punk—still in school," so the *Courier* sent its sports editor to bring her to the match.[14] After graduating from high school, she continued to work for the *Courier*, serving as editor, proofreader, and reporter: "[I] had a great career running around town looking into everything the law would allow and writing about it. I had a whole lot of comeuppances, and I found that I could make people laugh. I said, well that's fun, but I want to draw."[15]

Black newspapers were a significant part of Black life in a segregated America. Their impact and reach cannot be overstated. The *Chicago Defender* alone had a circulation of more than 150,000, with two-thirds of those copies sold outside of Chicago. By the late 1940s, Black newspapers had "developed networks of bureaus, zoned editions, and national editions."[16] The *Pittsburgh Courier*, which had begun as a four-page pamphlet, had fourteen regional editions and claimed to have a million readers at the height of its popularity. This figure may have been inflated; however, its readership was the largest in the nation, topping at least 300,000. Moreover, newspaper consumption was broader than could be accurately recorded because copies were often shared among readers. The mission of Black newspapers was distinct from that of white newspapers: they strove to "serve, speak and fight for the black minority," and nearly every column inch was used to that end.[17]

Drawing was Ormes's passion; and though she retained the eye of a reporter, she eventually maneuvered her way into the comics. But not immediately: soon after meeting a "soft spoken, gentle" man named Earl Ormes, the two were married in 1931, and her dreams of becoming a full-time comic artist at the *Courier* had to be put on hold. Earl was beginning a career at Steel City Bank and studying at the Pittsburgh School of Banking, and the couple became a fixture on the Black middle-class circuit of parties, benefits, and nightlife. Among their friends were the future bandleader Billy Eckstine and the aspiring actress Lena Horne, who was then living in Pittsburgh with her husband and children. Though the city was much smaller than New York or Chicago, it was a formidable and cosmopolitan center of Black politics, art, and culture. Numbers of well-known Black artists came from Pittsburgh, including the jazz pianist Billy Strayhorn and the photographer Charles "Teenie" Harris. The city was also home to the Pittsburgh Crawfords, who played in Greenlee Field, the first black-owned and -built baseball park in America. [18]

Several years into her marriage Jackie Ormes gave birth to the couple's only child, Jacqueline, much to their joy. But horror struck when the little girl was diagnosed with a brain tumor at the age of three. The child died soon after the devastating diagnosis, and Jackie refused to have any more children for fear of further heartache. Yet she would imbue her longest-running strip, *Patty-Jo 'n' Ginger*, with Jacqueline's spirit. Patty-Jo was wise, brave, outspoken, and full of spunk, and Ormes clearly saw these characteristics as appropriate and necessary aspects of Black girl- and womanhood.

In 1937, a year after Jacqueline's death, Ormes undertook her first thoughtful rendering of Black womanhood in her strip *Torchy Brown in "Dixie in Harlem."*[19] It follows the adventures of Torchy, a young Black woman who migrates from Mississippi to Harlem. The opening episode contextualizes Torchy's life in the South, where she knows little beyond the confines of her rural existence. Ormes narrated the character's desire to explore a wider world, though she mostly avoided a direct focus on the overt racial oppression that was pushing Black migrants North. *Torchy* ran for nearly twelve months, and over the course of the strip the character resists segregation laws by sitting in a whites-only train car, travels across the country, flies on an airplane, and works as a showgirl in exclusive New York City nightclubs. By the strip's end in April 1938, Torchy has gained fame and fortune and learned that her long-lost mother is a dead ringer for the international superstar Josephine Baker.[20]

Torchy's fanciful story was an exceptional life narrative for African American women during this era. Yet aside from the Baker embellishment, it was not entirely a dream. The performers Ethel Waters and Florence Mills had followed a similar trajectory, rising to prominence from obscurity and strategic migration. So did Cleo Hayes, a dancer who performed at the Cotton Club and the Apollo Theater during the 1930s and 1940s and appeared in the star-studded film *Stormy Weather*. As a teenager in the 1920s, Hayes had fled Greenville, Mississippi, and headed north. She exclaimed in an interview, "I don't have to tell you why I left! . . . . I had stars in my eyes. When I left Mississippi, I went to Chicago. Oh, I just thought that I had arrived, like I had stepped into another world."[21]

Like these real-life women, the fictional Torchy has good reasons for migrating. For young African American women in the South, securing a livelihood was difficult and uncertain in the late 1930s. In some ways, Torchy is more fortunate than most: when the narrative opens, she is living on a family farm with a caring aunt and uncle, an unusual situation in a country in which many Black farmers worked land that did not belong to them. Most African American women in the South lived in conditions not far removed from those of their formerly enslaved grandmothers. Two possibilities were open to them: agricultural work or domestic service. According to a 1937 report from the Women's Bureau, female cotton pickers earned a mere $41.67 a year in the Deep South.[22] Racial violence also routinely damaged prospects for Black men and women.

Black newspapers were a vital web of communication in local and national Black communities. They also were an influence on migration. Before the close of World War I, Robert Abbott, the founder of the *Chicago Defender*, had deliberately suggested that African Americans seek their fortunes and recover their dignity in the North.[23] In her work at the *Pittsburgh Courier*, Ormes was exposed to these complex economic and social pressures. She said later, "I had never been to Dixie, but I worked in a newspaper office. I read everything that was in that paper. It was a whole lot about struggles." The columns abutting the first *Torchy* strip report on the "plight of the Negro in the Depression" and the troubles stemming from racial segregation in Memphis.[24] Articles in subsequent issues call attention to the horrors of the South and trumpet the gains of "the race" in the North.[25]

There is a clear connection between the communities, businesses, institu-tions, and cultural environment that Black migrants slowly and painstakingly built during the Great Migration and the opportunities that the children of these "New Negroes" accessed. Ormes acknowledged this connection by having Torchy flee to Harlem, a reputed Black utopia, where she finds urban space, personal freedom, and a burgeoning Black modernity. Notably, Black women are key progenitors and harbingers of modernity in the strip. Torchy is encouraged to migrate by her glamorous cousin Dinah and by her own dreams of meeting her famous mother. Eventually, she herself becomes a link to urbanity for those who remain in her small southern town. Like the real-life Cleo Hayes, Torchy Brown represents the emerging modern African American woman. She is determined, fearless, and outspoken, a symbol of possibility, demanding freedom. Ormes instilled a Black feminist sensibil-ity within Torchy and all of her other Black female protagonists. They are independent and self-empowered, and each centers the experiences of Black women. Simultaneously, their success or failure does not depend on men or their proximity to masculinity.

By centering a Black female character drawn by a Black woman cartoon-ist, *Torchy Brown in "Dixie in Harlem"* brought a new perspective to the read-ers of Black newspapers. The *Courier* initially published the strip alongside Wilbert Holloway's *Sunny Boy Sam* and later the renowned cartoonist Sam Milai's *Society Sue and Family. Sunny Boy Sam*, one of the longest-running Black comics, revolves around a male comedic hustler who often plays into Black stereotypes: flashy, mischievous, and speaking in dialect. *Society Sue* features a woman as a main character, but she is mainly treated as a busybody, not imbued with the social awareness of Ormes's characters (though Milai would later publish more politically charged cartoons). Ormes recalled those early years: "Now there was a lot of news in the *Courier* about segregation and such, but these things never made it into the comics. They didn't deal with it at all."[26]

BRONZEVILLE AND THE POLITICS OF CARTOONING

In 1938, because of economic pressures linked to the Depression, Jackie and Earl Ormes moved to his hometown, Salem, Ohio. There she drew her last installments of *Torchy Brown in "Dixie in Harlem"* and ended its year-long run, probably due to the move. Salem was almost completely segregated, which meant that, like many educated Black men, Earl was forced to look for work outside his field. He spent four years as a crane operator at a mill until Ormes persuaded him to move to Chicago: "Earl wanted to be near his family. He wanted to feel secure–that was his big need. I needed Chicago. I talked him into it."[27] Perhaps Ormes was unhappy in Ohio because she had no opportunity to continue her career, though having any career at all was highly unusual for a woman at that time, even in the city.

In 1942, Chicago was a bustling metropolis with an established Black community that had been steadily increasing due to the Great Migration. Ormes's trajectory to the city was unusual: while she had traveled from the Mid-Atlantic to the Midwest, most African Americans who arrived in Chicago between 1915 and 1950 had come up from the oppressive and economically depressed South. So even though Chicago, like New York, was plagued by racial tension and stringent de facto segregation, it nonetheless embodied tremendous Black progress. In 1945, the sociologists St. Clair Drake and Horace Cayton published *Black Metropolis: A Study of Negro Life in a Northern City*, which outlines the ebb and flow of Black Chicago during the era:

> Here were colored policemen, fireman, alderman, and precinct captains, state representatives, doctors, lawyers, and teachers. Colored children were attending public schools and the city's junior colleges. There were fine churches in the Negro areas, and beautiful boulevards. It seemed reasonable to assume that this development would continue with more and more Negroes getting ahead and becoming educated. . . . On eight square miles of land, a Black Metropolis was growing in the womb of the white.[28]

Earl and Jackie Ormes settled in Bronzeville, the center of Chicago's Black metropolis, and Earl quickly found work as a manager at the prestigious DuSable Hotel and as an assistant comptroller for Supreme Life Insurance, a leading Black-owned company.[29] His position at the newly built hotel proved to be pivotal for the couple's personal and professional lives, not least because, as manager, it gave them housing.

With *Torchy Brown in "Dixie in Harlem,"* Ormes had a way to manipulate the popular image and representation of Black women. She had called on one layer of resistance (comic creation) to affect another (political commentary), and she had established a foothold as a cartoonist. In Chicago, Ormes began to work for the *Chicago Defender*, and the paper became the home of her next strip: *Candy*. In the character of Candy, she found an outlet for her growing interest in social commentary. Like her other strips, *Candy* incorporates Black feminist images and commentary, sharing portraits of Black life and African American women that were not routinely available in mainstream representations or elsewhere in the Black press.

During this period, there were many and varied voices in the Black press representing the diversity of their communities. White Americans had numerous specialized media venues through which to speak their multiplicities. Yet even when a Black weekly sought a middle ground or tried to eschew radicalism, mainstream observers treated the discussion of exigent issues impacting their readers as radical. It is true that Black newspapers were often necessarily (or willfully) confronting structural oppressions such as racism, classism, and sexism. The historian Fred Carroll notes that the papers' "outsized influence on black political life" led some publishers to include heavy coverage of "radical political views that were frequently at odds with their personal commitment to the national political system and its capitalist economy."[30] Ormes herself embraced and aided the popular and cultural fronts as well as the civil rights and early second-wave women's movements. This made her even more radical than some of her publishers and fellow cartoonists and journalists.

Candy is representative of her bent toward radicalism. The strip was short-lived, running only from March to July 1945, yet its representation of African American women had no equal in the comic pages, on stage, or on screen. In *Candy*, Ormes centered a Black woman domestic, drawing her in the pinup style of the moment and thus adding an important new expression of Black womanhood to confront the ill-defined white hegemony over 1940s American beauty standards.[31] The cartoon appeared on the editorial page, where the fictional Candy comments on the state of the country alongside Black opinion writers of the day. Topics include wartime shortages, a developing Black market for rationed products, so-called patriotic activities, and the complications of wartime Black womanhood.

Candy pits historical assumptions against American reality. In mainstream media, Black domestics were often portrayed as a docile, silent presence in white households, but this attested more to the needs of white America to perpetuate the mammy construction than to the women's actual feelings, resistance, and expressions.[32] Ormes modeled Candy after the living, breathing domestics she knew in Chicago and Pittsburgh, revealing, once again, her interest in portraying the interiority of Black women. Because she was working in the comic genre, she was able to take literary license, exaggerating Candy's agency in a white household in the 1930s and 1940s. Yet this very license shows that she was fully aware of the dangers that surrounded Black domestics at every turn.

There have been other outspoken Black female domestics in nineteenth- and twentieth-century popular culture. Hattie McDaniel's 1939 portrayal of Mammy in the film *Gone with the Wind* may have been based on the sassy yet subservient mammy stereotype, but McDaniel's humanistic acting constructed a wise and resistant character. In Alice Childress's 1956 novel, *Like One of the Family*, the servant Mildred exposes the hypocrisy of her white employers. In the 1970s television sitcom *The Jeffersons*, the maid Florence often refuses to cook, clean, or answer the door.[33] But Ormes's *Candy* stands alone. In the first episode of the strip, Candy instantly signals her superiority by announcing to her prospective employer, "Course, Mrs. Goldrocks, the first few weeks you'll be on probation!"[34] With the body of a pinup and the mind of an analytical Black feminist, Candy repeatedly calls out white hypocrisy and class privilege. She jokes, "There goes Mrs. Goldrocks bragging about her beautiful friendship with the butcher again. I wouldn't be surprised if she has him at her next dinner party!" But viewers understand that in real life Candy would be the one to have a relationship with the butcher and Mrs. Goldrocks would not be involved in the labor of shopping and cooking. In another episode, Candy, wearing her maid's uniform, holds up a piece of mail and says, "I'd better answer this GI mail for Mrs. Goldrocks so SHE'LL have something to brag about at her club meeting."[35] In yet another, Candy, looking down at a party from a stair landing, declares, "This job's good for me . . . the more I see of her friends, the more I appreciate my own."[36] Candy regularly stresses the significance of Black beauty in an era when it was often obscured or maligned. Standing in her employer's library in her uniform, she boldly reapplies her lipstick. With a side glance to the reader, she says, "So that's the great Swoona Stagrow! Hmmph . . . I've seen gals with more on accident than she's got on purpose!"[37] Ormes posited that this Black domestic possessed more beauty, as well as a deeper, more profound understanding of equality, freedom, democracy, and patriotism, than her elite white employer.

Candy's opinions would have resonated with Black women and the broader Black community. Women were working in a variety of jobs during the war: in factories, as nurses, and as servicemembers; as office workers, sharecroppers, and domestics.[38] While all endured racialized and gendered hell in their occupations, the hell of domestics was particularly familiar. Throughout the century, African American women had routinely served as domestics in both the North and the South. But during the labor vacuum created by the war, many families that had previously hired white women turned to Black women. By 1944, Black women made up 60 percent of all private household workers, up 13 percent from 1940 figures.[39] Still, even though Candy was a voice for these women, the strip's heavy emphasis on wartime issues may have triggered its demise. Germany surrendered to the Allied powers in May 1945, and *Candy* ended two months later.

Ormes's illustrations in *Torchy Brown in "Dixie in Harlem"* and *Candy* celebrate an independent Black feminist sensibility, but they also highlight how important it was for the Black press to provide images of Blackness that were not tied to the limitations of the white imagination. At prominent white mainstream newspapers, there were many steps between an artist's original conception and a finalized strip. Some papers bought syndicated comic strips; others hired a full staff of comic artists, and separate individuals would write the narrative, draw the strip, create the dialogue, and finalize the product. Usually, several people were involved in the creation of a single strip, making it difficult to maintain control over political or social commentary. In contrast, Ormes and other Black comic strip creators drafted their own narratives, drew their own images, and inserted their own text.[40] They managed their own content and maintained a sensitivity to the triumphs and struggles of their readership. Of course, not every strip in the Black press had political or social overtones. However, the omnipresence of inequity meant that such issues could never be avoided for long in any part of the paper. Ormes made them a fundamental part of her comics' narratives and politics.

PATTY-JO 'N' GINGER AND COLD WAR CIVIL RIGHTS

Ormes's longest-running and most famous strip, *Patty-Jo 'n' Ginger*, appeared in all editions of the *Pittsburgh Courier* between 1945 and 1956. No Black woman had ever before published a comic strip that would run fifty-two weeks a year for more than a decade. As the comic historian Trina Robbins writes, "it goes without saying that all those white-shirted men working for Disney were white, white-shirted men. If, after the war, action-oriented comics became a male-only domain, all nationally syndicated comics were, and had been, a white-only domain."[41] Ormes broke through the all-white, all-male precincts and used this hard-earned space as a platform for progressive, sometimes radical, journalism.

If *Candy* reflected the World War II moment, *Patty-Jo 'n' Ginger* represented the turbulent postwar era. Three pillars anchored the strip's political messaging: the lasting influence of the popular and cultural fronts, the rising civil rights movement, and the Cold War and anti-communism. The main character, Patty-Jo, is a little girl with big opinions, and Ormes was able to speak to significant issues of the day via her innocent musings. Ginger, Patty-Jo's always-silent teenage sister, is portrayed, as Candy was, in pinup style. Both sisters are beautifully drawn and wear the latest fashions. In the one-pane strip, Patty-Jo comments on everything from racial injustice, to the unequal treatment of women, to national and international politics. Her reflections are innocuous but have a bite. Although the cartoon prominently displays an aspirational middle-class lifestyle and its accoutrements, such as home ownership, access to quality education, and evidence of disposable income, it also repeatedly points to the conditions of the Black community as a whole and the national issues that faced Black America at midcentury.

In a pointed example from 1950, Patty-Jo stands in a room with leaky ceilings, broken windows, cracked and peeling walls, and falling rafters. It is the home of three poorly dressed kids and their mother, and Patty-Jo tells them facetiously. "Now you folks can REALLY stop worryin' . . . Uncle Sam's blowing our national wad on an H-bomb for your protection . . . course that don't spell HOUSING, but you gotta admit, it ain't HAY either!"[42] In this single image, Ormes succinctly called out the hypocrisy of pouring money into the arms race while neglecting domestic issues like urban blight in African American communities.

Even as the strip presents a middle-class construction of African American life, the reader is regularly reminded that Patty-Jo and Ginger live within a larger Black community that has little access to necessities. Patty-Jo has progressive opinions because she understands the complications of Black life, the impact of negligent political structures, and the fallout of race and gender inequality. Even in the context of its regular coverage of racial and class disparities, such stinging analysis was a radical statement for the *Courier*.

In the late 1940s and early 1950s, as African Americans pushed for equality and America entered the Cold War, Ormes centered her commentary on the changing political climate. The historian Mary Dudziak has explained how the standoff with the Soviet Union both opened the door to civil rights gains and limited their scope. Under a media spotlight and in a global race to install political democracies, the government was hobbled by disturbing civil rights coverage. The internal protests of civil rights activists were enhanced by international pressure, yet this took place in tandem with the national demonization of internationalism, communism, and radicalism. The situation led, Dudziak writes, to a "narrowing of acceptable Civil Rights discourse," which left many vulnerable to state attack.[43] Ormes's comics are remarkable because they detail this transformation under the cloak of the funny pages.

As I have discussed in previous chapters, the FBI and HUAC destroyed the lives and careers of countless men and women who were considered to be left-leaning during this period. Among them was the actor, singer, and athlete Paul Robeson, who would not be called before HUAC until 1956, well after damage had been done to his career. At one point his renown was so great that W. E. B Du Bois, called him "the best known American on earth."[44] Yet after the State Department revoked his passport in 1950 due to his prolific activism and communist associations, Robeson was unable to perform in the States or abroad. He became a prominent symbol of the price of Black communist affiliation and interracial radical activism. His 1958 memoir *Here I Stand* worked to rebut the accusations and slander that had felled him, and he took special care to outline the support of the Black press during his persecution by the government and the white press. In a list of excerpts from Black newspapers across the nation, he included a sample from an article published in the *Pittsburgh Courier* in July 1956: "There is a great fear that he would embarrass the U.S. abroad in regard to the negro question. This is sheer foolishness. The world is well aware of the treatment which America accords its Negro population. . . . This denial is robbing him of . . . years of his life."[45]

Through her critique of rising anti-radicalism and McCarthyism, Ormes worked in tandem with fellow journalists and artist-activists to condemn the brutal treatment of African American activists. Under the guise of fighting communism, HUAC was blacklisting Black organizations and labeling their members as radical. The activist Esther Cooper Jackson, a founding editor of *Freedomways* and an organizer of the Committee in Defense of Black Leadership, recalled that "there were several hundred African Americans who were either arrested or under contempt during the McCarthy era."[46] But at a time when many Black public figures feared making even a quiet critique of the anti-communism crusade, Ormes stepped directly into the fray. In her April

23, 1949, strip, Patty-Jo and Ginger are out for a spring walk, and Patty-Jo points to a manhole sign reading "Men at Work." She says to Ginger, "What'd I tell you. . . . . underground workers . . . jus' wait till the un-American Committee hears about this!"[47]

Ormes was unrelenting in her assault on fanatical anti-communism. In a July 24, 1948, strip, Patty-Jo, holding tight to her teddy bear, casually talks to her sister about her conservative friend Benjie: "Naw . . . I don't see much of Benjie anymore. His dad gave him an important job of pulling wings off of flies . . . Left Ones!"[48] Benjie is a friend of Patty-Jo's who often appears in the strip as a conservative counterweight to her radicalism. Undoubtably, Ormes included him as a direct response to rightwing readers.

Oliver Harrington, a fellow cartoonist for the *Courier*, was an early victim of the government's anticommunist witch hunt. Like Ormes, he had helped to craft the comics as a progressive extension of the political discussions in Black newspapers. Yale-educated, he was a multitalented artist, reporter, and writer. Before the war, he had published comics and articles for several African American papers, including the *People's Voice*, a radical weekly, and Harlem's mainstream *Amsterdam News*. After a break from the *Courier*, he returned in 1943 as a war correspondent and cartoonist.[49] Harrington created what was perhaps the most popular strip in Black comics at the time, *Dark Laughter*, with its unassuming silent protagonist—a middle-aged Black man named Bootsie. The character was an everyday everyman who acted as a witness to race and racism in addition to the ups and downs of Black American life.

Patty-Jo 'n' Ginger ran stacked or side by side with *Dark Laughter* in the late 1940s and early 1950s. Probably this was a layout decision as both comics were single panes, but the pairing was fortuitous as the strips raised many of the same social and political questions and critiques. But Harrington suffered years of governmental harassment due to his work with Du Bois and the NAACP and his role in the communist Benjamin Davis's campaign for New York City councilman. Finally, in 1951, he left America for France, never to live in his birth country again.[50]

Several national and international incidents deepened the Cold War and the communist hysteria. In October 1949, Russia detonated its first atomic bomb as a show of force. That same month, Mao Zedong founded the People's Republic of China, introducing another communist superpower into the delicate geopolitical balance. In January 1950, Alger Hiss, a high-ranking State Department official, was accused of espionage on behalf of the Soviet

Union and was subsequently convicted of perjury. In February, a little-known Wisconsin senator named Joseph McCarthy whipped the country into a frenzy when he claimed to possess of a list of 205 communist spies who had infiltrated the government. In June, the Korean War ignited, essentially a proxy war between the United States and the allied forces of China and the Soviet Union. Red-baiting, suspicion, and accusations of subversion settled over America like a fog. Ormes herself was fortunate not to suffer blacklisting at this time, although the FBI developed a keen interest in her activities.

In a March 1951 strip, published in the same year that Harrington had been forced to flee, Patty-Jo returns from church and reports to her sister: "So, like I said, the Rev. Mr. Holy was leading the congregation in prayer and got us into a wonderful chorus of PEACE MONGERING when Uncle Bootsie yelled 'Lawd an' MR. TRUMAN, TOO!'" . . . then a mother jumped straight up an' shouted AMEN . . . that's when the preacher stopped cold an' said: 'This is Easter, Brother Bootsie, let's keep it CLEAN. We don't want no FBI in here!'"[51] Ormes's brazen reference to Harrington's "Brother Bootsie" signaled the artist's solidarity with her fellow cartoonist.

The campaign to end progressive and radical organizing was widely effective. In place of the system-shifting popular and cultural front activism of the 1930s and 1940s, a more limited civil rights movement emerged, one with a narrower scope. Undiscouraged, Ormes published numerous strips that blatantly critiqued the government's treatment of her community and her friends. At the same time, her peace-mongering strip and others reminded readers that they were a part of a beloved Black world. When her characters leave their middle-class home, they exist in a mixed-income, segregated Black space, mirroring the experience of many African Americans at a time when there were few standalone middle- or upper-middle-class Black neighborhoods.

Because her papers have not been archived, Ormes's personal politics are hard to discern in full. What is clear is that she was involved in groups characterized as radical, and the worldview she articulated in her few interviews espoused elements of the popular and cultural fronts and the civil rights movement and was radical for its time. Her comics make this clear as well. In later strips, Ginger remains silent and reflective, but Patty-Jo becomes even more tenacious. In the October 8, 1955, strip, Patty-Jo walks in from the kitchen and tells her sister, "I don't want to seem touchy on the subject . . . but that new little white tea kettle just whistled at me!"[52] This remark is a reaction to the 1955 murder of Emmett Till, a fourteen-year-old who was abducted

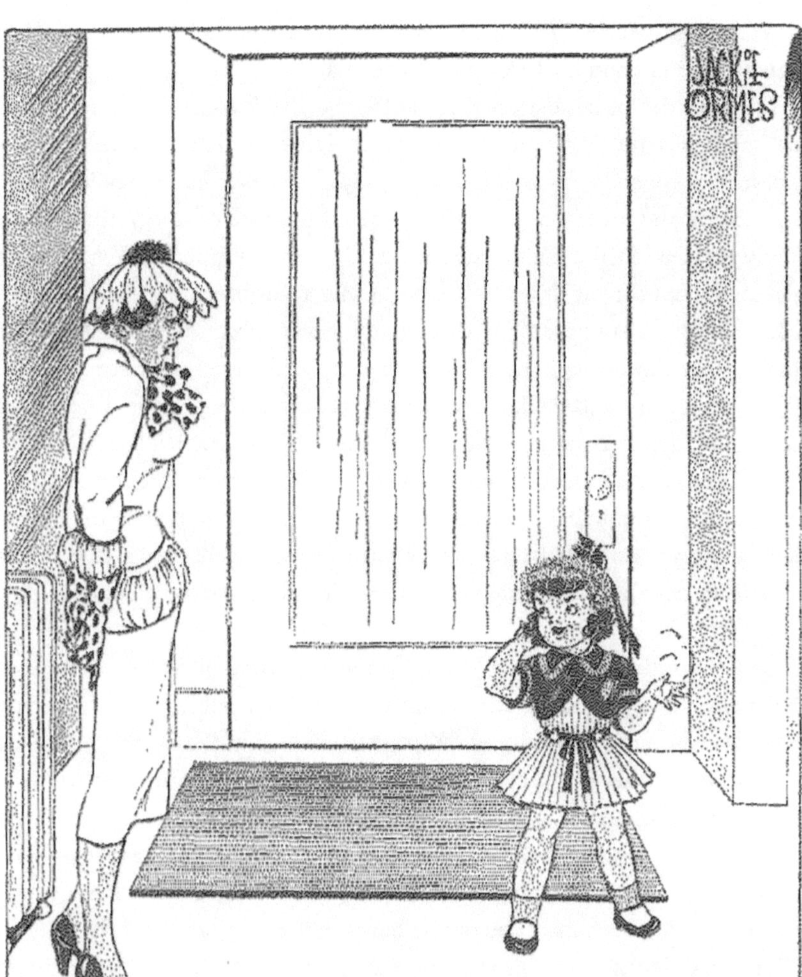

"So, like I said, the Rev. Mr. Holy was leading the congregation in prayer and got us into a wonderful chorus of PEACE MONGERING when Uncle Bootsie yelled 'LAWD an' MR. TRUMAN, TOO!' . . . then a mother jumped straight up an' shouted AMEN . . . that's when the preacher stopped cold an' said: 'This is Easter, Brother Bootsie, let's keep it CLEAN. We don't want no FBI in here!'"

FIGURE 12. Jackie Ormes, *Patty Jo 'n' Ginger*, *Pittsburgh Courier*, March 24, 1951. Courtesy of Nancy Goldstein.

from his uncle's Mississippi home, viciously beaten to death, then thrown into the river, his body weighed down by a cotton gin fan, allegedly because he had whistled at a white woman in a shop. African Americans reacted with horror and outrage. His death must have been even more distressing for the cartoonist because Till had lived with his mother in Chicago, where his funeral was held and his broken body viewed.

Till's murder became a touchstone for the Black community nationwide and marked a turning point for the civil rights movement, mostly due to widespread coverage by the Black press. *Jet*, the premier Black magazine, reported on the funeral and included explicit pictures of his mutilated body. Surely Ormes felt the heavy grief of her Chicago community. Yet Patty-Jo's response is not sorrow. It is ridicule at the vile absurdity of killing a fourteen-year-old boy for supposedly whistling at a grown white woman. Ormes was able to voice this by exploiting Patty Jo's youth and seeming innocence. Using the metaphor of a "little white tea kettle," she acknowledged the double standard embedded in American racial and sexual violence, which has historically beset Black people and gone unpunished.[53] Using the comic section of a Black newspaper as a political space, she delivered a scathing critique of segregation, miscegenation, and rape without triggering the backlash that similar sentiments may have prompted in other sections of the newspaper or in other media formats.

Ormes continued to insert Patty-Jo into the national conversation about civil rights throughout the strip's run. In an episode published on March 31, 1956, Patty-Jo crows to Ginger, "You guessed it! Bundle for the South . . . Montgomery, Ala., that is."[54] The little girl is carrying a pair of roller skates for shipping, and she is referring to the Montgomery bus boycott, which had started four months earlier when the activist and seamstress Rosa Parks refused to give up her seat to a white patron on a segregated bus. Parks's arrest led to a 381-day boycott of the public buses that began only months after the Till murder. Parks later said that she was thinking of Till during the pivotal confrontation.[55]

THE COSTS OF ON- AND OFF-THE-PAGE ACTIVISM

In 1953, Jackie Ormes was featured in *One Tenth of a Nation*, a newsreel series celebrating fourteen prominent African Americans. The short film shows her in her studio, meticulously drawing her popular comics.[56] At the time Ormes was approaching the zenith of her twenty-year career as a cartoonist in Black newspapers, but ironically the year also marked the moment when the FBI began taking an interest in her activities. As the civil rights movement gained momentum, Ormes's far-left activism was having consequences.

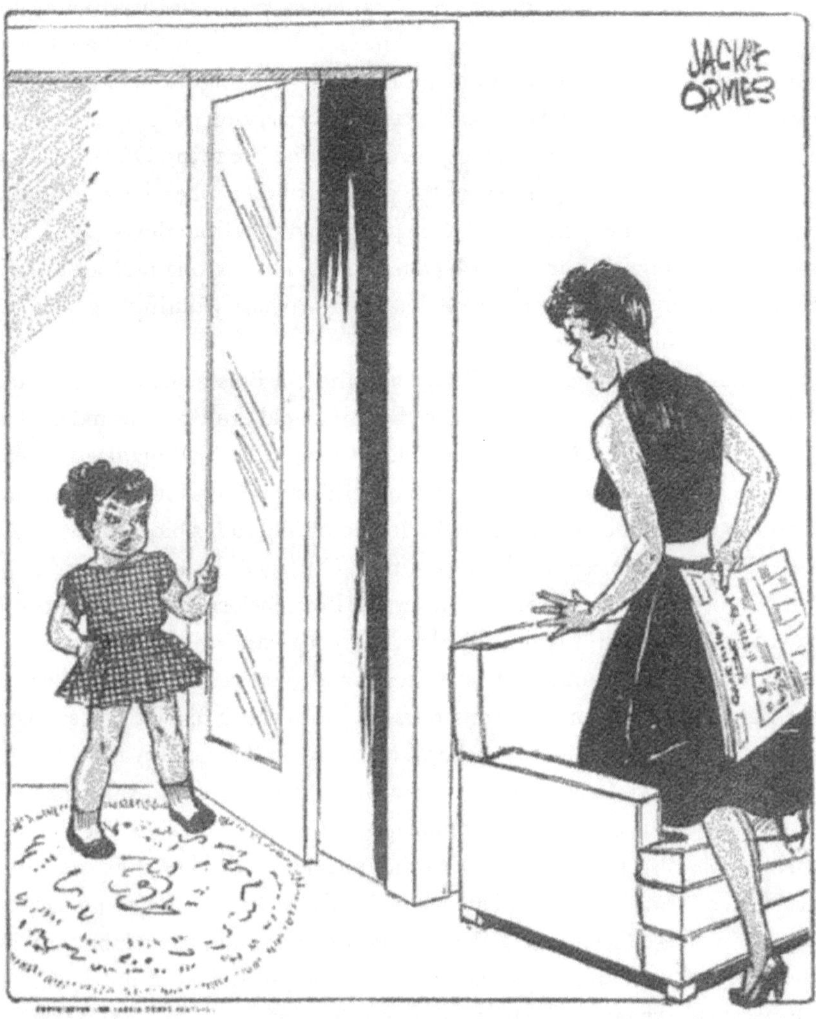

"I don't want to seem touchy on the subject . . . but, that new little white tea-kettle just whistled at me!"

FIGURE 13. Jackie Ormes, *Patty-Jo 'n' Ginger*, *Pittsburgh Courier*, October 8, 1955. Courtesy of Nancy Goldstein.

According to her FBI file, agents had been monitoring her activity since 1948, reportedly due to her attendance at a talk by several Communist Party USA members. After the war, the bureau, often in tandem with HUAC, was likely to investigate anyone involved in radical Black activism, and Ormes was under surveillance for at least the next five years. The FBI's biggest concern was her possible connection to the Communist Party and her friendships with influential activists such as Geraldine and Claude Lightfoot, Paul Robeson, and W. E. B. and Shirley Graham Du Bois.[57] The Lightfoots were deeply involved in the party: Claude as executive secretary of the Illinois branch, Geraldine as an active national organizer since the late 1930s. Du Bois would not become an official member of the party until 1961, when he was ninety-three years old. However, by the late 1940s, he had split from the NAACP and more closely aligned himself with communism. His lifelong radicalism kept him under continuous governmental attack, particularly during the McCarthy era, until his death in 1963.

Several letters suggest that Ormes and the Du Boises shared beliefs and connections. In early 1951, the eighty-three-year-old Du Bois was indicted in *U.S. vs. Peace Information Center* for failing to register as "an organization representing . . . a foreign power."[58] In response, his supporters formed a National Committee to Defend Dr. Du Bois with, according to his biographer, David Levering Lewis, "exceptional" support from Chicago.[59] In a letter dated September 30, 1951, Ormes wrote to Shirley Du Bois, enclosing a list of donors to the committee fund: "My dear Shirley . . . my regards to you and doctor. . . . I am wishing him a triumphant day in court, and great satisfaction that he is in the right, no matter what the consequences. With you at his side and so many souls behind him sharing his belief, I am truly optimistic. . . . Keep up the good fight!"[60] The letter's timing aligns with the publication of the *Patty-Jo 'n' Ginger* critique of the FBI and homage to Bootsie, so it is possible that the cartoon was also subtly referring to the injustice of the Du Bois trial. Two years later, Ormes received a letter from W. E. B. Du Bois, dated January 12, 1953, discussing a "lecture trip" that he and his wife would be making through the Midwest, including a planned stop in Chicago. The letter indicates that Ormes was in charge of hosting the couple, fundraising, and coordinating the lecture.[61] After the tour Du Bois followed up with a thank-you note, which included a nod to Ormes's activist labor. In the 1950s, he was not a popular figure among well-positioned liberal African Americans, many of whom (including Walter White of the NAACP) kept their distance.[62] So Ormes's assistance and support placed her in a cadre of activists who unashamedly positioned themselves on the courageous far Black left—a risky choice.

The FBI's investigation of Ormes was also linked to her regular participation in activist organizations. Like the artist Elizabeth Catlett, she was a member of both the radical South Side Community Arts Center and the

NAACP. She also supported community activities sponsored by the Freedom Associates, the Progressive Party, the American Peace Crusade, the Civil Rights Congress, and others. All were on the government's list of subversive organizations.[63] A number of scholars have published studies on the vital work of Black women who were in or associated with the Communist Party and larger radical freedom movements.[64] It is unclear whether Ormes formally belonged to this sisterhood, but her proximity to radicalism, radical organizations, and activists is clear. It is possible that she came to the government's attention as agents were tracking other radical activists. Whatever the case, something raised her profile.

Agents conducted four interviews with Ormes between 1953 and 1958; and if FBI memos are to be believed, she purposely worked to confuse, charm, and frustrate them.[65] According to her file, she evaded agents for as long as possible but was finally cornered at home on May 18, 1953. In her first interview, an agent asked questions that were "designed to give the subject an opportunity to express her views" about "Korea, Russia, the Smith Act, the Communist Party and the Negro question." These questions appear to be a litmus test for what passed as contemporary patriotism, as all were controversial topics linked to communist infiltration. On each subject, Ormes's response was polite but defiant. She said that America should not have been involved in the Korean conflict and that she saw Russia as advancing socially and culturally but posing no threat to the United States.[66]

Many individuals interviewed by the FBI firmly distanced themselves from the Communist Party and its philosophies. In contrast, Ormes remained unfazed and purposely enigmatic. In their reports, agents alternately described her as "well-read and intelligent" and "flighty." Perhaps they had a hard time seeing this petite, attractive comic artist as a viable threat, and no doubt she used such racist and sexist assumptions to her advantage. She freely expressed her political views and her evaluation of the Communist Party. In the interviews, she discussed its merits, though she denied being a member. On one occasion, she "engaged the agents in a rather lengthy discussion of the Communist movement. . . . She had stated she felt the Communist movement to be an innocuous one which . . . constituted no apparent threat to the continued existence of this country's form of government." She added that she believed "Communists were being investigated and persecuted because of their activities in breaking down racial barriers, exacting more benefits from capital interests for the working class," and she told another agent that she had worked "on the fringe" with many of the organizations in Chicago that were considered subversive by the FBI and said that "if her alignment with any such organization was considered tantamount to CPUSA membership by the FBI or CPUSA, she had no defense."[67]

Ormes's bold responses highlight the danger inherent in past or present association with the Communist Party USA and its allied organizations. They also reflect another reality. Many African Americans who engaged in social and political work viewed the party as a venue for activism while also having reservations about its motives in the Black community. Black-led organizations were always deeply involved in the fight for freedom and equality, and the party often joined movements or actions that Black leaders, local and national organizations, and everyday Black folks had begun. Chicago was the site of a busy Black activist front, including communist-affiliated organizations. According to the Black studies scholar Bill Mullen, the impact of Black organizing was so great in the city that it extended the popular and cultural fronts long after the party itself had begun to collapse.[68] The full history of the brave activism of African American men and women in Chicago is still unclear, as their connections to radical organizations were cloaked in secrecy or have been erased over time. Nonetheless, we do know that Ormes's comments would have drawn more attention from the FBI rather than less. So why did she escape the severe repercussions that were visited upon many other Black celebrities, artists, and activists in the era of the blacklist? Perhaps because the FBI decided she was benign. She also benefited from working and living in segregated spaces. The *Courier* was a Black newspaper with a Black staff funded by Black readership. She would not have lost significant numbers of readers based on governmental accusations. Her husband, Earl Ormes, the main economic earner in her home, was now managing the Sutherland Hotel, a posh establishment catering to African Americans.[69] These supports did not place her out of the reach of the government and its forces, but they did provide some cover.

Nancy Goldstein, Ormes's biographer, notes that if the FBI had wanted to discern her political views, all agents had to do was to thumb through the *Courier* and read her comics.[70] But despite government harassment, or maybe because of it, she continued to use them as a political platform from which to deliver powerful societal critiques. The FBI conducted formal interviews with Ormes on May 5 and July 29, 1953, and again on February 13, 1955, and February 13, 1956. But those interviews triggered little change in the political engagement in the panes of *Patty-Jo 'n' Ginger*. In fact, an astute reader may have noticed some real-time backtalk to the FBI on the topic of government suppression—a significant decision given that many people dissociated themselves from public political involvement for fear of incrimination. On May 4, 1953, the strip featured a portrait of Patty-Jo standing behind an X-ray machine, her skeleton visible through a screen. She says, "So locate the MARBLE, Doctor McCarthy an' lemme out of here . . . Anything else you might see is strictly personal, and after all, I got my RIGHTS!"[71]

Senator McCarthy dominated headlines and television news coverage as HUAC interrogated scores of people. During 1953 alone, he held 143 days of hearings and brought six hundred defendants before the committee.[72] Incredibly, Ormes's strip condemning this outrageous overreach was published the day before her first FBI interview. It seems unlikely that agents had reviewed her work before they spoke to her, or the outcome of the interview may have been very different. Ormes continued her critique in a June 1954 strip. As Patty-Jo and Ginger take a walk, Patty-Jo reflects, "Now take the sun f'rinstance . . . wouldn't you say it's a very welcome ambassador from the Far East? . . . Or will Mr. McCarthy have us viewing IT with alarm before summer's over?"[73] Ormes also published the October 1955 "tea kettle" strip during the period of her interrogation.

For Ormes, this unrelenting resistance was part of her engagement in a larger freedom struggle. In May 1954, the Supreme Court's historic *Brown v. Board* decision declared school segregation to be unconstitutional, and in July McCarthy was censured for overreach. The blacklist era did not end with his removal, and much damage had already been done. But the activism and protest of Ormes and her characters paved the way for the rising civil rights movement.

Her defiance endured. As *Patty-Jo 'n' Ginger* continued its run, Ormes created another dynamic, woman-centered comic. The full-page, full-color strip *Torchy in Heartbeats* appeared from 1950 to 1954 in the *Courier*'s Sunday edition, a sign of Ormes's hard-earned standing at the paper. Reimagined from her 1930s iteration, the modern Torchy is a single African American woman who travels the world, becomes involved in a slew of adventures, and practices several professions along the way. She is fearless and independent and uses her many talents to combat injustice. The strip freely deals with subjects that the FBI would have classified as subversive. Torchy combats bigotry and racial oppression, common topics among African Americans at midcentury. But she

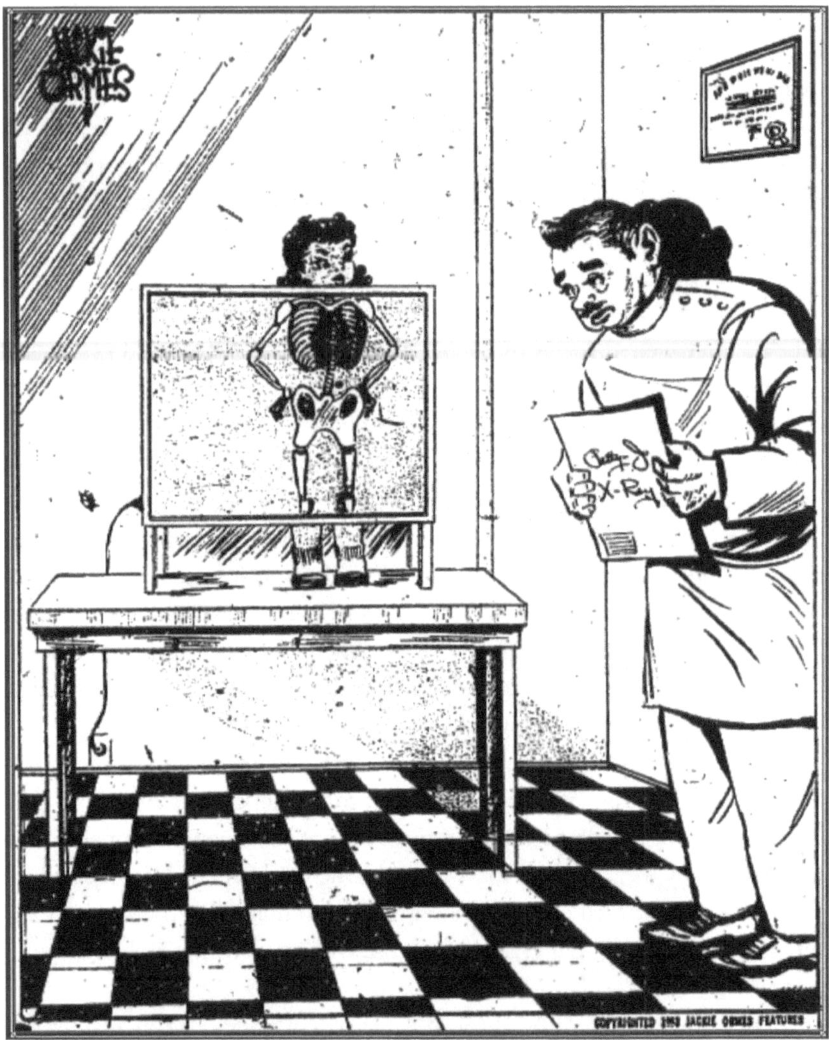

FIGURE 14. Jackie Ormes, *Patty-Jo 'n' Ginger*, *Pittsburgh Courier*, May 4, 1953. The caption reads, "So locate the MARBLE, Doctor McCarthy an' lemme out of here . . . Anything else you might see is strictly personal, and after all, I got my RIGHTS!" Courtesy of Nancy Goldstein.

goes further, tackling sexism, sexual harassment, and rape in the United States and abroad. In *Torchy in Heartbeats*, Ormes introduced discussions that would not enter the national consciousness or popular culture for decades, such as environmental racism and medical apartheid. In many ways, Torchy can be read as a precursor to the first African American female superhero.

As Ormes expanded her sites of resistance, Patty-Jo kept up her antics in her daily pane. But because of her constant drawing, Ormes had developed severe rheumatoid arthritis. She stopped producing her strips in 1956 and by her death in 1985 had lost much of the function in her hands.[74] This was ironic, given that they had been her principal weapons against the oppressions and repressions plaguing Black America and Black women. Her comics are a testament to the unique constructions of activism that African American women engaged in and the multipronged resistance that they waged. Ormes's political activist labor off the page and her radical messaging and image making within the panes of her comic strips reveal her layered resistance. She used her pioneering comics as progressive Black journalism, centering a Black female voice and citing Black women's concerns. Her chosen art form and its location in the funny pages of the Black press were made both subversive and radical in her hands.

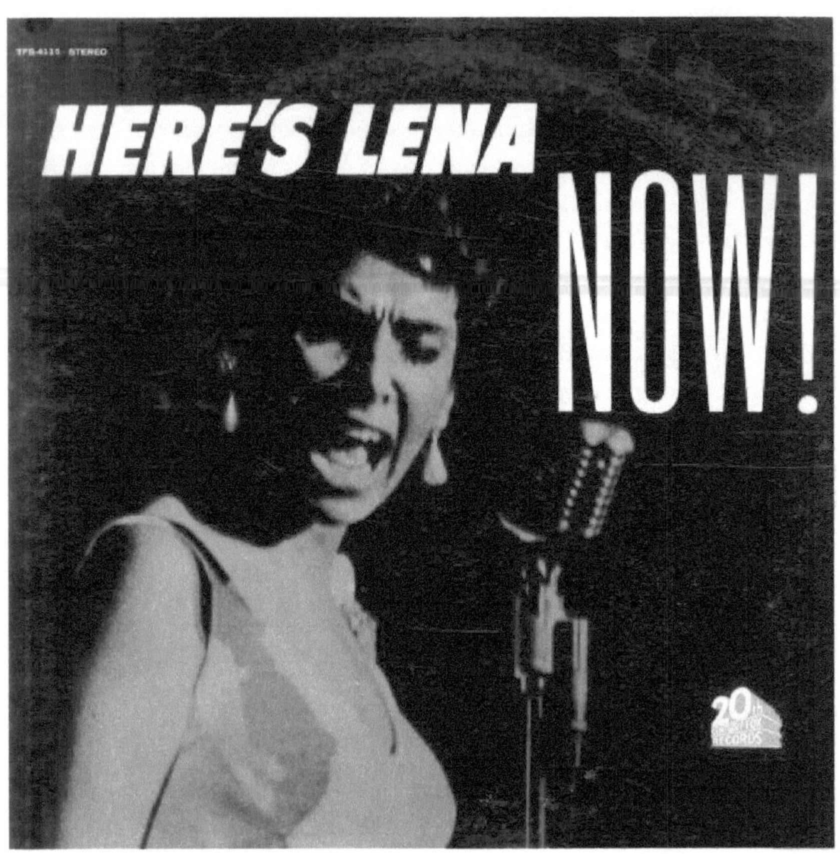

FIGURE 15. Lena Horne on the cover of her album *Here's Lena Now!*, 1963. Photographer unknown.

"You're Getting the Singer, Not the Woman"

Lena Horne in Three Acts

In 1981, Lena Horne lounged in an armchair on *The Dick Cavett Show*. She was in the midst of a press junket for her one-woman show, *The Lady and Her Music*. Cavett began his interview began by trying to ease her into comfort, but there was no need. Horne was ready to be open and transparent, more so than she had ever been before. She had found her voice. She told Cavett, "I was an introvert, I didn't become unintroverted until I was fifty! . . . I didn't talk. . . . I didn't have anything to say."[1]

Horne had become an introvert out of necessity. As the daughter of a renowned Black bourgeois family and a historicized symbol of Black stardom, she'd assumed that silence was the price of fame for a Black female celebrity: "I was behind a mask of what would not make me seem stereotypical of . . . a Black woman and the way that she was supposed to act, . . . [a] mask that erased everything . . . so that I couldn't be reached. I would not give myself easily."[2] As she had declared in her 1965 autobiography, *Lena*, "You're getting the singer, not the woman."[3]

Horne was an emblem of many things. At various moments she was seen as an undeserving, near-white ingénue; an adored Black star; a race woman bent on uplift; a sellout; a victim of the blacklist; a civil rights activist; and, eventually, proof of Black excellence, survival, and longevity. She was an enigma, often framed in ways that did not center her labor, challenges, or subjective articulations. But beginning in the early 1960s and continuing until her death in 2010, Horne became increasingly outspoken about her experiences.

Among the women celebrated in this book, Horne remains the most famous. In this chapter, I consider her as an empowered and defiant artist and performer who sometimes engaged in activism and, at other times, deliberately avoided it. However, her engagement with layered resistance was a consistent theme in her life. I begin with her childhood, then focus on her early career in the 1930s and 1940s, and end midcareer, in 1963, with the March on Washington and the release of her album *Here's Lena Now!*

ACT I: LENA CALHOUN

Lena Mary Calhoun Horne was born in 1917 into a first family of Brooklyn's Black bourgeoisie. The Hornes were exceptionally light-skinned, denoting their mixed-race heritage, and their high position in African American society was more related to skin tone and heritage than to finances. Her paternal grandfather, Edwin Fletcher Horne Sr., was a high-ranking official in the New York Department of Labor. His wife, Cora Calhoun Horne, was a community luminary and deeply involved in early civil rights activism, acting as a local leader in the Urban League, the YWCA, and the NAACP. She belonged to numerous uplift groups and organizations dedicated to improving conditions for her race, including the Colored Women's Clubs that arose at the turn of the twentieth century. These groups were led by moneyed Blacks who saw race advancement as their role. Thanks to her grandmother's standing, two-year-old Lena's portrait was featured in an NAACP branch bulletin.[4]

Lena seemed to be destined for a comfortable middle-class life. But her childhood was complicated by her aloof parents, Edwin Fletcher "Teddy" Horne Jr. and Edna Louise Scottron, who divorced when their only child was three, leaving her to the care of Teddy's parents.[5] Abandoning any status he might have held because of his family connections, Teddy Horne made a good living as a numbers banker, a card shark, and a hustler. An array of ticket stubs preserved in the Horne family archive attest to his carefree lifestyle, even during the Depression: attendance at the 1933 and 1934 National Colored All-Star baseball games, the 1949 World Series, and many, many boxing matches. He regularly watched the boxer Joe Louis in his heyday and considered him a friend.[6]

Unfortunately, this left Teddy little time for his daughter, and he was not consistently present in her life. Meanwhile, his ex-wife pursued a career in acting, becoming a member of the Lafayette Stock Company at the Lafayette

Theater. Over the decades, both the company and the theater became important sites for more than 250 Black productions, drawing actors such as Charles Gilpin, Rose McClendon, and Paul Robeson.[7] At first, Scottron had some success, performing leading roles in successful show productions of *Madame X* (1916–17) and *The Count of Monte Cristo* (1916–17). But even though she toured the country chasing her dreams, neither her talent nor her drive matched her ambitions.[8]

Among the subdued Black bourgeoisie, both Teddy and Edna were seen as heretics for rejecting their rarified birthright status. Yet as a man, Teddy was able to retain his male privilege and clout, even as a hustler. Edna, who had joined the theater, fled her family's class, and left behind motherhood and respectable Black womanhood, was thought of as a near-prostitute. Both of Lena's parents found ways to rebel against the burdens of race, class, and gender, and the weight of those expectations were very real. They dared to be independent spirits in an era when such freedom was uncommon for anyone, let alone Black Americans. Yet at the same time their connections to wealth and status surely helped them pursue their Jazz Age dreams.[9]

Their choices were bold, but their neglect made Lena Horne's childhood very unstable. While her mother was on tour, Lena shuttled among her grandparents' home, her mother's friends, distant relations, strangers, foster homes, and babysitters. Horne later described many of the caregivers as abusive or negligent, including her mother. One took to regularly beating Horne when she was wet and naked. Another was so neglectful that the child developed rickets, a condition linked to a lack of calcium and vitamin D—not likely to be a problem in most stable, middle-class Brooklyn homes.[10] The trauma of her childhood marked Horne for the rest of her life.

In 1929, the twelve-year-old gladly returned to the home in of her Horne grandparents, where Cora served as a steadying force. But within a few years both grandparents had passed away, and Horne needed to find a way to survive. She later recalled, "It became clear that the family's chief asset was me."[11] By this time Scottron had married Miguel Rodriguez, a white-presenting Cuban army officer, and Horne was reluctantly living with them.[12] In interviews, she described herself as knowing little about the world and possessing little talent for or interest in dancing or singing. But Scottron used her connections with the Cotton Club's chorus line captain to secure her daughter a job.[13] So in 1933, at age sixteen, Lena became a dancer, and her fast track into Brooklyn's elite Black society was permanently derailed: "Respectable girls were not supposed to go to work in Harlem nightclubs known to be owned by white hoodlums, or any other hoodlums for that matter."[14]

At the Cotton Club, Horne's star rose steadily, though she and those around her had misgivings about her talent. Other performers rightly assumed that most of her success was due to her light-skinned beauty, her mother's connections in the industry, and her father's connections to the mob. Although the club was known for hiring only the lightest of light-skinned chorus girls and it barred Black patrons, Black entertainers saw it as a plum gig. According to Horne, "it was the . . . showcase for Negro talent, and one had to have someplace to show one's creativity." She recalled seeing "Duke Ellington, Cab Calloway, and the great Ethel Waters . . . work[ing] under a roof in a cabaret that was a little better than a basement." Like other Black performers, she understood the contradictions of this Jim Crow environment: "I was torn because it was a dreadful place that was bad working conditions, little money, no respect paid to its creative people, and our own people couldn't come see us perform. . . . It was a trap."[15]

Through her exposure at the Cotton Club, Horne landed a gig as a featured singer with the Noble Sissle Orchestra. But just as her career in entertainment was beginning, it came to a halt. In 1937, after a short courtship, she married Louis Jones, a young printer from Pittsburgh. The marriage quickly foundered. Demanding and difficult, Jones pushed Horne to drop her career and become a traditional wife and mother. His granddaughter, Samadhi Jones, later described him as "a dyed-in-the-wool male chauvinist" who had "not won any kindness contests."[16] Quickly pregnant, Horne gave birth to a daughter, Gail. Then a few months later she was asked to star in a small low-budget Black film titled *The Duke Is Tops*.[17] The family's finances were dire, so she said yes. Although the job paid little and received scant attention, it further soured her marriage. Three years later, soon after giving birth to her son, Teddy, Horne boarded a train for New York City, leaving her small children in Pittsburgh with Jones and a live-in caretaker. After the divorce, he held on to the children for as long as he could, inflicting separation as a form of retribution. Eventually he did send Gail to Horne, but he kept Teddy, and that severance had an enduring impact on their mother-son bond.[18]

Motherhood, domestic turmoil, and divorce did not derail Horne's ambitions. Like the other women discussed in this book, she did not acquiesce to patriarchal or societal expectations, and her unapologetic rejection of traditional domesticity was a layer of her resistance. Her own mother, for all of her faults, was a model in this regard. When Horne returned to New York, she undertook her profession in earnest, first as a singer with Charlie Barnett's orchestra. Then, in 1941, she was offered a job at Café Society Downtown. Previously Hazel Scott had been the club's the main attraction. But when she moved to Café Society Uptown, Horne took over at the original site. She later called it "the sweetest job I ever got in my life." She remembered:

At that time Café Society was a gathering place for every great in jazz. . . . Teddy Wilson had the house band there, and he started out by trying to teach me how to carry a tune. . . . Around the corner . . . at . . . Nick's was Nat Cole. . . . A little further uptown was my beautiful sister Lady, Billie Holiday, then a little further on uptown was my other beautiful sister, Hazel Scott. So, you see, I was in the cream of everything that is wonderful in my profession.[19]

Horne's racial and political consciousness came to life in the club's radical atmosphere. Paul Robeson, an old friend of the Horne family, was a particular influence. He explained Black history and told her about her grandmother's activism as a race woman. "Paul taught me about being proud because I was a Negro. . . . I was getting more into that middle class trap with Negroes who . . . didn't speak about it."[20] She also befriended the singer and activist Josh White, who helped her develop her voice and deepened her understanding of racial oppression.[21]

Horne's short time at Café Society was an education in performance and politics. Thanks to her popularity there, she was invited to appear at more exclusive nightclubs, including the elite Savoy-Plaza Café Lounge, where she broke the color barrier. According to one newspaper, she "attracted capacity houses every single night . . . [and] the management . . . had to turn away up to 500 guests."[22] In these white-dominated venues, Horne's appearances would come to encompass more than her nightclub act. Undoubtedly, some audience members had never seen a Black woman perform before. Horne was on her way to becoming one of the biggest stars of the 1940s, and this meant she was pushing representations of African American women into national public space, a place that usually housed the worst aspects of the white imagination.

Although Horne's film appearances are still celebrated, her work as a nightclub singer is often forgotten. Yet it was the mainstay of her career. Audience members recall the coolness she exuded on stage. She excelled in intimate settings, and some critics and fans compared her performances to those of the Beat poets. Her signature technique was to sing quietly without a microphone,

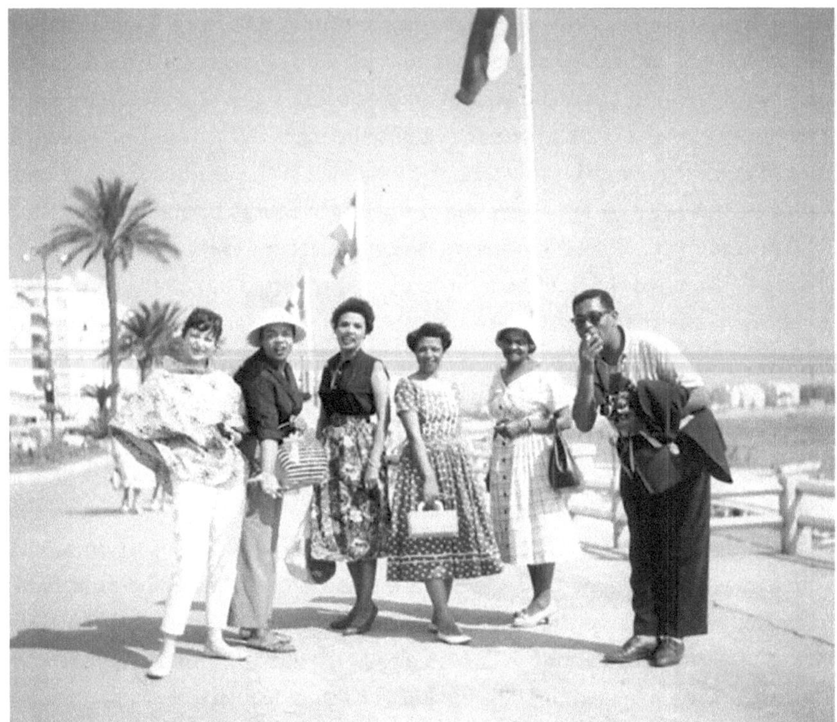

FIGURE 16. An excursion in Cannes in the late 1950s. From left to right, the British singer Annie Ross; Hazel Scott; Lena Horne; Dizzy Gillespie's wife, Lorraine Gillespie; a friend, L. B. Lucas; and the trumpeter Dizzy Gillespie. Horne met fellow performers such as Scott at Café Society and made lifelong friends. Courtesy of the photographer, Adam Clayton Powell III.

thus forcing her audience to listen closely in order to access her emotions. Her onstage delivery was an essential part of her layered resistance. She later said, "I had developed an isolation from the audience, that was probably a cover for hostility; most of them were so bemused by their own occupation with what a Negro woman should be onstage, and my difference from that preconception, that they did not see hostility. The image I gave them was exactly . . . that of a woman they could not reach."[23] Particularly in all-white spaces, the strategy of aloofness was an effort to exercise agency over the audience's intimacy with her. In the words of the scholar of performance studies Shane Vogel, she "renegotiated the fraught intimacies of the segregated cabaret stage."[24] Horne herself said, "In a funny way, the audience and I reversed roles. Usually, performers seek the audience's approval, but in my appearances, they, in a sense, had to seek mine." She recalled telling herself what she wanted to tell her listeners: "You're getting the singer, not the woman."[25] This strategy became embedded in her approach to performance. Thirty years later, in an interview in the early 1960s, she made it clear that she was still holding herself apart from her audiences: "I am too proud to let *them* think that they can have any personal contact with me. . . . I think many Negro performers feel much the same way, and they find their own methods of letting people know it. In other words, we all find our own means of rebellion."[26]

Horne insisted that she wanted to present "a different image of Negro women." For her white audiences, and sometimes also for her Black ones, that difference was often predicated upon her proximity to white beauty. For her, however, it was the ability to construct a popular yet enigmatic onstage representation of Black women. Her approach was exceptional in a national landscape marred by images of Black women as mammies, tragic mulattos, and Jezebels—all of whom were, by their very definition, accessible. Historically, openness was held up as a requirement for performers, particularly women, and especially Black women. Thus, Horne brandished her strategic lack of openness as a tool of resistance to white consumption.[27]

ACT II: HOLLYWOOD

Horne lamented, "I let some dude talk me into going to Hollywood!" In 1942, she signed a contract with Metro-Goldwyn-Mayer, thus ending her appearances at her beloved Café Society as well as other New York clubs where she regularly performed.[28] "The whole thing that made me a star was the war," she explained, "Of course, the black guys couldn't put Betty Grable's picture in their footlockers. But they could put mine."[29] The year 1943 was a major moment for Blacks in film, largely due to the release of two movies with an all-Black cast: *Cabin in the Sky* and *Stormy Weather*. Horne had starring roles in both.

In 1940, *Gone with the Wind* had featured iconic performances by Hattie McDaniel and Butterfly McQueen, each transforming the mammy role she'd been assigned. Unfortunately, such roles, along with Jezebels, were still the ones most available to African American women who wanted to work in the film industry.[30] Horne's 1943 roles also fit such stereotypes, but they did allow her a bit of room for reinterpretation. In *Cabin in the Sky*, she played Georgia Brown, a Jezebel character who steals another woman's husband. Although filmmakers were attempting to reveal Black modernity, the script was uneven, relying too much on familiar tropes, such as hyper-religiosity and ne'er-do-well Black masculinity. But with Georgia, Horne managed to embody the modernity that the film was seeking. The character seems to have blown into town from somewhere much more hip. Her presence allowed African Americans to enjoy the film with a measure of dignity.

Stormy Weather, conceived as a girl-meets-boy story-within-a-story set among touring performers, had much in common with the elaborate white musicals of the day. In it, Horne portrayed an independent woman who chooses her career over marriage. While the movie contains dozens of musical performances that put Black talent on display, its director did not stray far from the era's formulaic style, whose main aim was to distract viewers from the war. This may have contributed to its mass appeal: for a change, it did not saddle African Americans with a picture of themselves as a problem to be solved or force them to serve as benevolent sidekicks to white characters.[31]

With the release of these films, Horne's popularity expanded beyond the Black press. That year *Life*, *Look*, and *Harper's Bazaar* all featured her in dedicated photo layouts, and *Collier's* and *American Magazine* published long interviews with her. None of these magazines had ever promoted Black women in this way before. By 1947, *Life* was calling Horne the number-one nightclub singer in the country.[32]

She appeared in a string of all-star musicals in the 1940s, though usually as the sole Black character and never in a speaking role: *Thousands Cheer* (1943), *Broadway Rhythm* (1944), *Two Girls and a Sailor* (1944), *Ziegfeld Follies* (1946), *Till the Clouds Roll By* (1946), and *Words and Music* (1948). Many African Americans have since said that she was the first Black woman they remember seeing in the movies, although most of them had likely had glimpsed other Black women in more typical stereotyped roles. While the movie studios highlighted her light-skinned beauty and her soft singing voice, treating them as stand-ins for white approximation, Black people saw her as one of their own, regardless of her skin tone. Much has been made of her complexion and the concomitant neglect of darker-skinned women, yet as the actor Ossie Davis has said, "Lena for us was a part of our folk culture, you know, the things that we loved as a people, the collard greens, the Black Eyed Peas, you know, the pig's feet, whatever it was that was mashable and good. That made us feel, hey, this is home."[33]

There's no question that Horne was late to social activism and reluctant to engage in it. She only gradually moved toward publicly challenging racism and segregation and did not become fully involved with the civil rights movement until the 1960s. However, she was constantly defying American racial and gender hierarchies behind the scenes. Her campaign for better representations on stage and screen was a byproduct of her desire for better social and political conditions for Black Americans. Jim Crow attitudes made few distinctions based on status, class, gender, geography, or complexion; and like other Black artists and performers, Horne encountered bigotry beyond the comparatively safe space of New York City. In response, she, like Dunham and Scott, layered legal and extralegal confrontations with segregation into her resistance.

For instance, Horne forthrightly challenged segregated military performances. As a member of the Hollywood USO during the war, she was asked to perform at a show on a Little Rock, Arkansas, military base. When she got on stage, she saw that white troops had been seated immediately in front of her while African American soldiers had been relegated to the rear. Infuriated, she asked for permission to sing for Black troops in the mess hall the next morning. But to her shock, when she arrived, she discovered that German prisoners of war had been seated in front of the Black troops. In protest, Horne circled past the POWs and sang directly to the Black soldiers. Then, after hotly rushing away from the base, she headed for the nearest NAACP office, run by the chapter president, Daisy Bates, who would famously lead the Little Rock Nine during integration of the city's high school. Bates suggested that Horne lean on her celebrity status and publicize the soldiers' ill-treatment. Horne immediately resigned from the Hollywood USO and began discussing her experience in interviews. A media storm ensued.[34]

Since her days at Café Society, Horne had supported progressive causes. She had long been a member of a host of activist organizations, including the NAACP, the National Council of Negro Women, the American Committee for the Protection of the Foreign Born, and Women of Color for Peace.[35] But the USO incident marked her entry into modern civil rights movement activism. She joined other Black celebrities in their dangerous endorsement of Benjamin Davis as the first communist New York city councilman, and she became a member of the Council for African Affairs and the Joint Anti-Fascist Refugee Committee.[36]

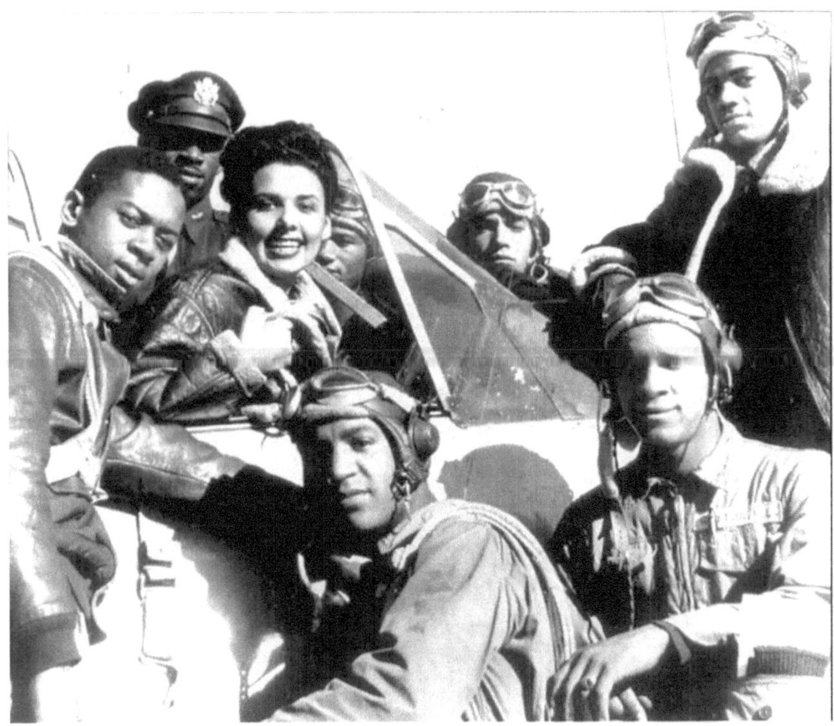

FIGURE 17. Lena Horne with the Tuskegee Airmen, January 1945. Photographer unknown.

Horne took legal action against more than one establishment that refused her service based on race. In 1949, for instance, when she and five friends were turned away at the door of Caruso's Restaurant in Chicago, she sued and won $500 in damages.[37] In 1955, she broke her engagement contract with Copa City, a club in Miami Beach, because of the treatment she and Black patrons had endured from high-end hotels on the strip. Before her arrival, she learned that the Urmey Hotel, where she had a reservation, had ejected twenty-five Black people who had been invited to the Lincoln Day dinner it was hosting for local Republicans. Her white Jewish husband then made a reservation at the Royal York Hotel, which canceled it and made an alternative booking at the all-Black Lord Calvert Hotel. The hotel denied that the cancelation was due to her race, and the white press painted her as overreacting. But the Black press recognized a link between Horne's racial consciousness and the refusal of accommodations.[38]

Horne was not a radical activist. Yet throughout her career she took activist stands that demonstrated her abhorrence of white supremacy, the denial of civil and human rights, and the perpetual construction of African Americans as subhuman. In 1951, as McCarthyism began to descend on the nation, she was blacklisted and kicked out of the Screen Actors Guild.[39] She would not be removed from the blacklist until 1956. Like many other Black artist-activists and performers, she saw much of her hard-earned celebrity washed away. Like Hazel Scott, she learned that her wartime activities around interracial harmony, once seen as high patriotism, were now marked as subversive.

Speaking of those days, Ossie Davis called performers such as Horne and Robeson "sacrificial lambs, . . . people who themselves paid a high personal price . . . for their freedom, . . . for their rights and defense of their rights"[40] Compared to many, Horne was fortunate: she retained her livelihood and her celebrity through limited engagements in America and extensive tours in Europe. But her career would never regain its momentum, and her layered resistance faltered. According to her biographer, Donald Bogle, Horne was booked for an appearance on *The Ed Sullivan Show* in September 1951, a year after her name had appeared in *Red Channels*.[41] After securing a few other television gigs, she thought she had overcome the stigma, until a few powerful media men publicly canceled her. In response, she appealed directly to Sullivan, who published a statement in which she disavowed communism and distanced herself from Robeson and others.[42]

Horne performed on Sullivan as planned, and on October 13, 1951, a headline in the *Amsterdam News* announced, "Lena Horne Cleared of Red Charge." According to the reporter, "Lena Horne's manager, Ralph Harris, verified reports this week that the famous singer had 'received a clean bill of health' from 'Counterattack' and 'Red Channels.'"[43] In her autobiography, Horne failed to address this episode with any depth, yet she must have had regrets, at least about her disavowal of Robeson. As the scholar Carol Sabile notes, Horne did publicly insist that "clearance" of her name would not stop her fight against injustice.[44] Likewise, Marvel Cooke of the *New York Daily Compass* reported that Horne had refused to name anyone she suspected of being a communist.[45]

Layered resistance was complicated, and for now accessing popular public space and continuing a career in image making had trumped Horne's dedication to progressive political agitation. Meanwhile, the public witch hunt had scarred the Black freedom movement. Once again movie screens filled with thin presentations of Blackness based on flawed white imaginings, and Black activism shift toward civil rights and away from the popular front's more humanist radicalism.

ACT III: BLACK WOMANHOOD, THE CIVIL RIGHTS MOVEMENT, AND *HERE'S LENA NOW!*

In the end, the blacklist did not curtail Horne's rebelliousness, and she would take much more definitive action during the civil rights movement of the late 1950s and 1960s. In her autobiography, she recalled this period as an extraordinary time of personal racial awakening. Horne's transition into active participation was prompted by several events that occurred in quick succession: the decision to end her nightclub career, a fateful meeting with Robert Kennedy, and the death of Medgar Evers. An incident in 1960 created a demarcation for her. In February, she was booked for a two-week engagement at the Cocoanut Grove in Hollywood. On her night off, she and her husband went to a nearby hotspot called the Luau to unwind. As a waiter headed to her table, another patron, a tipsy young white man, yelled at him for service. The waiter explained that he was about to serve "Miss Horne's" table. According to Horne, the patron retorted, "So what? Well, she's just another nigger. Where is she?" With this, Horne jumped up and held a light to her face: "Here I am, you bastard, the nigger you couldn't see!" After they traded more insults, the dispute reached a crescendo when he called her a "niggerbitch." Enraged, she threw a heavy ashtray and a table lamp at him.[46] The police were called, Horne was exculpated, and the man left with a gash over his eye and bruises on his body and his racist ego.

The aftermath of the incident was a revelation to Horne. African Americans poured out their admiration in the Black newspapers, by mail, and in person. Soon after the altercation, she went on vacation in the Caribbean vacation and was awed by the Black islanders' appreciation.[47] To Horne, the incident had been somewhat mundane, save for the ashtray throwing. She had always dealt with virulent racism on the club circuit—from fellow performers, to venue owners, to audience members.

She came to two realizations. First, "people thought because I was me that I wasn't catching hell." Second, they mistakenly believed that she did not consistently confront this ill-treatment.[48] Importantly, the incident made her feel more aligned with "her people." As a woman at the upper echelons of Black celebrity, she had achieved a unique isolation, and this had unwittingly distanced her from the Black community. At the same time, she understood that they saw her as an aspirational figure. She decided, "I wanted to re-identify myself with the Negro people. And yet I did not want to be forced into it . . .

by some external pressure. . . . I was determined not to be a symbol. I wanted my responses to be determined not by the symbolic me—and the protection of the same—but by the real me." [49]

So Horne announced her retirement from the nightclub circuit and began to shift her focus. Professionally, she had survived McCarthyism, but she no longer wanted to deal with the racialized and gendered mistreatment so prevalent in the clubs. Moreover, she recognized that the world was quickly changing. Writing for the *Amsterdam News*, Dave Hepburn speculated "the very fact that she wants to do work for sit-ins and freedom fighters is in itself proof that she does not really want to hang up her robes, but she does want her work to be meaningful."[50]

Over the next few years, Horne slowly increased her formal involvement with the civil rights movement, and in 1963 her activism took a major step forward. To call this a pivotal year for the movement is to wildly understate its significance: 1963 was a turning point for activists, their supporters, and their opponents. In that year Governor George Wallace stood before the doors of the University of Alabama's auditorium to block the entrance of two Black students who were attempting to register for classes, the activist Medgar Evers was assassinated in Jackson, Mississippi; the Ku Klux Klan bombed a Black church in Birmingham, Alabama, killing four girls and injuring nearly two dozen others; and the March on Washington drew an estimated 250,000 supporters of civil rights for all.[51]

The politeness of the 1950s was wearing off. Instead of transformation, protestors and activists were facing increased violence, especially in the South.[52] Racial violence in that region was as old as enslavement, but now many white southerners sensed that their segregated world was coming to an end. The idea of federally protected equal rights, particularly voting rights, brought out their fury. The activists, for their part, were steely in their determination to organize and push forward.

In May 1963, the writer James Baldwin invited Horne to meet with Robert Kennedy, the U.S. attorney general and the brother of President John F. Kennedy. The Kennedy administration was struggling to fathom the increasing anger and discontent of the Black community, and Robert hoped that a conversation with prominent Black professionals, celebrities, and activists would enlighten him.[53] In addition to Horne and Baldwin, the group included the playwright Lorraine Hansberry, the psychologist Kenneth Clark, the actor and singer Harry Belafonte, and a group of young activists from the Congress of Racial Equality (CORE) and the Student Nonviolent Coordinating Committee (SNCC). Belafonte was skeptical. He thought the participants were "a perfect coterie for a cocktail party" but not necessarily the best choice for briefing the attorney general on the state of "race relations."[54] He was also concerned that Kennedy was using the celebrity presence to sway the Black vote. In the end, however, the odd cross-section of Black America was advantageous. While participants approached the questions from many angles and social strata, all shared the same desires for freedom.

The conversation began as a civil exchange, until the participants realized that Kennedy believed that Blacks should be more grateful to the administration. Belafonte recalled, "He ticked off all the things that the administration had done to help our cause": he supported civil rights activists and tussled with staunch segregationists, such as Birmingham commissioner, Bull Conner. But he seemed completely out of touch with what the Black participants and their communities were actually experiencing. The attorney general was concerned that too much administrative action in support of civil rights would make southern Democrats flee from the party and doom the next election. He was also upset that many young African Americans were "heeding the radical message" of leaders such as Malcolm X.[55] He wanted to thwart such activity.

At this point, Jerome Smith, a CORE activist, interrupted the attorney general. He told the assembled group that he had endured brutal beatings. He had been jailed for a peaceful demonstration, and his family had been forcibly displaced because of his work with Black voter registration. He remained physically ill from past trauma and was tired of federal inaction. Horne later said that Smith "cut through the fog of statistical arguments, through the expression of this personal attitude and that one." He became "the soul of the meeting."[56] The other participants began echoing Smith's words, and Kennedy was taken aback. Exasperated and angry, he adjourned the meeting, and participants on both sides dispersed with an immense sensation of disenchantment. But the attorney general had gained a small but important insight into the mood of the African American community, and many believe the meeting directly affected the creation of the Civil Rights Act of 1964.[57]

For Horne, the meeting clarified her understanding of the movement and her place in it. A few months earlier she had told a reporter, "There's been the greatest upheaval of everyone's emotions in the past five years. The sit-ins, the Freedom Rides, the emerging African nations, the positive, progressive movements. . . . I never thought I'd see it. There's a new breed, a whole new breed, and what the oldtimers said just isn't applicable anymore; the mossbacks have had their day."[58] But the meeting had pushed her to confront her own lack of action. She returned to California and called the NAACP to inquire how she could support the movement in the South. Staff asked her to sing at a rally in Jackson on June 21, and she agreed, arriving with her friend Billy Strayhorn to accompany her on piano, her son Teddy Horne, and her friend Jean Noble.

Her meeting with Medgar Evers, the field secretary for Mississippi's NAACP office, was a highlight of the trip. Evers was a tireless leader in Jackson, spearheading voter registration and coordinating the NAACP's work with that of other national civil rights organizations. At this time only 3.75 percent of Black Mississippians were registered to vote.[59] But Evers had the rare his ability to balance older approaches to organizing with more radical strategies. He was the linchpin of the Mississippi branch of the movement.

His wife, the activist Myrlie Evers, recalled that one of the many tactics used to suppress Black people was to limit Black images and representation. Black Mississippians, she said, lived "behind the cotton curtain." Because state outlets refused to cover news of lynching and white brutality, that information had to be sent from the local branch to the national NAACP before being publicly released. Television shows that "included Lena Horne, Nat King Cole, . . . Roy Wilkins [the head of the NAACP]," or any other Black personality were blacked out mid-broadcast.[60] Thus, Horne's in-person performance was significant both symbolically and politically.

Medgar Evers met Horne and her party at the airport, and she was immediately struck by his bravery, kindness, and affability, even though by the summer of 1963 his life was under constant threat.[61] In fact, she remembered noticing that, unlike national leaders such as Martin Luther King Jr., he took little precautions for his own safety, despite the fact that his home (where he would he would have typically entertained a visiting Black celebrity) had recently been firebombed.[62]

Horne was scheduled to speak at a rally in the afternoon and to sing for the local community and movement organizers at a church that night. She told Evers that she was afraid of white violence but also even concerned that she might be rejected by the community that had been fighting so long for their rights while she had been living the life of a movie star. He calmed her fears. The courageous people surrounding her embraced her presence even as they educated her on the day-to-day work of the movement. She visited a class on nonviolent self-defense and talked to locals about their experiences: "To be in touch with that kind of purity, just for a moment, was a very great thing for me, after all the years I had wandered in the wilderness of my career, my personal preoccupations."[63]

Horne delivered a short address to the 2,000 people who had gathered at the rally and happily sang for organizers in the evening. In her own way, she had finally entered the fray, and she was filled with admiration and purpose. On June 12, she was scheduled to appear on *The Today Show* with Hugh Downs, and she now felt that she had an obligation to share what she had seen in Jackson with a national audience. Horne arrived at the New York City studio at 5 a.m. and learned that she had been moved to the show's second segment and that Roy Wilkins would be joining her. However, the staff member said he was running late, "considering what's happened." Horne did not understand. "Don't you know?" marveled the aide. "Medgar Evers was killed last night."[64]

On June 11, after a long day of meetings and errands, Evers had been shot in his driveway just after midnight. Myrlie Evers found him there, fallen and bleeding. Ironically, he had just been picking up a batch of sweatshirts emblazoned with "Jim Crow Must Go."[65] Horne had been with him in Jackson only a few days earlier, and she sat now in the studio, despondent and speechless. Later, she could barely remember anything she said on the show except for the conversation about the senseless killing.[66]

From the studio, Horne went to a previously planned luncheon in honor of Dr. King. The people in attendance were also devastated by Evers's murder, and they repeatedly attested to his leadership and importance in the movement. Horne thought to herself, "Whites tried to kill the meaning Medgar had for those [local] people, not [just] the larger cause."[67]

Medgar Evers's funeral attracted 6,000 mourners. Instead of intimidating Black Mississippians and civil rights organizers, his death had intensified their commitment. Those in attendance chanted, "After Medgar, no more fear!"[68] It had the same effect on Horne, deepening her resolve, increasing her bravery. Her biographer James Haskins writes, "For Lena, the Jackson rally with Medgar Evers was the apex of the Civil Rights Movement."[69] Learning of her growing involvement, King now asked her to appear at a protest rally in Atlanta. She agreed, and continued to assist and speak out boldly during that tumultuous year.

The March on Washington for Jobs and Freedom took place on August 28, 1963, just two months after Evers's death. It was a high point in the American civil rights movement, and Horne held it in comparable regard in her own history, even though the event was complicated by gender and gendered respectability. Her actions at the march expanded her personal resistance narrative, both as a supporter of civil rights and racial equity and a critic of sexism and gender inequality.

As reporters clamored to speak with the venerated male leaders at the march, Lena Horne instead introduced them to the civil rights pioneer Rosa Parks, the champion of the Montgomery bus boycott. Parks has too often been portrayed as a fed-up bystander who was drawn late into activism. But as the political scientist Jeanne Theoharis has shown, Parks's extensive history of organizing began long before the bus boycott.[70] Horne was exasperated that Parks wasn't being commemorated more widely. Gloria Richardson, the leader of the Cambridge Nonviolent Action Committee, recalled joining Horne and Parks as they walked to the press tents: "She was putting her in front of the foreign news crews and saying, 'This is the woman that started it!'"[71]

For the women leaders at the march, the day had been challenging. Although they, too, were joyous and triumphant, many also wrestled with disappointment. That shared weight had transformed Richardson and Horne into instant and unexpected allies. Horne was one of very few women who had been scheduled to perform, though, overwhelmed by the moment, she had only shouted a single word into the mic: "Freedom!"[72] The actress Ruby Dee emceed the event with her husband, Ossie Davis, and Marian Anderson, Odetta, and Mahalia Jackson sang. In full uniform, the performer Josephine Baker, who had been an agent for the French Resistance during World War II, delivered a moving, impromptu, two-minute speech, by far the longest presentation by a woman at the march and a complete accident of history. Otherwise, men dominated the program.[73] The lineup reinforced the idea that women were merely complements to the more serious intellectual male presence at the march and that women artists served a political purpose only as entertainers. None of this accurately represented the outsized role that women had really played in the movement and throughout history.[74]

As a concession to the complaints of women on the planning committee, officials had also added a brief "Tribute to Negro Woman Fighters for Freedom." It was supposed to feature Prince Lee, the widow of the activist Herbert Lee; Myrlie Evers; Diane Nash, the head of the SNCC; the journalist Daisy Bates; and the activists Rosa Parks and Gloria Richardson, who would each take a bow but not speak.[75] After much debate, one female speaker,

Myrlie Evers, was hastily added to the program and then replaced by Bates.[76] Eventually, after more struggle, each of the women was allowed one minute to speak.

The segment began when march organizer Bayard Rustin introduced Parks and Bates. Parks had time to say only one sentence, Bates a few more, before the next woman was introduced.[77] As far as organizers were concerned, Richardson was lucky to be on the program at all. A long-time activist and a member of SNCC's executive board, she had participated in the freedom rides and founded the radical Cambridge movement.[78] Her controversial approach was to mingle nonviolence with self-defense, many people treated her like a loose cannon. But she made her way onto the stage and eventually, after dealing with a snafu involving her missing chair, approached the podium. "Hello," she began, and then a marshal grabbed the microphone. She was sure that this had happened because the march's leaders were afraid she would not adhere to the liberal messaging. They were correct. She had planned to say, "Stay here until they pass that no-good civil rights bill!"[79] After she was escorted off the stage, Richardson rejoined Horne, who was still introducing Parks to the press. NAACP officials eventually approached the women and asked them to desist, claiming that they would "cause a mob," presumably due to Horne's celebrity and Richardson's notoriety.

Supposedly to "support" Richardson, Horne was put into a cab with her, and they were sent back to their hotels, just before King began his "I Have a Dream Speech."[80] Richardson said, "So . . . we heard just part of Martin's speech on the radio in the taxi. . . . In retrospect, I think it was because [Horne] was determined to see that Rosa Parks was recognized, and I had worn the denim skirt and hadn't dressed up properly and was a woman, and a series of things."[81]

During the march, Horne had leveraged her celebrity to highlight Parks's and Richardson's foundational contributions, seeking to disrupt the gendered narrative and correct civil rights history in real time. Although Black folks were well aware of women's centrality as local activists and supporters of the movement, many were uncomfortable about giving women national leadership roles, seeing this as a violation the code of respectability that governed such spaces. They were pleased to have Horne among them as a token of African American glamour and bourgeois success. They saw this as her role. But when she attempted to use her position strategically to thwart a gender imbalance, she was circumvented.

Another area of resistance for both Horne and Richardson concerned image and representation. Many civil rights workers wore jeans in the field for practicality, safety, and comfort. But according to the scholar Tanisha Ford, SNCC women also used denim to signify "political radicalism and an alternative definition of gender."[82] Richardson had been warned that "it was not appropriate for her to wear jeans to the march instead of the hat, gloves, and dress they expected [her] to wear."[83] So she decided to wear a jean skirt, partly in defiance of what she saw as an antiquated and gendered request, partly as a practical act. As it happened, she didn't have any easy time finding one: "I had to run all over the Eastern Shore [of Maryland] in search of a jean skirt."[84] During the event, she mused over what the other women were wearing and later recalled thinking, "I sure would like to see the police running them down the street with stockings and dress shoes and fancy hats on."[85] In the end, the March on Washington turned out to be a peaceful event, but at the time no one knew exactly what would unfold. Richardson's concrete thinking stemmed from memories of the violence that had greeted civil rights protestors elsewhere around the country. Nonetheless, such practicality made no impression on the gendered status quo. After the march, the *Chicago Defender* published a photo of Richardson. In it, she sits between two male leaders, her hand on her head in thought. The caption reads, "Mrs. Gloria Richardson, heroine of Cambridge." The headline, however, exclaims, "Oh This Hair."[86] For the Black press, the state of her hair trumped her value as a leader.

Horne's dress was also pragmatic, but she did avoid the scrutiny that Richardson endured. Photographs show that she strategically obscured her glamorous image behind large sunglasses, tucking her hair into a cap emblazoned with "NAACP" and tying a yellow scarf under her chin. Her goal for the momentous day was to function as an activist, not as a turned-out Hollywood star. Black-and-white photos of the march eliminate even the pop of color, leaving Horne the activist unadorned. Neither her look nor Richardson's met organizers' expectations. Instead, like Black women throughout history, they aligned their image and conduct with oppositional self-definition.[87] Although the women worked and lived in separate spheres, both engaged in multi-terrain resistance at the March on Washington, confronting sexism and racism via appearance, acceptable decorum, and approximation to leadership. Still, while Horne's autobiography reflects on her involvement in the civil rights movement, it includes no discussion of the march, perhaps because she was never able to fully excavate her relationship with it.

Perhaps Horne's most overlooked act of resistance was her 1963 album *Here's Lena Now!*, released just a year before Nina Simone's single "Mississippi Goddam" and Sam Cooke's "A Change Is Gonna Come," both also inspired by the events of 1963. While Horne's album may have been in conversation with Max Roach and Abbey Lincoln's very different 1960 *We Insist! Freedom Now Suite*, it arose specifically from a set of 1960 benefit concerts at Carnegie Hall, produced by Harry Belafonte and also featuring Frank Sinatra.[88] The proceeds would be donated to the performers' preferred charities, which for Horne included the SNCC and the Gandhi Society for Human Rights, a fundraising arm for the Southern Christian Leadership Conference's civil rights activism. All were controversial organizations at that time, and the FBI was compiling a file on Horne.

The first night of the benefit, October 5, was Horne's; the second, Sinatra's, who had chosen to donate his proceeds to the Foundation for International Child Health. At first, sales for his night far outstripped Horne's, for obvious reasons—Sinatra's dizzying fame and Horne's choice of charities.[89] In 1962 alone, he had released six hit albums, including the critically lauded *Sinatra*

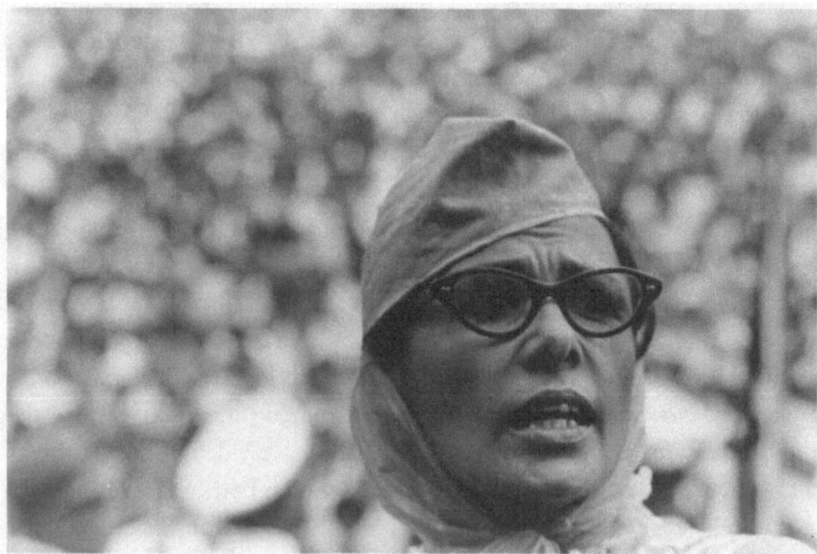

FIGURE 18. Lena Horne at the March on Washington, August 28, 1963. Photograph by Rowland Scherman. Courtesy of U.S. Information Agency, Press and Publications Service, Washington, D.C.

and Strings. So for her night occasion, Horne also chose to introduce new songs, both of which would form the basis for *Here's Lena Now!* One was the title track, "Now!"; the other was "Silent Spring."[90]

The album's title is its own proclamation, signifying the arrival of a more boldly progressive Lena Horne. The recast of her representational image and announced her alignment with the freedom movement. The word *Now* was key. The rallying cry of the civil rights movement was "Freedom Now!" and by the early 1960s, the phrase had become ubiquitous, a way to push back against white America's resistance to equality and change. Yet in this moment, the struggle felt stalled. In his 1963 "Letter from Birmingham Jail," King wrote, "Maybe I was too optimistic. Maybe I expected too much. I guess I should have realized that few members of a race that has oppressed another race can understand or appreciate the deep groans and passionate yearnings of those that have been oppressed, and still fewer have the vision to see that injustice must be rooted out by strong, persistent, and determined action."[91]

In this climate, Horne, like many others, added her voice to the chorus. Each side of *Here's Lena Now!* functions as an arc that ends with a blistering statement on civil rights. At first glance, the album's track list may seem benign and familiar:

Side 1	Side 2
Great Day (Rose-Eliscu-Youmans)	Blowin' in the Wind (Dylan)
Once in a Lifetime (Bricusse-Newley)	Distant Melody
The Eagle and Me (Harburg-Arlen)	(Comden-Green-Styne)
Tomorrow Mountain	Wouldn't It Be Loverly
(Latouche-Ellington)	(Lerner-Loewe)
Lost in the Stars (Anderson-Weill)	Meantime (Allen-Stillman)
Now! (Comden-Green-Styne)	The Best Things in Life Are Free
	(DeSylva-Henderson-Brown)
	Silent Spring (Arlen-Harburg)[92]

But in fact Horne chose the songs as a deliberate response to the social and political moment. As a traditional pop and jazz artist, she worked within her style while also interrogating her musical persona. She later wrote, "The great protest songs are coming from the Southern students. I can't sing *these* songs, but I think songs can be written . . . which simply put the Negro in context of the world. . . . It is the great chance of my generation to . . . express this."[93] In other words, *Here's Lena Now!* was a way for her to demonstrate the desire of the older generation to join the *now*—in message, if not in style.

On the album, Horne reworked popular standards so that they served as both social commentary and direct statements on freedom, racism, and civil rights. The songwriters may have originally framed *freedom* as nebulous and fanciful, but her delivery reimagined it as deeply urgent. Some songs, such as "Silent Spring," express the weight of racial violence. Others, such as "Tomorrow Mountain," verge on the fantastical. But all entreat listeners to recognize that African Americans should have the freedom to experience life in all its fullness.

In Horne's interpretation, "The Eagle and Me" took on a special meaning in the early 1960s. Written for the 1944 Broadway play *Bloomer Girl* (1944), it was originally designed to be sung by Pompey, an enslaved runaway, and some consider it to be "the first theater song of the fledgling civil rights movement."[94] She sings, "We gotta be free / The eagle and me."[95]

In contrast, Horne transformed "Tomorrow Mountain" and "Lost in the Stars," once applicable to anyone's experience, into songs that spoke directly to African American life in this moment. "Tomorrow Mountain," for instance, offers the hope for an easier tomorrow.[96] "Lost in the Stars" was originally from a 1948 musical of the same title, based on Alan Paton's novel *Cry, The Beloved Country*, set in early apartheid South Africa. It had become a popular song by the 1960s and had lost some of its underlying racialized meaning. But Horne reestablished its anti-oppression origins, emphasizing the line, "And the lord God hunted through the wide night air for the little dark star." God makes a special promise that it will not "get lost again."[97] The lyric acts as a not so subtle code for Black people and the conditions that they endured.

Among the twelve songs on *Here's Lena Now!*, "Silent Spring" and "Blowin' in the Wind" offer the most incisive political commentary. But "Now!" was the album's controversial underground hit. It was written for Horne by Betty Comden and Adolph Green and set to the tune of the Jewish celebration song "Hava Nagila" as a purposeful sign of solidarity with the civil rights movement. The song is raucous, and Horne's voice is powerful: "The message of this song's not subtle / No discussion, no rebuttal." "Now!" forthrightly demands equal access, equal rights, and full freedoms. Horne snaps: "People all should love each other / Just don't take it literal."[98] Such searing pronouncements were too hotly political for radio stations to play, even if they'd wanted to. The track was immediately banned by stations across the country, including seven of Los Angeles's eleven, one of New York City's eleven, and every station in the South. Regardless, as a single, it sold 185,000 copies within its first three days of release and made the top twenty on Cash Box's R&B chart.[99]

The single's B side, "Silent Spring," which referred to the bombing of the 16th Street Baptist Church in Birmingham, on Sunday, September 15, 1963, only deepened the force of the full-length record.[100] Harold Arlen wrote the song specifically to honor the four girls—Addie Mae Collins, Cynthia Wesley, Carole Robertson, and Carol Denis McNair—who were killed in the explosion as well as the many people who were injured.[101] On the album, Horne softly sang: "Is this the land where flags are flown? / to bring this hopeful world a dream of spring unknown?"[102] Her lament calls to account not only the perpetrators but also the nation.

The brutality of 1963 had an intense effect on Black artists. Nina Simone remembered, "I heard about the bombing of the church in which the four little black girls were killed in Alabama. . . . Medgar Evers had been recently slain in Mississippi. At first, I tried to make myself a gun. . . . I gathered some materials. I was going to take one of them out."[103] Fortunately, her husband talked her out of violence, and she wrote "Mississippi Goddam" instead. Nonetheless, her visceral response reveals the well of anger within the Black community. *Here's Lena Now!* was part of that response. Though it was a departure within Horne's discography, it embodied her complicated transformation and became an essential layer of her resistance. The album is significant musically as well: an example of how Black protest music could be forged from traditional tools and thus serve as a bridge on which older African Americans, mired in respectability, could meet their younger, bolder descendants.

Epilogue

In September 2024, the largest and most comprehensive exhibition of Elizabeth Catlett's life's work started its journey through museums across the country. The exhibition's title, *Elizabeth Catlett: A Black Revolutionary Artist and All That It Implies!*, arose from a quote that Catlett used to describe herself and her artwork. It opened at the Brooklyn Museum and from there moved to the National Gallery of Art in Washington, D.C. One of its three curators, Dalila Scruggs, is currently the inaugural Augusta Savage Curator of African American Art at the Smithsonian American Art Museum. In that capacity she has brought a rare Black woman's presence to national fine art administration.[1] The spectacular show owes much to the labor of all of its curators. However, Scruggs's curatorial appointment and the display at the National Gallery represent a full circle moment for Black women artist-activists. Catlett was dogged in her insistence that Black women deserve to be, and see themselves as, the subject of fine art, and her strivings lifted many flesh-and-blood as well as spiritual sisters up to the seat of American art and culture. With the Catlett exhibition, the long Black freedom movement bore glorious fruit, but this would not have been possible without Black feminists and their layered resistance to the historical and present-day oppressions that plague Black women.

But as has happened so often over the course of American history, forces determined to upend progress and deny Black humanity have challenged this triumphant moment. By late summer 2025, the presidential administration was actively removing representations that it has labeled *anti-American*.[2] The exact definition of the term is deliberately vague and unrefined, but the list of what it wants to celebrate is short: white, cisgender, heterosexual, native-born, male-dominant, Christian; scrubbed clean of critique, historical scrutiny, and diverse contributions. As museum workers were packing the Catlett exhibit and the outlines of her sculpture still lingered in memory, the engines that had pushed her out of America were regaining their strength.

Inhumanity attempted to erase the cultural and political labor of Catlett, Dunham, Horne, Ormes, and Scott, and our alarming political present reminds us that the struggles of the Fierce Five are far from over. In such climates, layered resistance, no matter how constant, becomes obscured, attacked, and minimized. It is no small irony that life-shaking events such as the Great Depression, the end of World War II, and the March on Washington took place even as radical advocates for equality and freedom were being repudiated. The activism in which these women engaged and their layered resistance made them heroines of the long Black freedom movement, yet they were also blacklisted and had complicated relationships with the politics of respectability and gender.

Most of the women I discuss in this book would not have identified their cultural and political work as radical but as a natural outgrowth of the needs of their communities. Yet much like today's political repression, the small-minded ideology that led to the Red Scare targeted activism and difference of any kind. Each woman suffered the wrath of the anticommunist-antiradical crusade, which sought to arrest her artistic production at the height of her career and rob the world of her full artistic possibility.

Katherine Dunham encountered the conservative backlash of the 1950s near the end of her grueling twenty-year dance career. The added weight of scarce funding, along with audience preferences for staid European-derived dance and white Americana, precipitated the demise of her company. She eventually moved to East St. Louis, where she drew on the layered resistance she'd honed in the 1940s and became a local community activist. She opened the Katherine Dunham Centers for Arts and Humanities in her neighborhood, and it remains open today, more than twenty years after her death.

Scott settled in New York City upon her return from France. She faced a new America in the sixties. She had been away from the rising civil rights movement but understood the integrationist and radical impulses of both eras. She continued as a performer and, until her death in 1981, always reminded people of her and her sister compatriots' forgotten activist labor.

Lena Horne toured abroad and nationally after donating her time to the movement. She became the most well known of the five, making appearances on Broadway, television, and film until her death in 2010.

Jackie Ormes's contributions persisted through her community work on the South Side of Chicago and her beloved cartoons. She died in 1985, the least known of the women under study. However, as more people discover her art and activism, her work is being resurrected.

Elizabeth Catlett moved to Mexico in the mid-1940s and became a citizen, remaining there until her death in 2012. She was the first woman to head the department of sculpture at the National Autonomous University of Mexico. Throughout her long and prolific career, she continued to make art that spoke to the overlooked humanity of African American and Mexican people. Her focus on elevating the image of Black women in fine art never relented. She is regarded as one of the greatest artists of the century.

With their layered politics of resistance, these women were both ahead of their time and the radical daughters of their foremothers. Their work forever altered the landscape and possibilities of African American women's resistance, image, and representation, on film, in dance, on stage, in art, and in popular media. They laid the groundwork for the many African American women activist artists of the 1950s and 1960s—among them, the singer and actress Abbey Lincoln, the actress Ruby Dee, and the artist Faith Ringgold, to name only a few. Yet they also continued the legacy of a web of female artist-activists of the 1930s and 1940s. The Fierce Five left a blueprint of resistance, complicating imposed images and representations even as they meticulously constructed new ones, in a not-too-distant past and a never-ending present.

Notes

INTRODUCTION

1. Maureen Honey, *Bitter Fruit: African-American Women in World War II* (Columbia: University of Missouri Press, 1999), 2.
2. Art Taylor, *Notes and Tones: Musician-to-Musician Interviews* (New York: Da Capo, 1993), 266.
3. Hazel Scott, autobiography (1979), Hazel Scott Papers, Library of Congress. Dwayne Mack ("Hazel Scott: A Career Curtailed," *Journal of African-American History* 91, no. 2 [2006], 153–70); and Karen Chilton (*Hazel Scott: The Pioneering Journey of a Jazz Pianist from Cafe Society to Hollywood to HUAC* [Ann Arbor: University of Michigan Press, 2008]) are pioneering researchers on Scott who have helped bring her story and words into the spotlight. Both recount this 1943 narrative of resistance on the set as exemplifying Scott's resistance in Hollywood.
4. Scott, autobiography.
5. Scott, autobiography.
6. See Maureen Honey, *Bitter Fruit: African American Women in World War II* (Columbia: University of Missouri Press, 1999), 28–29; Donald Bogle, *Bright Boulevards, Bold Dreams: The Story of Black Hollywood* (New York: One World/Ballantine, 2005); and Donald Bogle, *Brown Sugar: Over One Hundred Years of America's Black Female Superstars* (New York: Continuum, 2007).
7. See Kimberlé Crenshaw, *On Intersectionality: Essential Writings* (New Press, 2019); Frances M. Beale, "Double Jeopardy: To Be Black and Female," *Meridians* 8, no. 2 (2008): 166–76; and Deborah K. King, "Multiple Jeopardy, Multiple Consciousness: The Context of a Black Feminist Ideology," *Signs* 14, no. 1 (1988): 42–72.

8. Claudia Jones, *An End to the Neglect of the Problems of the Negro Woman!* (New York: Communist Party USA, National Women's Commission, 1949), 467.

9. Ruth Feldstein, *How It Feels to Be Free: Black Women Entertainers and the Civil Rights Movement* (Oxford, UK: Oxford University Press, 2013), 8.

10. According to E. Frances White, African Americans sometimes create restrictive narratives that overemphasize respectability to counter oppressive and racist constructions of what constitutes blackness. Degrading portraits of African American life and culture plague these oppressive constructions (*Dark Continent of Our Bodies: Black Feminism and Politics of Respectability* [Philadelphia: Temple University Press, 2001]).

11. Several books provide an overview of the work of African Americans in the civil rights movement, including the way in which their activism stretched back into the 1940s. See, for instance, Danielle L. McGuire, *At the Dark End of the Street: Black Women, Rape, and Resistance. A New History of the Civil Rights Movement from Rosa Parks to the Rise of Black Power* (New York: Knopf, 2010); Barbara Ransby, *Ella Baker and the Black Freedom Movement: A Radical Democratic Vision* (Chapel Hill: University of North Carolina Press, 2003); and Vicki L. Crawford, Jacqueline Anne Rouse, and Barbara Woods. *Women in the Civil Rights Movement: Trailblazers and Torchbearers, 1941–1965* (Brooklyn, NY: Carlson, 1990).

12. Honey's *Bitter Fruit* (28–29) discusses the representations and images of Black women as they are propagated nationally, looking at the importance of Black women artists and entertainers in this image production and speaking directly of the image production of Dunham, Scott, and Horne. Also see Jacqueline Jones (*Labor of Love, Labor of Sorrow: Black Women, Work, and the Family from Slavery to the Present* [New York: Basic Books, 1985], 232–74), which examines African American women, including artists, and their increased visibility in nontraditional roles and as image producers.

13. Deborah Elizabeth Whaley, *Black Women in Sequence: Re-inking Comics, Graphic Novels, and Anime* (Seattle: University of Washington Press, 2016), 47. Nancy Goldstein was Ormes's first biographer: *Jackie Ormes: The First African American Woman Cartoonist* (Ann Arbor: University of Michigan Press, 2008). All indications are that Goldstein was the first to request her file through the Freedom of Information Act. Future researchers owe her a debt for this thorough research.

14. Michael Denning, *The Cultural Front: The Laboring of American Culture in the Twentieth-Century* (London: Verso, 1996), xix.

15. Monica Hairston, "Gender, Jazz, and Front," in *Big Ears: Listening for Gender in Jazz Studies*, ed. Nichole T. Rustin and Sherrie Tucker (Durham, NC: Duke University Press, 2008), 64–89.

16. Dayo Gore, *Radicalism at the Crossroads: African American Activists in the Cold War* (New York: NYU Press, 2011), 30.

17. Lena Horne and Richard Schickel, *Lena* (Garden City, NY: Doubleday, 1965), 117.

18. H. Zahra Caldwell, interview with Elizabeth Catlett, April 23, 2011; Wanda Davis, interview with Frances Dunham Catlett (2002), Oral History Collection, MS 191, African American Museum and Library, Oakland Public Library; H. Zahra Caldwell, interview with Marie-Christine Pratt, July 27, 2011.

CHAPTER 1

1. "They Will Show New Yorkers the Haitian Dances," *Baltimore Afro American*, March 6, 1937; John Martin, "The Dance among Educators," *New York Times*, March 7, 1937.

2. *Concert dance* refers to the performance of dance on the stage, separate from other forms of entertainment. Until the late 1920s and early 1930s, dance was presented only in order to augment comedy routines, music concerts, variety shows, or drama, not alone as a staged art form. Black concert dance, although stifled, developed alongside a burgeoning interest in white concert dance. For more, see James Haskins, *Black Dance in America: A History through Its People* (New York: Harper Trophy, 1992); and John O. Perpener, *African American Concert Dance: The Harlem Renaissance and Beyond* (Urbana: University of Illinois Press, 2001).

3. Edna Guy, letter to Katherine Dunham, January 9, 1937, Katherine Dunham Papers, Special Collections Research Center, Morris Library, Southern Illinois University, Carbondale (hereafter cited as Dunham Papers); Joyce Aschenbrenner, *Katherine Dunham: Dancing a Life* (Urbana: University of Illinois Press, 2002), 107–8.

4. Guy to Dunham.

5. Susan Manning, *Modern Dance, Negro Dance: Race in Motion* (Minneapolis: University of Minnesota Press, 2004), 94–101.

6. Julia L. Foulkes, *Modern Bodies: Dance and American Modernism from Martha Graham to Alvin Ailey* (Chapel Hill: University of North Carolina Press, 2002), 52.

7. Perpener, *African American Concert Dance*, 17.

8. John Martin, "Dance Recital Given by Negro Artists" *New York Times*, April 30, 1931.

9. Foulkes, *Modern Bodies*; James Haskins, *Katherine Dunham* (New York: Coward, McCann, and Geoghegan, 1982), 70.

10. Foulkes, *Modern Bodies*; Madison Davis Lacy, dir., *Free to Dance* (New York: National Black Programming Consortium, 2001), first broadcast on PBS in 2001.

11. Lacy, *Free to Dance*.

12. Haskins, *Dunham*, 62–63; Martin, "The Dance among Educators"; Lacy, *Free to Dance*.

13. Frederic L. Orme, "The Negro in the Dance as Katherine Dunham Sees Him," *American Dancer* 11, no. 5 (1938): 61–62; Aschenbrenner, *Dancing a Life*, 110.

14. Perpener, *African American Concert Dance*, 158.

15. For details about Dunham, see Katherine Dunham, Vèvè Clark, and Sarah East Johnson, eds., *Kaiso! Writings by and about Katherine Dunham* (Madison: University of Wisconsin Press, 2005). This is the definitive collection on Dunham's contribution to dance.

16. Aschenbrenner, *Dancing a Life*, 17–18.

17. Katherine Dunham, *A Touch of Innocence: Memoirs of Childhood* (New York: Harcourt, Brace, 1959), n.p.

18. Albert Dunham Jr., letter to Katherine Dunham (1931), Dunham Papers.

19. Dunham, *A Touch of Innocence*, 194

20. Dunham, *A Touch of Innocence*, 190–92.

21. Bill Mullen, *Popular Fronts: Chicago and African American Cultural Politics, 1935–46* (Urbana: University of Illinois Press, 1999), 5.

22. Katherine Dunham, "Minefields" in Dunham et al., *Kaiso!*, 109; Aschenbrenner, *Dancing a Life*, 20,25; Albert Dunham Jr. to Dunham.

23. Katherine Dunham, "Survival," in Dunham et al., *Kaiso!*, 110.

24. Aschenbrenner, *Dancing a Life*, 83.

25. Dunham, "Minefields," 104.

26. St. Clair Drake and Horace R. Cayton, *Black Metropolis: A Study of Negro Life in a Northern City*, rev. ed. (Chicago: University of Chicago Press, 1993), xvii.

27. Haskins, *Katherine Dunham*, 40.

28. Aschenbrenner, *Dancing a Life*, 29–30.

29. Katherine Dunham's grade record, Northwestern University, 1934–35, Dunham Papers.

30. Aschenbrenner, *Dancing a Life*, 31

31. Aschenbrenner, *Dancing a Life*, 44–45.

32. This narrative of events seems to have had its origins in Luther Davis and John Cleveland, "Partly Primitive: Katherine Dunham, the Marian Anderson of Dance," *Collier's*, January 11, 1941, 22–23. It is difficult to identify which are direct Dunham quotes and which have been imagined by the writer. Dunham disputed this story in several later interviews, including in Lacy, *Free to Dance*.

33. Ruth Beckford, *Katherine Dunham: A Biography* (New York: Dekker, 1979), 28; Katherine Dunham, *Dances of Haiti* (Los Angeles: University of California, Center for Afro-American Studies, 1983), xxii.

34. Amy Porter, "Anthropological Katie," *Collier's*, February 24, 1945, 69.

35. Aschenbrenner, *Dancing a Life*.

36. Katherine Dunham, *Island Possessed* (Chicago: University of Chicago Press, 1994), 23.

37. Beckford, *Katherine Dunham*, 36.

38. Dunham, *Island Possessed*, 3, 11–13.

39. Katherine Dunham, letter to Melville Herskovits, November 11, 1935, Dunham Papers.

40. Wendy Perron, "Katherine Dunham: A One-Woman Revolution, in Art and in Life," *Dance* 74, no. 8 (2000): 42.

41. Although employing a different approach, Zora Neale Hurston, a contemporary of Dunham's, similarly understood anthropology. Both saw it as an avenue to prove the equality of African American and other African-derived peoples. The anthropologist A. Lynn Bolles writes: "Both Zora Neale Hurston and Katherine Dunham must be counted among some of the true innovators in cultural anthropology—Hurston for her reflexive ethnographic method used decades before anthropologists or postmodernists embraced it, and Katherine Dunham for creating the field of dance anthropology" ("Seeking the Ancestors: Forging a Black Feminist Tradition in Anthropology," in *Black Feminist Anthropology: Theory, Politics, Praxis, and Poetics*, ed. Irma McClaurin [New Brunswick, NJ: Rutgers University Press, 2001], 30–31). Also, like Hurston, Dunham was the student of a founding anthropologist who had traveled to the Caribbean. (Hurston was a student of Frank Boas.) Although Dunham and Hurston were known to have a sometimes contentious relationship, Hurston spied in her great potential and ability. In her 1947 review of Dunham's short book on her month with the maroons, she wrote that "Katherine Dunham's *Journey to Accompong* is a lively and word-deft account of a thirty days visit to Accompong. . . . Miss Dunham's book is very readable: in addition to the lively style and the part observations on the doings of the men, women, and children of Accompong." Hurston's description of Dunham could very easily be used to describe her engaging style of ethnography. See Zora Neale Hurston, "Thirty Days among the Maroons," *New York Herald Tribune*, January 12, 1947.

42. Elizabeth Catlett, interview with the author, April 23, 2011.

43. Dunham, "Minefields," 85.

44. Dunham, "Survival," 87, 101.

45. Joanna Dee Das, *Katherine Dunham: Dance and the African Diaspora* (Oxford, UK: Oxford University Press, 2017), 3.

46. Dunham, "Survival," 90.

47. Aschenbrenner, *Dancing a Life*, 115.

48. Irma McClaurin, *Black Feminist Anthropology: Theory, Politics, Praxis, and Poetics* (New Brunswick, NJ: Rutgers University Press, 2001), 9.

49. Vèvè Clark, "Performing the Memory of Difference in Afro-Caribbean Dance: Katherine Dunham's Choreography, 1938–1987," in Dunham et al., *Kaiso!*, 331.

50. Haskins, *Katherine Dunham*, 73; Haskins, *Black Dance*, 40.

51. Marie-Christine Dunham Pratt, interview with the author, March 10, 2011.

52. "Ballet Fedre Is Fine WPA Theatre Production," *Chicago Defender*, February 5, 1938, 2.

53. "Sugar Hill Opens Run in Chicago," *Philadelphia Tribune*, February 3, 1938.

54. Gwendolyn Hale, "Dunham's Creative Dance Ability Impress Writer," *Pittsburgh Courier*, January 13, 1945.

55. Dunham, "Minefields," 100.

56. John Pratt was an established member of Chicago society, a gallery artist, and a fixture on the creative scene, having worked as a designer with dancers such as Agnes de Mille.

57. Pratt, interview with the author; John Pratt, letter to Katherine Dunham, August 14, 1943, Dunham Papers.

58. Harry Hopkins, letter to Katherine Dunham, April 28, 1938, Dunham Papers.

59. Mary McLeod Bethune, letter to Katherine Dunham July 3, 1938, Dunham Papers.

60. Arthur W. Mitchell, letter to Katherine Dunham July 8, 1938, Dunham Papers.

61. Gerald Horne, *Race Woman: The Lives of Shirley Graham Du Bois* (New York: NYU Press, 2002), 73.

62. Lauren Rebecca Sklaroff, *Black Culture, and the New Deal: The Quest for Civil Rights in the Roosevelt Era* (Chapel Hill: University of North Carolina Press, 2009), 216.

63. Aschenbrenner, *Dancing a Life*, 121.

64. Charles S. Johnson, letter to Katherine Dunham, March 1, 1938, Dunham Papers; Katherine Dunham, letter to Sue Bailey Thurman, April 3, 1938, Dunham Papers; Katherine Dunham, letter to Eleanor Roosevelt, May 2, 1938, Dunham Papers.

65. Aschenbrenner, *Dancing a Life*, 108.

66. Pratt, interview with the author.

67. Lacy, *Free to Dance*.

68. Katherine Dunham, "Survival: Chicago after the Caribbean," in *Kaiso!*, 105.

69. Aschenbrenner, *Dancing a Life*, 120; press release, Windsor Theater, January 31, 1940, Dunham Papers.

70. Edward Thorpe, *Black Dance* (Woodstock, NY: Overlook, 1990), 126.

71. Perron, "Katherine Dunham," 43; press release, Windsor Theater.

72. Dunham, "Minefields," 117.

73. Perron, "Katherine Dunham," 43.

74. Dunham, "Minefields," 119.

75. Hazel V. Carby, "'It Jus Be's Dat Way Sometime': The Sexual Politics of Women's Blues," *Radical America* 20, no. 4 (1987): 8–12.

76. John Martin, "Dance: A Negro Art," *New York Times*, February 14, 1932.

77. Dunham, "Minefields," 119.

78. Peter Barry, "K. Dunham's Hips Are Sociological," *DC Compass*, April 15, 1950; Robert Wahls, "La Dunham Comes Back Still Sexy and Sizzling," *Sunday News*, December 11, 1955.

79. Contract with Katherine Dunham, Actor's Equity Association, September 18, 1940, Dunham Papers.

80. Aschenbrenner, *Dancing a Life*, 124.

81. Dunham was continuously at odds with Ethel Waters, who was known to be difficult on set, often treated younger actresses with contempt, and wanted full star treatment. She and Dunham had several run-ins during the production. One issue was the amount of press that Dunham received for her part. Both *Time* and *Collier's* coverage barely mentioned Waters and did not print her picture. Apparently, Waters also made friends with some of the dancers and attempted to steal them away from Dunham (Dunham, "Minefields," 148–49). See Donald Bogle, *Heat Wave: The Life and Career of Ethel Waters*, (New York: HarperCollins, 2011).

82. Perpener, *African American Concert Dance*. 145–46.

83. Zita Allen, James Hatch, and Arthur Smith, interview with Tally Beatty (1981), 11–12, Hatch Billops Collection, Schomburg Center for Research in Black Culture, New York; Perpener, *African American Concert Dance*, 146.

84. Constance Valis Hill, "Collaborating with Balanchine on *Cabin in the Sky*," in *Kaiso!*, 235. Dance scholar Constance Valis Hill debates this characterization of the collaboration as fraught, instead seeing *Cabin in the Sky* as an important collaboration between the two choreographers.

85. Haskins, *Katherine Dunham*, 70. This protest preceded Hazel Scott's similar on-set rebellion against racial stereotyping in 1943.

86. Allen et al., interview with Beatty, 6–7.

87. Aschenbrenner, *Dancing a Life*, 127.

88. Claude Barnett, letter to Katherine Dunham, November 18, 1941, Dunham Papers; Katherine Dunham, letter to Claude Barnett, October 20, 1941, Dunham Papers.

89. Barnett to Dunham; Dunham to Barnett. The Good Neighbor Policy arose after World War II as a U.S. effort to strengthen alliances with South American countries. The policy called for nonintervention in the domestic affairs of those countries and pushed for economic exchange. It heavily affected the movie industry, where it was often used as a tool of propaganda and an avenue to increase American profit.

90. Barnett to Dunham; Dunham to Barnett; contract between Katherine Dunham and Felix Young, December 4, 1941, Dunham Papers.

91. Haskins, *Katherine Dunham*, 73.

92. Todd Vogel, ed., *The Black Press: New Literary and Historical Essays* (New Brunswick, NJ: Rutgers University Press, 2001), 107. Shane Vogel provides an excellent overview of the history of the song "Stormy Weather" and the various productions in which it was incorporated. He identifies how Ethel Waters, Lena Horne, and Katherine Dunham reinterpreted the song to create a marker of Black modernism ("Performing 'Stormy Weather': Ethel Waters, Lena Horne, and Katherine Dunham," *South Central Review* 25, no. 1 [2008]: 93–113).

93. Katherine Dunham, letter to Yvonne Wood, August 21, 1943, Dunham Papers.

94. Vogel, *The Black Press*, 107.

95. Gene Kelly and Stanley Donen, dirs., *Singin' in the Rain* (Hollywood, CA: Metro-Goldwyn-Mayer, 1952).

96. John Pratt's induction papers, July 9, 1943, Dunham Papers.

97. Pratt to Dunham.

98. Louis [last name unknown], letter to John Pratt, November 6, 1941, Dunham Papers.

99. In one well-known case, in 1936, Jessie Owens and his wife were denied a hotel room in New York City on the night he returned from winning four gold medals in Berlin and doing considerable damage to the Nazi claim of white supremacy. He had to lodge above 125th Street, in the heart of Black Harlem. America reserved little to no star treatment for its Black celebrities.

100. Lacy, *Free to Dance*.

101. Aschenbrenner, *Dancing a Life*, 133; Valerie Linson, interview with Carmencita Romero (1981), 153, Hatch Billops Collection; Harry Belafonte and Michael Shnayerson, *My Song: A Memoir* (New York: Knopf, 2011), 193.

102. Katherine Dunham, "Brazil: Jaime Crow," *Time*, July 31, 1950.

103. Alexander Sterne, letter to Katherine Dunham, September 6, 1943, Dunham Papers. "The Four Freedoms" refers to Franklin Delano Roosevelt's appeal for human rights in his 1941 state-of-the-union address, in which he called for freedom of speech, freedom of worship, freedom from want, and freedom from fear.

104. Katherine Dunham, letter to Annette Dunham, November 16, 1943, Dunham Papers.

105. Joyce Aschenbrenner, "Katherine Dunham: Anthropologist, Artist, Humanist," in *African American Pioneers in Anthropology*, ed. Ira E. Harrison and Faye Venetia Harrison (Urbana: University of Illinois, 1999), 137.

106. Katherine Dunham, "Comment to a Louisville Audience," Dunham et al., *Kaiso!*, 255.

107. Pratt, interview with the author.

108. Helen Tamiris, letter to Katherine Dunham, October 21, 1943, Dunham Papers; Edna Thomas, letter to Katherine Dunham, January 17, 1941, Dunham Papers.

109. Edward C. Carter, letter to Katherine Dunham, April 3, 1942, Dunham Papers.

110. Constance Valis Hill, "Katherine Dunham's 'Southland': Protest in the Face of Repression," *Dance Research Journal* 26, no. 2 (1994): 1–10.

111. Valis Hill, "Katherine Dunham's 'Southland,'" 4–5.

112. Ian Zack, "Julie Robinson Belafonte, Dancer, Actress and Activist, Is Dead at 95," *New York Times*, March 21, 2024.

113. Valis Hill, "Katherine Dunham's 'Southland,'" 5.

114. Dale [probably Dale Wasserman], letter to Katherine Dunham, February 2, 1953, Dunham Papers. Wasserman was Dunham's stage director.

115. Valis Hill, "Katherine Dunham's 'Southland,'" 5.

116. Aschenbrenner, *Dancing a Life*, 150–51.

117. Perron, "Katherine Dunham," 45.

118. Federal Bureau of Investigation, memo, special agent in charge, Washington Field Office, to special agent in charge, New York Field Office, March 2, 1967, Katherine Dunham File, 161-4870-39, 3/2/67, New York Field Office Records.

119. Thorpe, *Black Dance*, 130. This was the last performance of the intact Dunham Company. However, Dunham would continue to work with different members throughout the rest of her life.

120. Aschenbrenner, *Dancing a Life*, 161, 173.

CHAPTER 2

1. Langston Hughes, "To Be Somebody," *Phylon* 11, no. 4 (1950): 311. Hughes wrote this poem in honor of Hazel Scott and Joe Louis. The title points to the postwar aspirations of African Americans on the verge of the civil rights movement.

2. Luther Davis, "Hi Hazel," *Collier's* 109, no. 2 (1942): 16; Karen Chilton, *Hazel Scott: The Pioneering Journey of a Jazz Pianist from Café Society to Hollywood to HUAC* (Ann Arbor: University of Michigan Press, 2008), 9–10; Donald Bogle, *Primetime Blues: African-Americans on Network Television* (New York: Farrar, Straus, and Giroux, 2001), 15.

3. Adam Clayton Powell III, interview with the author, April 11, 2008.

4. Maureen Honey, *Bitter Fruit: African-American Women in World War II* (Columbia: University of Missouri Press, 1999), 2. Histories of the era often focus exclusively on white American women's labor and economic advancement: on assembly lines, serving their country in the Women's Army Corps, filling traditionally male jobs. These discussions neglect the experiences of Black women. Here, Honey emphasizes not only African American women's vast contributions to the war effort but also their manipulation of public space, drawing on accounts in Black newspapers of Black women's accomplishments and activism in various professions, including as artists and performers.

5. Powell, interview with the author; "Hazel Scott," *Current Biography, 1943* (New York: Wilson, 1943), 678; "Hazel Dorothy Scott," *American National Biography*, ed. John A. Garraty, Mark C. Carnes, and American Council of Learned Societies (New York: Oxford University Press, 1999), 491.

6. Arna Wendell Bontemps, *We Have Tomorrow* (Boston: Houghton Mifflin, 1945).

7. Nigel O. Bolland, "Race and Class Struggles in a Colonial State: Trinidad, 1917–1945, Review," *The Americas* 51, no. 4 (1995): 615–16. On social and class categorization

in the Caribbean, see George Simpson, "Social Stratification in the Caribbean," *Phylon* 23, no. 1 (1962): 29–46. During this period, Trinidad, like many other islands in the Caribbean, had a complex ethnic-racial structure in which skin complexion often correlated to class status. That status was also most often hereditary. However, Trinidad's racial-ethnic social caste system was more fluid than, say, India's.

8. Eric Eustace Williams, *From Columbus to Castro: The History of the Caribbean, 1492–1969* (New York: Harper and Row, 1971), 444, 456.

9. Chilton, *The Pioneering Journey*, 5.

10. "Hazel Scott," *Current Biography, 1943*, 678.

11. James Weldon Johnson, *Black Manhattan* (New York: Da Capo, 1991), 153.

12. Scholars widely identify 1925 as the beginning of the Harlem Renaissance, when Alain Locke released *The New Negro*, a compilation of Black writing (1925; reprint, New York: Simon and Schuster, 1997). See David L. Lewis, *When Harlem Was in Vogue* (New York: Books, 1997).

13. Arthur P. Davis and J. Saunders Redding, eds., *Cavalcade: Negro American Writing from 1760 to the Present* (Boston: Houghton Mifflin, 1971), 429.

14. Stephen Tuck, *We Ain't What We Ought to Be: The Black Freedom Struggle from Emancipation to Obama* (Cambridge, MA: Belknap/Harvard University Press, 2010), 176; Cheryl Lynn Greenberg, *"Or Does It Explode?": Black Harlem in the Great Depression* (New York: Oxford University Press, 1991), 32–35.

15. "Little Miss Hazel Scott, Child Wonder Pianist," poster, Hazel Scott Papers, collection of Adam Clayton Powell III (hereafter cited as Hazel Scott Papers).

16. "Hazel Scott," in *Current Biography, 1943*, 678.

17. Chilton, *Pioneering Journey*, 14; Will Haygood, *King of the Cats: The Life and Times of Adam Clayton Powell, Jr.* (New York: Amistad, 2006), 121.

18. Margo Jefferson, "Great (Hazel) Scott!" *Ms.* 3 (November 1974): 23.

19. For an excellent discussion of this subculture as well as the character, composition, and challenges of these female bands, see Sherrie Tucker, *Swing Shift: "All Girl" Bands of the 1940's* (Durham, NC: Duke University Press, 2000).

20. Haygood, *King of the Cats*, 121; Bontemps, *We Have Tomorrow*, 95.

21. Chilton, *Pioneering Journey*, 30.

22. Art Taylor, *Notes and Tones: Musician-to-Musician Interviews* (New York: Da Capo, 1993), 255; "Hazel Scott," in *African-American Women: A Biographical Dictionary*, ed. Dorothy C. Salem (New York: Garland, 1993), 444–45.

23. Linda Dahl, *Stormy Weather: The Music and Lives of a Century of Jazzwomen* (New York: Limelight, 1989), 23, 25.

24. Jefferson, "Great (Hazel) Scott!," 25.

25. Tucker, *Swing Shift*, 6.

26. Taylor, *Notes and Tones*, 262–63; Jefferson, "Great (Hazel) Scott!," 25.

27. Billie Holiday, with William Duffy, *Lady Sings the Blues* (New York: Harlem Moon,

2006), 103. Scott described Holiday as quitting her gig at Café Society specifically so that Scott could then be hired at Holiday's request (Hazel Scott, autobiography [1979], Hazel Scott Papers).

28. "African-American all-woman bands may have been unique in their ability to link expressions of the political desire of race women with the sensual desire of Blueswomen" (Tucker, *Swing Shift*, 10). This was yet another trait that Scott would share with these women.

29. Adam Clayton Powell Jr., "My Life with Hazel Scott," *Ebony* (January 1949): 45.

30. Hazel Scott, "I Found God in Show Business," *Ebony* (May 1956): 41–42.

31. Chilton, *Pioneering Journey*, 39.

32. Davis, "Hi Hazel," 56. Angela Davis notes that there are multiple and simultaneous African American feminist traditions, many of which have been overlooked by scholars, who depict feminist history as overwhelmingly white. This leaves the majority of history books largely bereft of a Black feminist/womanist presence. Davis explains that early twentieth-century blueswomen, including Ma Rainey, "although prefeminist in a historical sense, . . . were acknowledging and addressing issues central to contemporary feminist discourse" (*Blues Legacies and Black Feminism: Gertrude "Ma" Rainey, Bessie Smith, and Billie Holiday* [New York: Pantheon, 1998], xix).

33. "Hazel Scott," in *Current Biography, 1943*, 445

34. Taylor, *Notes and Tones*, 253.

35. "Alpha Kappa Presents Hazel Scott," program, 1948, 5–6, 16, Hazel Scott Papers.

36. "Alpha Kappa Presents Hazel Scott," 16–17; Jefferson, "Great (Hazel) Scott!," 25.

37. Davis, "Hi Hazel," 16.

38. Amiri Baraka, *Blues People: Negro Music in White America* (New York: Morrow, 1999), 218.

39. Kathryn M. Talalay, *Composition in Black and White: The Life of Philippa Schuyler* (New York: Oxford University Press, 1995); Marilyn Richardson, "The Child Prodigy Who Grew Up," *Women's Review of Books* 13, no. 7 (1996): 9. Schuyler was born in 1931 to the conservative Black journalist George Schuyler and Josephine Cogdell, a white Texas heiress and painter. The child's upbringing was an experiment in interracial unity for her parents. The Schuylers believed that raising a biracial child on a strict dietary and educational regimen would draw out the best of both races and instill superior abilities. Young Philippa was fed a diet of raw vegetables and raw meat and allowed to read only advanced subjects, such as classical literature. To supplement this rigorous education, she was taught to play the piano, in which she excelled.

40. Kathryn M. Talalay, "Philippa Duke Schuyler, Pianist/Composer/Writer," *Black Perspective in Music* 10 (February 1982): 43.

41. Linda Dahl, *Morning Glory: A Biography of Mary Lou Williams* (New York: Pantheon, 1999), 1:3–10.

42. Dahl, *Morning Glory*, 1:37–38, 109–11.

43. Bill Chase, "All Ears," *New York Amsterdam News*, December 10, 1938; "Notes at Random," *New York Amsterdam News*, November 12, 1938; "High Priestess," *New York Amsterdam News*, November 19, 1938; Chase, "All Ears"; "Mistress of Swing," *New York Amsterdam News*, March 19, 1938.

44. "Hot Classicist," *Time*, October 5, 1942, 89; Hazel Scott," in *Current Biography, 1943*, 678.

45. Bontemps, *We Have Tomorrow*, 97–98; Holiday, *Lady Sings the Blues*, 102–3; "Hazel Scott Succeeds Billie Holiday at Café Society," *New York Amsterdam News*, November 18, 1939.

46. David W. Stowe "The Politics of Cafe Society," *Journal of American History* 84, no. 4 (1998): 1384.

47. Helen Lawrenson. *Whistling Girl* (Garden City, NY: Doubleday, 1978), 86–89.

48. Stowe, "Politics of Café Society," 1384–95.

49. Tuck, *Black Freedom Struggle*, 182.

50. Photograph of Café Society attendees, n.d., Hazel Scott Papers; Barney Josephson and Terry Trilling-Josephson, *Cafe Society: The Wrong Place for the Right People* (Urbana: University of Illinois Press, 2009), 150.

51. Stowe, "Politics of Café Society," 1389, 1394; David W. Stowe, *Swing Changes: Big-Band Jazz in New Deal America* (Cambridge, MA: Harvard University Press, 1994), 66–67.

52. Mark Naison, *Communists in Harlem during the Depression* (Urbana: University of Illinois Press, 1983), 211.

53. Sondra Lomax and George Jackson, "Reviews: National," *Dance* 67, no. 3 (1993): 80.

54. "London Swing Critic Lines Up Mixed British Swing Ork Here," *New York Amsterdam News*, December 2, 1939; "Hazel Scott Signs to Make Recordings, " *Afro-American*, November 30, 1940; "Café Society's Greatest Swing Show to Do Spirituals to Swing, "*New York Amsterdam News*, December 23, 1939; Chilton, *Pioneering Journey*, 56.

55. "Four Pictures—$4,000 a Week,"*Afro-American*, December 30, 1944; "Hazel Scott Is NYU's 'Queen of Prom,'" *Afro-American*, May 17, 1941; "People Are Talking About . . . ," *Vogue*, June 15, 1940, 85; "Hazel Scott Tested for 'Panama Hattie,'" *Afro-American*, August 30, 1941; "Will It Be Lil or Hazel?," *Afro-American*, October 18, 1941; "Hazel Dorothy Scott," 491.

56. Bogle, *Primetime Blues*, 15–16.

57. Gene Caldwell, interview with the author, April 29, 2008.

58. James Agee, *Agee on Film: Criticism and Comment on the Movies* (New York: Modern Library, 2000).

59. Rebecca Evans Carroll, "Relation of Social Environment to the Moral Ideology and the Personal Aspirations of Negro Boys and Girls," *School Review* 53, no. 1 (1945): 30–38.

60. Carroll, "Relation of Social Environments," 34–35.

61. Michael Carter, "Tells How She Became a $4000 a Week Pianist," *Afro-American*, December 30, 1944.

62. Carter, "Tells How She Became a $4000 a Week Pianist."

63. Darlene Clark Hine, *Hine Sight: Black Women and the Re-Construction of American History* (Brooklyn, NY: Carlson, 1994) 34.

64. "Hot Classicist," 89; Davis, "Hi Hazel," 67.

65. Hazel Scott, "The Truth about Me," *Ebony* (September 1960): 142–43.

66. Hine, *Hine Sight*, 37.

67. Roy Coverley, "Queen of Café Society," *Chicago Defender*, November 1948.

68. Chilton, *Pioneering Journey*, 61.

69. Josephson, *The Wrong Place*, 138.

70. Carter, "Tells How She Became $4000 a Week Pianist."

71. Vincente Minnelli, dir., *I Dood It* (Hollywood, CA: Columbia, 1943).

72. Roy Del Ruth, dir., *Broadway Rhythm* (Hollywood, CA: Metro-Goldwyn-Mayer, 1943).

73. Henry Myers, Edward Eliscu, and Jay Gorney, "The White Keys and the Black Keys" (New York: Mills Music, 1944).

74. Sondra Gorney, *Brother, Can You Spare a Dime?: The Life of Composer Jay Gorney* (Lanham, MD: Scarecrow, 2005); Nichole T. Rustin and Sherrie Tucker, *Big Ears: Listening for Gender in Jazz Studies* (Durham, NC: Duke University Press, 2008), 65.

75. Scott, autobiography (1979).

76. Chilton, *Pioneering Journey*, 87.

77. "Hazel Scott Signed as Gershwin's Inspiration in 'Rhapsody'," *Afro-American*, September 18, 1943.

78. Phil Carter, "Hazel Scott Is Queen Once More in Warner's 'Rhapsody in Blue,'" *Chicago Defender*, September 1, 1943.

79. David Platt, "Hazel Scott's Role in Film Heavily Chopped in Memphis," *Daily Worker*, February 3, 1946.

80. Holiday, *Lady Sings the Blues*, 136.

81. Bruce Tyler, *From Harlem to Hollywood: The Struggle for Racial and Cultural Democracy, 1920–1943* (New York: Garland, 1992).

82. Haygood, *King of the Cats*, 80–85.

83. Haygood, *King of the Cats*, 98; Martha Biondi, *To Stand and Fight: The Struggle for Civil Rights in Postwar New York City* (Cambridge, MA: Harvard University Press, 2003), 11.

84. Ernest E. Johnson, "New York Masses Protest for Democracy," *Chicago Defender*, June 27, 1942.

85. Haygood, *King of the Cats*, 89.

86. Kenneth O'Reilly and David Gallen, *Black Americans: The FBI Files* (New York: Carroll and Graf, 1994).

87. Haygood, *King of the Cats*, 98–99.

88. Powell, "My Life with Hazel Scott," 42; Chilton, *Pioneering Journey*, 98–99.

89. Scott, autobiography.

90. Norma Jean Darden, "Hazel Scott: Up Tempo," *Essence* (November 1978): 148.

91. Adam Clayton Powell III, *Adam by Adam: The Autobiography of Adam Clayton Powell, Jr.* (New York: Dial, 1971), 223–24.

92. Abe Hill, "Adam Kisses Women Guests at Reception," *New York Amsterdam News*, August 2, 1945.

93. Hill, "Adam Kisses Women."

94. Bogle, *Primetime Blues*, 16.

95. Powell, *Adam by Adam*, 224.

96. Powell, interview with the author.

97. Scott, "I Found God in Show Business," 41

98. Powell, interview with the author.

99. Scott, "I Found God in Show Business," 50.

100. Scott, autobiography.

101. Constance Curtis, "Hazel Scott Expects Baby Next Summer," *New York Amsterdam News*, January 1, 1945.

102. Scott, autobiography.

103. Scott, autobiography; Haygood, *King of the Cats*, 233; Powell, interview with the author. Her son remembers his mother opening her house in Paris to women who had been abused by their husbands and boyfriends. Undoubtedly, her experience in her marriage to Powell made her empathetic to other women suffering similar abuse.

104. I include this behind-the-scenes narrative of their marriage to deepen readers' understanding of Scott's challenges and triumphs, not to disparage the legacy of either as luminaries.

105. "Negro Freedom Rally Program," *New York Times*, June 12, 1945; "Freedom Rally Set for Garden Airing," *Afro-American*, June 23, 1945.

106. Gerald Horne, *Black Liberation/Red Scare: Ben Davis and the Communist Party* (Newark: University of Delaware Press, 1994), 108. According to her son, Scott was involved in numerous groups, particularly African American women's organizations, but was not usually a formal member (Powell, interview with the author).

107. Carter, "Tells How She Became a $4000 a Week Pianist," 5; Salem, "Hazel Scott," 342; Powell, interview with the author.

108. Dwayne Mack, "Hazel Scott: A Career Curtailed," *Journal of African-American History* 91, no. 2 (2006): 156; "Tea for Fifty Ladies," *Newsweek*, October 22, 1945.

109. "Hazel Scott to Tour Nation in Fight against Jim Crow," *Chicago Defender*, December 1, 1945.

110. Scott, autobiography; Salem, "Hazel Scott," 445–46.

111. "Hazel Scott to Tour Nation in Fight against Jim Crow."

112. Howard B. Woods, "Hazel Scott Jim Crowed Again; St. Louis Café Bars Pianist," *Chicago Defender*, October 27, 1945.

113. "Nina Mae McKinney Beaten Up in Dixie," *New York Amsterdam News*, January 13, 1940.

114. Powell, interview with the author; Tony Cox, "Before Oprah, TV Audiences Cozied Up to Hazel," *News and Notes*, January 26, 2009, National Public Radio; "Marian Anderson, Hazel Scott Split on Jim Crow Issue," *Chicago Defender*, March 19, 1949.

115. "Hazel Scott Balks at University of Texas Jim Crow," *Afro-American*, November 27, 1948.

116. "Damages of $250 for Hazel Scott," *Spokesman Review*, December 30, 1949; Scott, autobiography.

117. Langston Hughes, "It Is Criminal to Refuse Any Person Food Who Has the Cash," *Chicago Defender*, March 12, 1949.

118. "Hazel Scott Wins Suit," *New York Times*, April 20, 1950; Chilton, *Pioneering Journey*, 138–39; Mack, "Career Curtailed," 160.

119. C. H., "14,000 at Stadium Hear Hazel Scott," *New York Times*, June 20, 1948.

120. Mack, "Career Curtailed," 160.

121. Albert Fried, ed., *McCarthyism: The Great American Red Scare* (New York: Oxford University Press, 1997), 119.

122. Fried, *McCarthyism*, 16, 24–25. HUAC was formed in 1938. It was dormant through World War II but would become a vehicle for the political career of Senator Joseph McCarthy and destroy many people's lives after its revival in 1947.

123. Cox, "Before Oprah."

124. Hazel Scott Powell, testimony before the House Un-American Activities Committee, U.S. House of Representatives, 81st Cong., 2d sess., September 22, 1950 (Washington, DC: Government Printing Office, 1950), 3617.

125. Carol A. Stabile, *The Broadcast 41: Women and the Anti-Communist Blacklist* (London: Goldsmiths, 2018) 121.

126. Hazel Scott, "What Paris Means to Me," in *A Stranger in the Village*, ed. Farrah Jasmine Griffin and Cheryl Fish (Boston: Beacon, 1993), 187.

127. Louie Robinson, "Hazel Scott Comes Home to the 'Action,'" *Ebony* (March 1968): 102.

128. The era of Scott's heyday preceded the period traditionally associated with the modern civil rights movement. For scholarship that connects wartime and postwar

civil rights, see Peniel Joseph's *Waiting 'Til the Midnight Hour* Joseph, (New York: Holt, 2006).

CHAPTER 3

1. Samuella Lewis, *The Art of Elizabeth Catlett* (Claremont, CA: Handcraft Studios, 1984), 11.
2. Elizabeth Catlett, interview with the author, April 23, 2011.
3. Kellie Jones, "Swimming with E. C.," in *Women and Migration: Responses in Art and History*, ed. Deborah Willis, Ellyn Toscano, and Brooks Nelson (Cambridge, MA: Open Book, 2019), 219–20.
4. Catlett, interview with the author.
5. Catlett, interview with the author.
6. Lewis, *The Art of Elizabeth Catlett*, 2.
7. Catlett, interview with the author.
8. Catlett, interview with the author.
9. Glory Van Scott, "Interview of Elizabeth Catlett by Glory Van Scott, December 8, 1981," in *Artist and Influence* ed. James V. Hatch and Leo Hamalian (New York: Hatch Billops Collection, 1991), 10:5.
10. Elton Fax, *Seventeen Black Artists* (New York: Dodd, 1971), 17.
11. Catlett, interview with the author.
12. Fax, *Seventeen Black Artists*, 17.
13. Steven Lafer, "DC Sculptress Unveils Work," *Daily World*, June 29, 1976.
14. Catlett, interview with the author.
15. Melanie Herzog, "Elizabeth Catlett in Mexico: Identity and Cross-Cultural Intersections in the Production of Artistic Meaning," *International Review of African American Art* 11, no. 3 (1994): 19.
16. David Levering Lewis, *When Harlem Was in Vogue* (New York: Penguin, 1997) 12; Catlett, interview with the author.
17. Maryemma Graham, *The House Where My Soul Lives: The Life of Margaret Walker*, (New York: Oxford University Press, 2022), 220–22.
18. Phoebe Farris, *Women Artists of Color: A Bio-Critical Sourcebook to 20th Century Artists in the Americas* (Westport, CT: Greenwood, 1999), 253.
19. Catlett, interview with the author.
20. Herzog, "Elizabeth Catlett in Mexico," 21.
21. Thalia Gouma-Peterson, "Elizabeth Catlett: 'The Power of Human Feeling and of Art,'" *Woman's Art Journal* 4, no. 1 (1983): 49.
22. Bill Mullen, *Popular Fronts: Chicago and African American Cultural Politics, 1935–46* (Urbana: University of Illinois Press, 1999), 75–76.
23. Lisa Farrington, *Creating Their Own Image: The History of African-American Women Artists* (Oxford, UK: Oxford University Press, 2011), 105–6.

24. Savage's experience is detailed in Jeffreen M. Hayes, *Augusta Savage: Renaissance Woman* (London: Giles, 2018), 25.

25. Farrington, *Creating Their Own Image*, 8.

26. According to Nicholas Mirzoeff, visual culture is best understood as the study of the functions of the world addressed through pictures, images, and visualizations rather than through texts and words (*An Introduction to Visual Culture* [London: Routledge, 1999]), 1–2.

27. The Delgado Museum was later renamed the New Orleans Museum of Art.

28. Catlett, interview with the author; Lewis, *When Harlem Was in Vogue*, 16.

29. Catlett, interview with the author.

30. Christina Heatherton, *Arise!: Global Radicalism in the Era of the Mexican Revolution* (Berkeley: University of California Press, 2022) 155. Heatherton interviewed the well-known New Orleans artist Willie Birch, who spoke of Catlett and her artistic influence in New Orleans.

31. Joshua Cohen, "Picasso's African Influences," in *The "Black Art" Renaissance: African Sculpture and Modernism across Continents* (Berkeley: University of California Press, 2020), 55–93.

32. Lewis, *The Art of Elizabeth Catlett*, 16.

33. Catlett, interview with the author.

34. Hayes, *Augusta Savage*, 27.

35. Mullen, *Popular Fronts*, 81.

36. Catlett, interview with the author.

37. Heatherton, *Arise!*, 158. In my interview with Catlett, she did not discuss communist membership, although she was greatly involved with institutions and organizations that were connected to the party.

38. Herzog, "Elizabeth Catlett in Mexico," 39; Mary Helen Washington, *The Other Blacklist: The African American Literary and Cultural Left of the 1950s* (New York: Columbia University Press, 2014), 80.

39. Glory Van Scott, "Interview of Margaret Burroughs by Glory Van Scott, June 6, 1975," in *Artist and Influence*, ed. James V. Hatch and Judy Blum (New York: Hatch Billops Collection, 2005), 24:43.

40. Heatherton, *Arise!*, 158

41. Washington, *The Other Blacklist*, 77.

42. Stacy Morgan, *Rethinking Social Realism: African American Art and Literature, 1930–1953* (Athens: University of Georgia Press, 2004), 48–52.

43. Clifton Johnson, interview with Elizabeth Catlett, January 7, 1984, audiotape, Elizabeth Catlett Papers, Amistad Research Center, New Orleans.

44. Fax, *Seventeen Black Artists*, 17; Lisa Farrington, *African American Art: A Visual and Cultural History* (New York: Oxford University Press, 2017), 169–70.

45. Lewis, *The Art of Elizabeth Catlett*, 17.

46. Lewis, *The Art of Elizabeth Catlett*, 17.

47. Sarah Kelly Oehler, "Socialist Networks in Chicago and New York," in *Elizabeth Catlett: A Black Revolutionary Artist and All That It Implies!*, ed. Dalila Scruggs (Chicago: University of Chicago Press, 2024), 83.

48. Catlett, interview with the author.

49. Jonathan Gill, *Harlem: The Four Hundred Year History from Dutch Village to Capital of Black America* (Berkeley, CA: Grove, 2011).

50. Catlett, interview with the author.

51. Fax, *Seventeen Black Artists*, 22.

52. Washington, *The Other Blacklist*, 85; Earnestine Lovelle Jenkins, *Black Artists in America: From the Great Depression to Civil Rights* (New Haven, CT: Yale University Press). White's mural is still in place and has undergone preservation; see Melanie Rock, "A Fragile but Important Artwork at Hampton University Gets a Boost," *Preservation* (Spring 2022), https://savingplaces.org.

53. Catlett rendered Harriet Tubman several times during her career, attesting to her admiration for freedom fighters.

54. Catlett, interview with the author; Herzog, "Elizabeth Catlett in Mexico," 34–36; Vanessa Cross, "Charles White: The Art of a Chicago Son Beautifies Experiences of Common Black Folk," *Afrique* (June 1996): 196.

55. George Washington Carver School, course catalog (Fall 1945), Schomburg Clippings Collection, Robert Frost Library, Amherst College, Amherst, Massachusetts.

56. Ramona Lowe, "Harlem's Carver School Draws Capacity Classrooms," *Chicago Defender*, February 5, 1944.

57. Carver School, course catalog, 13.

58. Lowe, "Harlem's Carver School," 18.

59. Catlett, interview with the author.

60. Catlett, interview with the author.

61. Catlett, interview with the author.

62. Catlett, interview with the author.

63. Catlett, interview with the author. For a fuller description of the symphony, which was inspired by the 1941 Nazi siege of Leningrad, see Heatherton, *Arise!*, 165.

64. Fax, *Seventeen Black Artists*, 23.

65. Catlett, interview with the author.

66. Bill Chase, "Judge Delany Is Married," *New York Amsterdam Star-News*, September 26, 1942; Catlett, interview with the author.

67. Catlett, interview with the author.

68. Bill Chase, "Meet Mr., Mrs. Charles White," *New York Amsterdam Star-News*, September 5, 1942.

69. Florence Davies, "Wife of the Master Mural Painter Gleefully Dabbles in Works of Art," *Detroit News*, February 2, 1933.

70. Herzog, "Elizabeth Catlett in Mexico," 47.

71. Romare Bearden and Harry Henderson. *A History of African-American Artists: From 1792 to the Present* (New York: Pantheon, 1993), 398.

72. Morgan, *Rethinking Social Realism*, 46–47.

73. Morgan, *Rethinking Social Realism*, 32–33.

74. Rebecca M. Schreiber, "The Politics of Form: African American Artists and the Making of Transnational Aesthetics," in *Cold War Exiles in Mexico: U.S. Dissidents and the Culture of Critical Resistance* (Minneapolis: University of Minnesota Press, 2008), 28.

75. Theodore Cohen, *Finding Afro-Mexico: Race and Nation after the Revolution* (Boston: Cambridge University Press, 2020), 37.

76. Paul Ortiz, *An African American and Latinx History of the United States* (Boston: Beacon, 2018), 13.

77. Ortiz, *An African American and Latinx History*, 46.

78. Tiffany Ruby Patterson and Robin D. G. Kelley, "Unfinished Migrations: Reflections on the African Diaspora and the Making of the Modern World," *African Studies Review* 43, no. 1 (2000): 16.

79. Cohen, *Finding Afro-Mexico*, 128.

80. Herzog, "Elizabeth Catlett in Mexico," 5.

81. Patterson and Kelley, "Unfinished Migrations," 20.

82. Ernest Hamlin Baker, portrait of Joseph Stalin, "Man of the Year, 1939," *Time*, January 1, 1940, front cover; Boris Artzybasheff, portrait of Joseph Stalin, "Man of the Year, 1942," *Time*, January 4, 1943, front cover.

83. "Six Directors Quit," *New York Times*, December 18, 1943.

84. "Policies for Carver Called Nonpartisan," *New York Times*, December 24, 1943.

85. Catlett, interview with the author; Herzog, "Elizabeth Catlett in Mexico," 78–79.

86. David Craven, *Art and Revolution in Latin America, 1910–1990* (New Haven, CT: Yale University Press, 2002), 67. The institutions and organizations to which Catlett belonged were well aware that the Mexican School extended beyond the muralists, in part due to the TGP's prints. For more on the history of the TGP, see Gustavo Quintero, "Visual Dimensions of Social Unrest: Posters and Flyers of Taller de Gráfica Popular and Taller," *DiáLogo* 22, no. 2 (2019): 7–19; Dina Comisarenco Mirkin, "A Collective Roar from the Taller de Gráfica Popular: Mariana Yampolsky, Elizabeth Catlett, Fanny Rabel, and Celia Calderón," *Artelogie* 17 (2021), https:// journals.openedition.org; and Schreiber, "The Politics of Form," 29. Herzog's *Elizabeth Catlett* and Heatherton's *Arise!* also contain extensive discussions of the TGP.

87. Farrington, *African American Art*, 183.

88. Schreiber, "The Politics of Form," 28.

89. The series is also known as *The Black Woman Series*.

90. Catlett, interview with the author.

91. Camille O. Cosby, interview with Elizabeth Catlett (2004), National Visionary Leadership Project Interviews and Conference Collection, American Folklife Center, Library of Congress, Washington, DC.

92. Ella Baker and Marvel Cooke, "The Bronx Slave Market," *The Crisis 42* (November 1935): 330–31. Cooke later wrote about her own experiences as a domestic in "I Was a Part of the Bronx Slave Market," *New York Daily Compass*, January 8, 1950.

93. See Gayle Wald, *Shout, Sister, Shout!: The Untold Story of Rock-and-Roll Trailblazer Sister Rosetta Tharpe* (Boston: Beacon, 2007).

94. Herzog, "Elizabeth Catlett in Mexico," 155.

95. Yohuru Williams and Michael G. Long, "Raise a Fist of Solidarity!," *Progressive*, January 7, 2021.

96. This linocut calls up a famous image of Rosa Parks, the civil rights activist and icon, whose refusal to be removed from her seat on a segregated Montgomery, Alabama, bus sparked a renewed wave of freedom movement activity. Parks was photographed at the conclusion of the Montgomery bus boycott, sitting on the bus quietly looking out the window. The photo shows her seated in a row *in front of* a white man, signaling the impact of the civil rights movement as well as the ways in which Black women acted as its engine. Catlett's 1946 print was produced nearly a decade before the incident but captured the historic and harsh conditions that would give rise to the movement.

97. Susan Saulny, "At Housing Project, Both Fear and Renewal," *New York Times*, March 18, 2007.

98. Catlett, interview with the author.

99. Elizabeth Catlett, speech (1970), Elizabeth Catlett Papers, Amistad Research Center, New Orleans.

CHAPTER 4

1. Langston Hughes, "Colored and Colorful," *Chicago Defender*, June 26, 1948.

2. David Jackson, "The Amazing Adventures of Jackie Ormes," *Reader: Chicago's Free Weekly* 14, no. 46 (1985): 24.

3. Fredrik Stroemberg, *Black Images in the Comics: A Visual History* (Seattle, WA: Fantagraphics, 2003), 23–24.

4. Maurice Horn, *Women in the Comics* (New York: Chelsea House, 1977), 92.

5. All-American News, founded in 1942, was the sole newsreel company that produced "news and feature material calculated to be of particular interest to black citizens." Its films ran in 365 of the nation's 451 Black theaters, and the Office of War Information believed that 85 percent of Blacks in the five largest cities received much of their news from them. That claim failed to take Black newspapers into account, the sources from which Black people probably received most of their news, but

certainly the newsreels were also significant. See Raymond Fielding, *The American Newsreel, 1911–1967* (Norman: University of Oklahoma Press, 1972), 187–88.

6. Henry T. Sampson, *That's Enough, Folks: Black Images in Animated Cartoons, 1900–1960* (Lanham, MD: Scarecrow, 1998), 2–3. See also Christopher P. Lehman, *The Colored Cartoon: Black Presentation in American Animated Short Films, 1907–1954* (Amherst: University of Massachusetts Press, 2009).

7. Fredrik Stromberg, *Black Images in the Comics: A Visual History* (Seattle: Fantagraphics, 2003), 81.

8. Thomas Cripps, *Slow Fade to Black: The Negro in American Film, 1900–1942* (Oxford, UK: Oxford University Press, 1993), 305.

9. Sampson, *That's Enough, Folks*, 11, 12, 65.

10. U.S. Bureau of the Census, "1910 (Thirteenth) Census of the United States, Pittsburgh Ward 5, Allegheny, Pennsylvania," http://ancestry.com.

11. William Winfield Jackson, draft registration card (1917–18), Draft Board, Allegheny County, Pennsylvania, National Archives and Records Administration, Washington, DC; Pennsylvania had a surprising number of Black-owned businesses. A 1909 survey identified at least eighty-five. See Joe William Trotter and Eric Ledell Smith, *African Americans in Pennsylvania: Shifting Historical Perspectives* (Harrisburg: Pennsylvania State University Press, 1997), 410.

12. Nancy Goldstein, *Jackie Ormes: The First African American Woman Cartoonist* (Ann Arbor: University of Michigan Press, 2008), 1–9. Goldstein's biography, the only full-length work on Ormes's life, includes interviews with her sister Delores, who died soon after the book's publication. They are among the few sources on Ormes's early and later life. See also Frank E. Bolden, "The First Hundred Years," *Pittsburgh Courier*, April 1, 1950.

13. Jackson, "Amazing Adventures," 18.

14. Jackson, "Amazing Adventures," 18.

15. Jackson, "Amazing Adventures," 18.

16. Gene Roberts and Hank Klibanoff, *The Race Beat: The Press, the Civil Rights Struggle, and the Awakening of a Nation* (New York: Knopf, 2007), 16.

17. Roland Edgar Wolseley, *The Black Press, USA* (Ames: Iowa State University Press, 1990), 3–4; Mark Whitaker, *The Untold Story of Smoketown: The Other Great Black Renaissance* (New York: Simon and Schuster, 2018), xvi.

18. Whitaker, *The Untold Story of Smoketown*, xvi.

19. Goldstein, *Jackie Ormes*, 16–17; Jackson, "Amazing Adventures," 18, 24.

20. Goldstein, *Jackie Ormes*, 74.

21. Heather Lyn MacDonald, dir., interview with Cleo Hayes, in *Been Rich All My Life* (New York: First Run Features, 2005), DVD.

22. Jacqueline Jones, *Labor of Love, Labor of Sorrow: Black Women, Work, and the Family, from Slavery to the Present*, rev. ed. (New York: Basic Books, 2010), 169.

23. Ira Berlin, *The Making of African America: The Four Great Migrations* (New York: Viking, 2010), 158–59.

24. "Plight of the Negro in the Depression," *Pittsburgh Courier*, May 1, 1937.

25. Ethan Mitchell, *The Defender: How the Legendary Black Newspaper Changed America, from the Age of the Pullman Porters to the Age of Obama* (Boston: Houghton Mifflin Harcourt, 2016), 242–68.

26. Jackson, "Amazing Adventures," 24.

27. Jackson, "Amazing Adventures," 20.

28. St. Clair Drake and Horace R. Cayton. *Black Metropolis: A Study of Negro Life in a Northern City* (New York: Harper and Row, 1962), 80.

29. Roi Ottley, "Owners Invest $300,000 to Give South Side a First Class Hotel," *Chicago Daily Tribune*, April 15, 1956.

30. Fred Carroll, *Race News: Black Journalists and the Fight for Racial Justice in the Twentieth Century* (Urbana: University of Illinois Press, 2017), 5.

31. Alice Childress created a Black women domestic as a character in her serial *Conversations from Life*, which appeared in the Black Marxist newspaper *Freedom* between 1951 and 1955. The serial was later published as the novel *Like One of the Family: Conversations from a Domestic's Life* (1956; reprint, Boston: Beacon, 1986).

32. Micki McElya discusses America's obsession with the mammy construction in *Clinging to Mammy: The Faithful Slave in Twentieth-Century America* (Cambridge, MA: Harvard University Press, 2007).

33. Childress, *Like One of the Family*.

34. Jackie Ormes, *Candy*, *Chicago Defender*, March 24, 1945.

35. Ormes, *Candy*, July 21, 1945.

36. Ormes, *Candy*, April 7, 1945.

37. Ormes, *Candy*, April 21, 1945.

38. Maureen Honey details the roles and voices of African American women during World War II as revealed in African American newspapers (*Bitter Fruit: African American Women in World War II* [Columbia: University of Missouri Press, 1999]).

39. Jones, *Labor of Love, Labor of Sorrow*, 201.

40. Goldstein, *Jackie Ormes*, 63.

41. Trina Robbins and Kristy Valenti, *Pretty in Ink: North American Women Cartoonists, 1896–2013* (Seattle, WA: Fantagraphics, 2013), 105.

42. Ormes, *Patty-Jo 'n' Ginger*, *Pittsburgh Courier*, February 11, 1950.

43. Mary Dudziak, *Cold War Civil Rights: Race and the Image of American Democracy* (Princeton, NJ: Princeton University Press, 2000), 13.

44. Paul Robeson, *Here I Stand* (Boston: Beacon, 1988), x.

45. Robeson, *Here I Stand*, 43.

46. Mary Helen Washington, "Alice Childress, Lorraine Hansberry, and Claudia Jones: Black Women Write the Popular Front," in *Left of the Color Line: Race, Radicalism,*

and Twentieth-Century Literature of the United States, ed. Bill Mullen and James Edward Smethurst (Chapel Hill: University of North Carolina Press, 2003), 185.

47. Ormes, *Patty-Jo 'n' Ginger*, April 23, 1949.

48. Ormes, *Patty-Jo 'n' Ginger*, July 24, 1948.

49. Thomas Inge, ed., *Dark Laughter: The Satiric Art of Oliver W. Harrington* (Jackson: University Press of Mississippi, 1993), xviii–xxviii.

50. Inge, *Dark Laughter*, xxxiv–xxxv; Herb Boyd, "Ollie Harrington, in Memoriam," *Black Scholar* 26 (Winter/Spring 1996): 74. Harrington continued to send correspondence, art, and comics from abroad. He was a steady presence in the Black press into the 1980s, despite his exile.

51. Ormes, *Patty-Jo 'n' Ginger*, March 24, 1951.

52. Ormes, *Patty-Jo 'n' Ginger*, October 8, 1955.

53. Danielle L. McGuire details the racialized violence that beset Black women during the civil rights movement in *At the Dark End of the Street: Black Women, Rape, and Resistance—A New History of the Civil Rights Movement, from Rosa Parks to the Rise of Black Power* (New York: Vintage, 2011).

54. Ormes, *Patty-Jo 'n' Ginger*, March 31, 1956.

55. Jeanne Theoharis, *The Rebellious Life of Mrs. Rosa Parks* (Boston: Beacon, 2013), 62.

56. Fielding, *The American Newsreel*, 187–88.

57. Federal Bureau of Investigation, memo, special agent in charge, Chicago Field Office, to director, Washington, DC, February 27, 1956, Jackie Ormes File, Chicago Field Office Records.

58. David Levering Lewis, *W. E. B. Du Bois: A Biography* (New York: Holt, 2009), 548.

59. Levering Lewis, *W. E. B. Du Bois*, 550.

60. Jackie Ormes, letter to Shirley Graham Du Bois, September 30, 1951, W. E. B. Du Bois Papers (MS 312), Special Collections and University Archives, University of Massachusetts Libraries, Amherst.

61. W. E. B. Du Bois, letter to Jackie Ormes, January 12, 1953, W. E. B. Du Bois Papers (MS 312) Special Collections and University Archives, University of Massachusetts Libraries, Amherst.

62. Levering Lewis, *W. E. B. Du Bois*, 550–52.

63. Federal Bureau of Investigation, memo, February 27, 1956.

64. Ormes was in good artistic and journalistic company. In *Radicalism at the Crossroads: African American Women Activists in the Cold War* (New York: New York University Press, 2011), the feminist historian Dayo Gore unearths the forgotten labor of radical Black women activists, emphasizing the groundwork they laid and the activist networks they built, including the central roles they played in the Communist Party USA and radical Black left freedom movements (22–23). Among them was the editor Marvel Cooke, who personified radical journalism and worked for, among other outlets, the *People's Voice* alongside Oliver Harrington. The

historian Erik McDuffie also refutes the idea that these women were anomalous, situating them as "part of a community of Black women radicals" whose activism spanned a good part of the twentieth century (*Sojourning for Freedom: Black Women, American Communism, and the Making of Black Left Feminism* [Durham, NC: Duke University Press, 2011], 7).

65. For important analyses of the FBI file, see Goldstein, *Jackie Ormes*, 29–31; and Deborah Elizabeth Whaley, *Black Women in Sequence: Re-inking Comics, Graphic Novels, and Anime* (Seattle: University of Washington Press, 2016), 57.

66. Federal Bureau of Investigation, memo, special agent in charge, Chicago Field Office, to director, Washington, DC, May 18, 1953, Jackie Ormes File, Chicago Field Office Records.

67. Federal Bureau of Investigation, memo, May 18, 1953.

68. Bill Mullen, *Popular Fronts: Chicago and African American Cultural Politics, 1935–46* (Urbana: University of Illinois Press, 1999), 5.

69. Ottley, "Owners Invest $300,000 to Give South Side a First Class Hotel."

70. Goldstein, *Jackie Ormes*, 31.

71. Ormes, *Patty-Jo 'n' Ginger*, May 4, 1953.

72. Rebecca Raines, "The Cold War Comes to Fort Monmouth: Senator Joseph R. McCarthy and the Search for Spies in the Signal Corps," *Army History* 44 (Spring 1998): 10–12.

73. Ormes, *Patty-Jo 'n' Ginger*, June 12, 1954.

74. Jackson, "Amazing Adventures," 23.

CHAPTER 5

1. *The Dick Cavett Show* (New York: American Broadcasting Corporation), November 5, 1981.

2. *The Dick Cavett Show.*

3. Lena Horne and Richard Schickel, *Lena* (Garden City, NY: Doubleday, 1965), 197.

4. Gail Lumet Buckley, *The Hornes: An American Family* (New York: Knopf, 1986), 81.

5. "Lena Horne Is Still on the Way Up," *PM*, December 15 1942.

6. Teddy Horne, ephemera, Sc MG 327, Horne Family Research Collection, Schomburg Center for Research in Black Culture, New York Public Library; Buckley, *The Hornes*, 93–94, 110.

7. Cary D. Wintz and Paul Finkelman, *Encyclopedia of the Harlem Renaissance* (New York: Routledge, 2004), 94–95; M. Francesca Thompson, "The Lafayette Players, 1917–1922," in *The Theater of Black Americans: A Collection of Critical Essays*, ed. Errol Hill (Englewood Cliffs, NJ: Prentice-Hall, 1979), 216–22.

8. Horne and Schickel, *Lena*, 94.

9. Buckley, *The Hornes*, 77, 94, 84.

10. Horne and Schickel, *Lena*, 37, 26.

11. Horne and Schickel, *Lena*, 47.

12. Buckley, *The Hornes*, 112.

13. Barney Josephson and Terry Trilling-Josephson, *Café Society: The Wrong Place for the Right People* (Urbana: University of Illinois Press, 2009), 120.

14. Horne and Schickel, *Lena*, 48, 61.

15. "Lena Horne: In Her Own Voice," *American Masters (Boston: WGBH Television*, 1997).

16. James Gavin, *Stormy Weather: The Life of Lena Horne* (London: Simon and Schuster, 2010), 62.

17. "Lena Horne, a Girl from Brooklyn Became This Season's Biggest Nightclub Hit . . . And How She's Quietly Using Her Unrehearsed Success to Win Respect for Her People," *PM*, January 10, 1943.

18. Seymour Peck, "Calling on Lena Horne: The Star of Jamaica Reflects on Career and Marriage" *New York Times*, October, 27, 1957; Horne and Schickel, *Lena*, 102–3; Josephson and Josephson, *Café Society*, 129–30.

19. Lena Horne, *Live on Broadway. Lena Horne: The Lady and Her Music* (New York: Rhino/Warner Records, 1981).

20. "Lena Horne: In Her Own Voice."

21. In 1950, at the zenith of his career, Josh White was listed prominently in *Red Channels*. He appeared before HUAC in September of that year, where he defended himself but criticized Robeson. He was eventually blackballed by both progressives and anticommunists (Elijah Wald, *Josh White: Society Blues* (Amherst: University of Massachusetts Press, 2000), 193–98).

22. "Lena Horne Is Still on the Way Up."

23. Horne and Schickel, *Lena*, 197.

24. Shane Vogel, "Lena Horne's Impersona," *Camera Obscura* 23, no. 67 (2008): 11–44.

25. Michiko Kakutani, "Lena Horne: Aloofness Hid the Pain until Time Cooled the Anger," *New York Times*, May 3, 1981; Horne and Schickel, *Lena*, 197.

26. Lena Horne, "I Just Want to Be Myself," *Show* (September 1963): 62.

27. Horne's apparent accessibility and actual lack of openness can also be seen as a form of resistance. See Darlene Clark Hine's *Hine Sight: Black Women and the Re-Construction of American History* (Brooklyn, NY: Carlson, 1994), 37–38.

28. Lena Horne, *Live on Broadway*.

29. Aljean Harmentz, "Lena Horne, Singer and Actress, Dies at 92," *New York Times*, May 10, 2010.

30. Charlene B. Regester discusses the roles that African American women were repeatedly assigned and the history surrounding them (*African American Actresses: The Struggle for Visibility, 1900–1960* [Bloomington: Indiana University Press, 2010]).

31. Donald Bogle's *Toms, Coons, Mulattoes, Mammies, and Bucks: An Interpretive History of Blacks in American Films* (New York: Continuum, 2001) remains the definitive discussion of the tropes that African Americans have been forced into throughout movie history. His chapter on the 1940s is an important overview of the roles that dominated that decade, including the troubling portrayals of African Americans (particularly biracial Black people) as problems to be solved or as perpetual servants.

32. "Lena Horne, a Girl from Brooklyn . . . ," *PM*, January 10, 1943.

33. "Lena Horne: In Her Own Voice."

34. Alfred E. Smith, "Lena Horne Quits Tour in Row over Army Jim Crow," *Chicago Defender*, January 6, 1945; Horne and Schickel, *Lena*, 175–77.

35. "Lena Horne: In Her Own Voice"; Carole A. Stabile, *The Broadcast 41: Women and the Anti-Communist Blacklist* (London: Goldsmiths, 2018), 60; "Lena Horne Joins NAACP" *Pittsburgh Courier*, July 31, 1943.

36. Ted O. Thackery, "Lena Horne and the Smear," *Daily Compass*, September 11, 1951.

37. "Lena Horne Sues, Says Chicago Restaurant Barred Her," *PM*, September 20, 1949.

38. "Lena Horne Cancels Contract because of Hotel Jim Crow," *Afro-American*, February 26, 1955; "Lena Horne Cancels Miami Engagement," *Atlanta Daily World*, February 19, 1955; Kae Williams, "On the Air," *Philadelphia Tribune*, February 26, 1955.

39. Thackery, "Lena Horne and the Smear."

40. "Lena Horne: In Her Own Voice."

41. Hazel Scott, Langston Hughes, and Fredi Washington were also listed among others artist-activists (*Red Channels: The Report of Communist Influence in Radio and Television* [New York: American Business Consultants, 1950]).]

42. Donald Bogle, *Lena Horne: Goddess* Reclaimed (Philadelphia: Running Press, 2023), 170–71.

43. "Lena Horne Cleared of Red Charge," *Amsterdam News*, October 13, 1951.

44. Stabile, *The Broadcast 41*, 128.

45. Marvel Cooke, "Lena Horne's Manager Says She'll Refuse to 'Name Names,'" *Daily Compass*, October 11, 1951.

46. Horne and Schickel, *Lena*, 272–74, 296–97; "Lena Hurls Objects in Offense to Man's Slurs," *Chicago Defender*, February 17, 1960.

47. "Lena Horne Hurls Lamp at Diner in Racial Slur," *New York Herald Tribune*, February 17, 1960; Horne and Schickel, *Lena*, 296–97.

48. Gavin, *Stormy Weather*, 297.

49. Horne and Schickel, *Lena*, 274.

50. Dave Hepburn, "In the Wings," *Amsterdam News*, March 23, 1963.

51. "1963: The Year of Murders and Assassinations," *Chicago Defender*, December 28, 1963.

52. On the civil rights movement, see, for example, Lynne Olson, *Freedom's Daughters: The Unsung Heroines of the Civil Rights Movement from 1830 to 1970* (New York: Scribner's, 2001); Taylor Branch, *Parting the Waters: America in the King Years, 1954–63* (New York: Simon and Schuster, 1989); and Traci Parker and Marcia Walker-McWilliams, *The New Civil Rights Movement Reader: Resistance, Resilience, and Justice* (Amherst: University of Massachusetts Press, 2023).

53. Layhmond Robinson, "Kennedy Fails to Sway Negroes at Secret Talks Here" *New York Times*, May 26, 1963.

54. Harry Belafonte and Michael Shnayerson, *My Song: A Memoir* (New York: Knopf, 2011), 267.

55. Belafonte and Shnayerson, *My Song*, 267.

56. Horne and Schickel, *Lena*, 280.

57. Larry Tye, *Bobby Kennedy: The Making of a Liberal Icon* (New York: Random House, 2016), 199.

58. Morton Cooper, "Lena Bids Farewell to Nightclubs," *Chicago Defender*, March 8, 1963.

59. Myrlie Evers-Williams and Manning Marable, *The Autobiography of Medgar Evers: A Hero's Life and Legacy Revealed through His Writings, Letters, and Speeches* (New York: Basic Civitas Books, 2005), 201; Gavin, *Stormy Weather*, 316.

60. Evers-Williams and Marable, *The Autobiography of Medgar Evers*, 8.

61. "1963: The Year of Murders and Assassinations."

62. Horne and Schickel, *Lena*, 282.

63. Horne and Schickel, *Lena*, 284; Gavin, *Stormy Weather*, 316–17.

64. Horne and Schickel, *Lena*, 285.

65. Branch, *Parting the Waters*, 824–25.

66. Horne and Schickel, *Lena*, 285.

67. Horne and Schickel, *Lena*, 286.

68. Evers-Williams and Marable, *The Autobiography of Medgar Evers*, 201.

69. James Haskins, *Lena Horne* (New York: Coward-McCann, 1983), 132.

70. On Parks's life of activism, see Jeanne Theoharis, *The Rebellious Life of Mrs. Rosa Parks* (Boston: Beacon, 2013).

71. Amy Goodman, "Civil Rights Pioneer Gloria Richardson, 91, On How Women Were Silenced at 1963 March on Washington," *Democracy Now!*, August 27, 2013; Janet Dewart Bell, "Gloria Richardson," in *Lighting the Fires of Freedom: African American Women in the Civil Rights Movement* (New York: New Press, 2018), 169–91.

72. Meghan Weaver, "'Freedom!': Black Women Speak at the March on Washington for Jobs and Freedom," https://kinginstitute.stanford.edu.

73. Faith S. Holsaert, *Hands on the Freedom Plow: Personal Accounts by Women in SNCC* (Urbana: University of Illinois Press, 2010), 287–88.

74. Many scholars have noted that women provided an overwhelming share of the

movement's membership and labor. They were local and national organizers and administrators and contributed both strategy and day-to-day support. See Olson, *Freedom's Daughters*; and Holsaert, *Hands on the Freedom Plow*.

75. Olson, *Freedom's Daughters*, 278–90.

76. Much of women's formal participation at the event was made possible because women organizers pressed male leaders for inclusion. Dorothy Height was the sole woman member of the "Big Six" event organizers. The others were Martin Luther King Jr., John Lewis, James Farmer, A. Philip Randolph, Roy Wilkins, and Whitney Young. Anna Arnold Hedgeman of the National Council of Churches, who was on the march's administrative committee, was one of those who pushed for women's proper inclusion.

77. Olson, *Freedom's Daughters*, 288.

78. The Cambridge movement was based in Cambridge, Maryland, not far from the site of the March on Washington. It was dedicated to breaking down the city's rigid segregation. Richardson and the Black community triggered the wrath of local whites as well as leaders of the civil rights movement by publicly arming themselves at demonstrations.

79. Bell, "Gloria Richardson."

80. Goodman, "Civil Rights Pioneer Gloria Richardson"; Holsaert, *Hands on the Freedom Plow*, 287–93.

81. Goodman, "Civil Rights Pioneer Gloria Richardson."

82. Tanisha Ford, *Liberated Threads: Black Women, Style, and the Global Politics of Soul* (Chapel Hill: University of North Carolina Press, 2015), 79–80.

83. Joseph R. Fitzgerald, *The Struggle Is Eternal: Gloria Richardson and Black Liberation* (Lexington: University Press of Kentucky, 2018), 125.

84. Olson, *Freedom's Daughters*, 287.

85. Holsaert, *Hands on the Freedom Plow*, 288.

86. "The Defender Marched . . . As Did Others but in Penna., Race Hate Exploded," *Chicago Defender*, September 3, 1963.

87. Patricia Hill Collins discusses Black women's self-definition as an expression of Black feminist thought in *Black Feminist Thought: Knowledge, Consciousness, and the Politics of Empowerment*. (Abingdon, UK: Routledge, 2000).

88. Bob Hunter, "Lena Horne's Battle against Jim Crow," *Chicago Defender*, September 18, 1963.

89. "Lena Horne's Daughter Hits Sinatra Hypocrisy," *Chicago Defender*, November 2, 1963.

90. Haskins, *Lena Horne*, 131–33.

91. Martin Luther King Jr., "The Negro Is Your Brother" ["Letter from Birmingham Jail"], *Atlantic Monthly* 212 (August 1963): 78–88.

92. Lena Horne, *Here's Lena Now!* (Los Angeles: 20th Century–Fox Records, 1963).

93. Horne and Schickel, *Lena*, 281.

94. Harold Myerson and Ernie Harburg, with Arthur Perlman, *Who Put the Rainbow in "The Wizard of Oz"?: Yip Harburg, Lyricist* (Ann Arbor: University of Michigan Press, 1993), 196–97.

95. Myerson et al., *Who Put the Rainbow*, 96–97.

96. Horne, *Here's Lena Now!*

97. Horne, *Here's Lena Now!*

98. Horne, *Here's Lena Now!*

99. "Lena's Song Banned," *Arizona Tribune*, November 8, 1963.

100. *Silver Spring* was also the title of Rachel Carson's 1962 groundbreaking study of human-linked environmental devastation. Clearly, there was an intersectional understanding of social concerns during the era.

101. Sara Bullard, *Free at Last: A History of the Civil Rights Movement and Those Who Died in the Struggle* (Oxford, UK: Oxford University Press, 1993), 62–63.

102. Horne, *Here's Lena Now!*

103. LaShonda Barnett, *I Got Thunder: Black Women Songwriters on Their Craft* (New York: Thunder's Mouth Press, 2007), 149.

EPILOGUE

1. Francesca Aton, "Smithsonian American Art Museum Hires Dalila Scruggs as First African American Art Curator," *Art News*, March 11, 2024.

2. Kimberlé Crenshaw and Jason Stanley, "Why Trump's 'Anti-Woke' Attack on the Smithsonian Matters," *The Guardian*, August 25, 2025.

H. ZAHRA CALDWELL, PhD, is an Associate Professor in Ethnic and Gender Studies at Westfield State University. She is an educator and cultural historian who teaches in the fields of History, Black Studies, and Women's Studies. Her community and academic work focus on unpacking and expanding the definition of resistance, as discussed within the long struggle for Black freedom, particularly as it relates to African American women, culture, art, and inventive activism.